# INNOVATIONS IN THE REFLECTING PROCESS

# INNOVATIONS IN THE REFLECTING PROCESS

## The Inspirations of Tom Andersen

edited by

*Harlene Anderson & Per Jensen*

Systemic Thinking and Practice Series

Series Editors

*David Campbell & Ros Draper*

Routledge
Taylor & Francis Group
LONDON AND NEW YORK

Chapter 1 excerpted from L. Hoffman, "The Art of Withnessing", in: H. Anderson & D. Gehart (Eds.), *Collaborative Therapy: Relationships and Conversations That Make a Difference* (New York: Routledge, 2006), copyright © 2006. Reproduced by permission of Routledge/Taylor & Francis Group, LLC.

First published 2007 by Karnac Books Ltd.

Published 2019 by Routledge
2 Park Square, Milton Park, Abingdon, Oxon OX14 4RN
52 Vanderbilt Avenue, New York, NY 10017

First issued in hardback 2019

*Routledge is an imprint of the Taylor & Francis Group, an informa business*



**British Library Cataloguing in Publication Data**

A C.I.P. for this book is available from the British Library

ISBN 13: 978-0-367-10575-4 (hbk)
ISBN 13: 978-1-85575-487-4 (pbk)

Edited, designed, and produced by Communication Crafts

*Dedicated to all who have contributed to,*
*and who have been a part of,*
*the reflecting processes movement*

# CONTENTS



**Innovations**

# *SERIES EDITORS' FOREWORD*

This is an important book for our Series. It brings together people who have either previously contributed books to this Series or have been "present" in many volumes through the force and influence of their ideas. The book engages the reader at two levels. On one level, it demonstrates how the ideas that Tom Andersen promulgates can be developed, or, as it seems in several chapters, how they can act as a springboard for other major contributors to the family therapy field such as Hoffman, Seikkula, Shotter, and Harlene Anderson to develop and refine their own theoretical positions. Central to these authors are Andersen's notion of respect, resourcefulness of clients, collaborative relationships, dialogue, and, of course, the well-known reflecting process, but because these authors are sharpening the cutting edge of their own thinking, they are bringing fresh ideas for contemporary therapists.

And on another level, this volume illustrates Andersen's passion for inspiring and supporting local efforts to transform mental health services throughout the world. Many chapters by lesser-known authors describe projects in their local communities, in places as diverse as Africa, South America, and Central Europe, in which they have creatively applied some of Andersen's ideas to change the way services are delivered and the way patients are understood and addressed. The experience of reading these chapters is of understanding the local context, then rolling up your sleeves and tackling real-world problems. One of the striking things about these chapters is that many projects were inspired by personal contact with Tom Andersen and supported by his continuing interest in the projects.

The book is well framed by the two editors, who have known and worked with Tom for many years, yet they have avoided any urge to deify him. Instead they give a clear-eyed description of Tom's place in the field and the relevance of his ideas for systemic therapists and consultants. And in spite of some of the weighty and thoughtful contributions, the book also has a lighter touch and is sprinkled with humour and personal memories of Tom Andersen as a friend, colleague, and teacher.

*David Campbell*
*Ros Draper*
London, November 2006

# ABOUT THE EDITORS AND CONTRIBUTORS

## Editors

**Harlene Anderson (USA)** is a Founding Member of the Houston Galveston Institute and Assistant Professor of Psychology, Our Lady of the Lake University–Houston. She is the author of *Conversations, Language and Possibilities: A Postmodern Approach to Therapy* and coeditor of *Collaborative Therapy: Relationships and Conversations that Make a Difference*. She is internationally recognized as a leader in the field of family therapy and for her postmodern collaborative approach to therapy and education.

**Per Jensen (Norway)** is an Associate Professor, Masters Programme in Family Therapy and Systemic Practice, Diakonhjemmet University College, Oslo, Norway. He is the author of *Ansikt til ansikt* [Face to Face: Systems and Family Perspectives as Frameworks for Clinical Nursing Practice] and co-author of *Familien—pluss en* [The Family—Plus One: Introduction to Family Therapy].

## *Contributors*

**Pål Abrahamsen (Norway):** Psychiatrist, private practice, Oslo, Norway; working simultaneously in forensic psychiatry and as a consultant to child psychiatry, Family Department, Karasjok, Norway.

**Eva Albert (Norway):** University of Tromsø Medical School, Tromsø, Norway since 1980; specializing in gynaecology and obstetric medicine; senior consultant in palliative medicine in Kristiansand, Norway, since 2002.

**Rebekka Alne (Norway):** Social worker in child welfare and social welfare; currently working as a technical adviser in the rehabilitation unit of the Psychiatric Centre, University Hospital of Northern Norway, Tromsø, Norway.

**Gry Årnes (Norway):** Nurse in Karlsøy and Tromsø, Norway; working in district community health care, specializing in helping people with mental disorders.

**Nelly Chong (Peru):** Clinical Psychologist and Family Therapist; Director of Instituto Familiar Sistémico de Lima (IFASIL), Lima, Peru.

**Barbro Collén (Sweden):** Psychologist and clinical psychologist-educator in systemic organizational theory, family therapy, and leadership; Director of Strategic Development, Centre for Habilitation and Technical Aids, Uppsala, Sweden.

**Helena Maffei Cruz (Brazil):** Psychologist and family therapist; Founding Member, Instituto FAMILIAE, São Paulo, Brazil.

**Liv Marit Edvardsen (Norway):** Psychiatric nurse in Karlsøy, Tromsø; formerly a public health nurse and currently working in district community health care, specializing in helping people with mental disorders.

**Heidi Susann Emaus (Norway):** Psychiatric nurse; working in the emergency unit (Akuttenheten) of the Psychiatric Centre for Tromsø and Karlsøy at the University Hospital of Northern Norway, Tromsø, Norway.

**Eugene Epstein (Germany):** Psychologist and social worker; working as chief psychologist in an outpatient clinic for child and adolescent psychiatry and psychotherapy in Wilhelmshaven; supervisor and trainer in narrative and reflecting practices.

**Margit Epstein (Germany):** Psychologist; working in private practice as psychologist and psychotherapist in Oldenburg; trainer and a lecturer at the University of Onsabruck, Onsabruck, Germany.

**Tone Vangen Fagerheim (Norway):** Psychiatric nurse in Tromsø, Norway; lead nurse in a psychiatric unit at the University Hospital of Northern Norway, Tromsø, Norway.

**Anna Margrete Flåm (Norway):** Psychologist at the Child Guidance Clinic, Tromsø University Medical Hospital; member of reflecting processes and reflecting teams connected to the work.

**Adela G. Garcia (Argentina):** Psychologist and family therapist; Founding Member and Director, Centro de Estudios Sistémicos, Buenos Aires, Argentina; Coordinator of The South Triangle Network.

**Anki Godø Giæver (Norway):** Teacher, Karlsøy, Tromsø, Norway; currently specializing in work with adult refugees.

**Åsrun Gjølstad (Norway):** Psychiatric nurse, in Tromsø, Norway; working in the twenty-four-hour unit (Døgnenheten) of the Psychiatric Centre for Tromsø and Karlsøy at the University Hospital of Northern Norway, Tromsø, Norway.

**Trygve Grann-Meyer (Norway):** Bachelor of Economic Science, Tønsberg, Norway.

**Lino Guevara (Argentina):** Psychiatrist, supervisor, and trainer in collaborative, narrative, and reflecting practices; member of the South Triangle Network; Coordinador del Equipo de Orientación y Mediación Familiar de la Fundación Retoño; and Coordinador Docente del Centro de Estudios Sistémicos, Buenos Aires, Argentina.

**Kirsti Ramfjord Haaland (Norway):** Founder and Chair of the Norwegian Association for Family Therapy for fourteen years; assistant professor, Department of Psychology, University of Oslo, and clinical psychologist, Østensjø Family Clinic, Oslo, Norway.

**Magnus Hald (Norway):** Chief psychiatrist, Psychiatric Centre of Tromsø and Karlsøy, Psychiatry Department, University Hospital of Northern-Norway; Founding Member of the North Calotte Network.

**Lynn Hoffman (USA):** Social worker and family therapy historian; Adjunct Lecturer, Department of Marriage and Family Therapy, St. Joseph's College, West Hartford, Connecticut.

**Georg Høyer (Norway):** Professor of Social Medicine, University of Tromsø, Tromsø, Norway.

**Berit Ianssen (Norway):** Physiotherapist living in Levanger, Norway; educated in Norwegian psychomotor physiotherapy; working in a clinic with patients and with physiotherapists learning psychomotor physiotherapy; co-authored *Movements of Life* together with Tom Andersen and colleagues in 1997.

**Arlene Katz (USA):** Instructor in Social Medicine, Harvard Medical School, Boston, Massachusetts; family therapist; and author of "Afterwords" chapter in Tom Andersen's 1990 book, *The Reflecting Team*.

**Eva Kjellberg (Sweden):** Consultant and Head of the Outpatient Clinic for Child and Adolescent Psychiatry, Gällivare, North Sweden; Swedish representative in the management group for the North Calotte Project.

**Anders Lindseth (Norway):** Philosophical practitioner/counsellor; Professor for Practical Philosophy, Centre for Practical Knowledge, Bodø, Norway, and at the Medical Department, University of Tromsø, Tromsø, Norway.

**Knut Beine Lykken (Sweden):** Paediatrician, health care for children, and mountain guide, Arvika, Sweden.

**Hans Christian Michaelsen (Norway):** Director, LEON (an institute for family therapy and rehabilitation); Chairperson of the Norwegian Family Therapy Association, Oslo, Norway.

**Gudrun Øvreberg (Norway):** Physiotherapist living in Harstad, Norway; learned Norwegian psychomotor physiotherapy from

Aadel Bülow-Hansen; working in a clinic with patients and with physiotherapists learning psychomotor physiotherapy; co-authored *Movements of Life* together with Tom Andersen and colleagues in 1997.

**Peggy Penn (USA):** Honorary Associate, Taos Institute; Faculty, Ackerman Institute for eighteen years and Training Director for nine years, New York.

**Marília de Freitas Pereira (Brazil):** Psychologist and family therapist; Founding Member, Instituto FAMILIAE, São Paulo, Brazil.

**Judy Rankin (South Africa):** Psychologist, Buffalo City, Eastern Cape of South Africa; work includes academic, professional training, community development, and relational therapist in private practice.

**Eli Rongved (Norway):** Physiotherapist; educated in Norwegian psychomotor physiotherapy and living in Melbu, Northern Norway; working in a clinic with patients and with physiotherapists learning psychomotor physiotherapy; co-authored *Movements of Life* together with Tom Andersen and colleagues in 1997.

**Jaakko Seikkula (Finland):** Clinical psychologist and professor, Department of Psychology, University of Jyväskylä, Jyväskylä, Finland, and part-time at the Institute of Community Medicine, University of Tromsø, Tromsø, Norway .

**John Shotter (England):** Emeritus Professor of Communication, Department of Communication, University of New Hampshire, Durham, New Hampshire; associate of the Kensington Consultation Centre Foundation, London, England.

**Pål Talberg (Norway):** Educational Family Therapist, Child Guidance Clinic Tromsø, Norway; founding member of the June Seminars and the North Calotte Network.

**Madeleine Thörnlund (Sweden):** Sociologist with further education in systemic organizational theory and work; quality controller, The Centre for Habilitation and Technical Aids, Uppsala County Council, Uppsala, Sweden.

**Judit Wagner (Sweden):** Licensed psychotherapist and social worker; working with central issues in the reflecting process among the criminal justice system and the common health care system, Kalmar, Sweden

**Curt Westin (Sweden):** Psychologist, educator, and systemic family therapist; also working in the area of organizational theory and leadership; Assistant Director of Child and Adult Habilitation Services, The Centre for Habilitation and Technical Aids, Uppsala, Sweden.

**Manfred Wiesner (Germany):** Psychologist; working as chief psychologist in an inpatient clinic for child and adolescent psychiatry and psychotherapy in Wilhelmshaven; supervisor and trainer in reflecting practices and constructionist ideas.

**Roxana Zevallos (Peru):** Clinical psychologist and family therapist; Academic Director of Instituto Familiar Sistémico De Lima (IFASIL), Lima, Peru.

# PREFACE

The passion to continually be on the move to seek new understanding has been a characteristic of the field of family therapy and systemic thinking over the last forty years. Many professionals have moved around, more or less freely, in and out of this field. Some have made footprints that will last for a long time. One of these is Tom Andersen. From a position as Professor in Social Psychiatry at the University of Tromsø in Northern Norway, he has moved around the world participating with other professionals in their efforts to develop their work and seek wider horizons.

This book, this *Festschrift,* honours Tom Andersen and his enormous courageous, creative, and committed contributions to psychiatry and psychotherapy. Most importantly, it is a gift basket for the reader. The basket is filled with *inspirations*: a collection of articles and greetings that capture and exemplify the broad range of innovative ways in which therapists around the world have been inspired by Tom Andersen and his *reflecting conversations process*. It is filled with stories about the authors' daily work and the influence of their histories with Tom. Little-seen glimpses, outside Norway, give the reader a sense of Tom: ideas and practices do not emerge out of the blue but are closely connected to the person—the person's values, context, history, relationships, and so forth. We are privileged to edit this book and to have its authors join us in saying "thank you" to Tom for his unselfish generosity.

It is about the same distance from Oslo to Tromsø as from Oslo to Italy. When we (Per and colleagues) started the Family Therapy Education programme at Diakonhjemmet University College in Oslo in 1990, we asked Tom Andersen to come as a visiting professor and teach us. In the years since, and several times a year, we have continued to learn from and with him. Harry Goolishian used to say that the Gulf Stream started at his dock in Galveston and flowed all the way to Northern Norway, warming it and connecting the faraway Galveston and Tromsø groups. There were two main commonalities in this connection: first, our (Harry and Harlene) being uncomfortable with psychiatric practices and understandings of human beings that "patients" said—in their words and actions and with which we concurred—were not helpful; second, our longing to connect with others who were challenging and offering alternatives to the traditions of psychiatry and family therapy. Tom Andersen and his colleagues provided fellowship and conversations that were encouraging and through which new ideas would begin to form, take shape, and be clarified. Many of this book's contributors share this same experience with Tom: he comes from far away and inspires us.

We hope that those readers who know Tom Andersen will be reminded of the gatherings with Tom, both personally and with his texts. If this is your first meeting with Tom, you will also meet many of his colleagues and friends and gain a glimpse of how he has inspired us. Inspiration is not only something spiritual or intellectual; it is connected to the verb "to inspire", to draw one's breath. One of Tom's main sources of inspiration was Norwegian physiotherapist Aadel Bülow-Hansen, who worked with the body and the breath in a way that invited new understandings of family therapy: we experience "seeing" and "hearing" through the body.

The reflecting conversation process was formed when a team of therapists, within the therapy session, began to ask family members if they would like to listen to what the team members behind the mirror thought about as they were listening to the therapy conversation between the family members and the therapist. This began a process of dialogues about dialogues that enabled new conversations, giving time and space for speaking and listening to the unspoken, and giving family members the choice to respond and how to respond.

In the first section of the book, the authors' stories vividly portray the usefulness of reflecting processes and their multiple variations across cultures, contexts, and languages. These stories are followed by an accounting of seminars organized by Tom and his colleagues that brought together people interested in exploring and developing what is now referred to as dialogical or conversational practices. An interview with Tom is then followed by greetings that capture Tom's touching, unforgettable warmth and care and his steadfast, sometimes provocative, commitment to challenge many of our cultural, political, and ethical traditions.

We very much want to thank David Campbell and Karnac Books for saying, without any hesitation, yes to publishing this book. We also very much want to express our gratitude to Kerstin Hopstadius and Michaele Ramberg for editing and referencing and to Diakonhjemmet University College in Oslo, Norway, for their support and contributions to the project.

*Harlene Anderson* (Houston) & *Per Jensen* (Oslo)
November 2006

# INNOVATIONS

CHAPTER 1

# Practising "withness": a human art

*Lynn Hoffman*

## *The first rays*

I had been to the North of Norway on numerous occasions, mostly at the Summer Solstice, but Tom Andersen kept telling me that I must come in the "Darktime". So he invited me for the first day of spring, just as the sun was going to appear. Tom took me to his top-floor office at the University of Tromsø the morning of the conference, and out the window I saw the first rays. They appeared in the cleft of two snow-covered mountains, then faded away, followed by colours of pink, mauve, and gold that lit up the edges of landscape and sky.

From time to time as I have passed through the history of this field, I have been given the chance to see such first rays. And I have in some way known or guessed which newcomer approaches would establish themselves and persist. One is taking shape now, like a ship hull-up on the horizon and coming closer. Roger Lowe (2005), in a recent article, has referred to it as the "Conversational" or "Dialogical therapies". More interesting, perhaps, Lowe distinguishes between "Structured-Question" approaches, like Narrative (White, 1995) and Solution-Focused (de Shazer, 1994) work, and what he calls, following John Shotter (Shotter & Katz, 1998), a "Striking Moments" approach. By this description, we seem to have discovered a territory that relies on a relational version of static electricity for its effects rather than a technology that is imposed from outside. Using this new measure, the Collaborative perspective of Harry Goolishian and Harlene Anderson, and the Reflecting Process of Tom Andersen, are being joined by a new band of travelling players who have related, but different, songs to sing.

As part of this thinking, we have been introduced to a cornucopia of philosophical treasures based on the writings of Ludwig Wittgenstein and Mikhail Bakhtin. We have a new "in-house philosopher" in social thinker John Shotter (1993), who has described how these writers can help us understand what Bakhtin (1981) calls "dialogicality". We are beginning to have new terms for what we do, like Tom Andersen's idea of "Withness Practices". Finally, we have some unusual examples of these ideas embedded in the work of innovators such as Jaakko Seikkula and his colleagues in Finland (Seikkula & Olson, 2003; Seikkula et al., 1995), who have been developing an approach called "Open Dialogue". Finally, let me mention Chris Kinman (2001) in Vancouver, who has been experimenting with a Language of Gifts that is producing an entire system change. But being one of the historians of this field, I am interested in establishing a train of forebears for these new additions. So let me go back in time and start with the early genius who (for me) began it all: Gregory Bateson.

## *Bateson and "syllogisms in metaphor"*

Bateson's daughter Catherine tells us that, at the end of his life, when he and she were working on *Angels Fear* together (Bateson & Bateson, 1987), her father was excitedly focusing on what he was calling "syllogisms in metaphor". This focus, she explained, tied together his lifelong interest in the forms of sublingual communication that are common to religion, humour, playfulness, some forms of madness, animal communication, and art. Catherine saw his goal as putting together "the beginning of a Creatural grammar". Her father had used Jung's term, the "Creatura", to describe the world of the living, as opposed to the "Pleroma", meaning Newton's world of force and mass. The Pleroma has no mental process, no names, no classes. The Creatura, on the other hand, is founded on pattern and communicates through "as-if" language, using similitude and metaphor in a variety of embedded and embodied ways.

So what might that mean? In contrasting the truths of logic with the truths of metaphor, Bateson explains that classical logic describes causal word structures called syllogisms that are built on classification and follow the form, "if this is true, then that is true":—if Socrates is a man, and if all men die, then Socrates will die. But there is another word structure that Bateson describes that is built on likeness, the example for which is: "Grass dies, Men die, [therefore] Men are grass." Logicians disapprove of this kind of syllogism because it does not make sense (they call it "affirming the consequent"), but Bateson believed that this formula indicated the way the natural world communicated. He fires off this ringing salvo:

> The whole of animal behaviour, the whole of repetitive anatomy, and the whole of biological evolution—each of these vast realms is within itself linked together by syllogisms in grass—whether the logicians like it or not. . . . And it became evident that metaphor was not just pretty poetry, it was not either good or bad logic, but was in fact the logic on which the biological world had been built, the main characteristic and organizing glue of this world of mental process that I have been trying to sketch for you. . . . [Bateson & Bateson, pp. 26–30]

This statement thrilled me. It felt accurate, and it justified the enormous importance my community of relational therapists placed on sensory pathways and emotional gestures in the work we did. The preverbal, analogical vision of Bateson seemed especially pertinent to the project of psychotherapy, because it indicated that advice and expertise were not enough—you had to reach for connection at levels that lay beyond the scope of words. I felt that Bateson was saying that there is a hidden language that had to do with what Pascal called "reasons of the heart". Current researchers in neurology (Damasio, 1994) have pointed to a specific area of the brain—the amygdala, also called the "emotional brain"—saying that this is the brain's "smoke alarm", because this is where the intense memories are stored that warn us away from bad things and towards good ones. It makes sense to believe that messages directed towards this area have to use this ancient grammar of Nature or they will not be recognized. Of course, when Bateson talked about syllogisms in metaphor, he did not mean that we should literally use figures of speech, but, rather, that sensory and feeling-level channels do best in carrying messages of life importance, as the channels of reason and logic are untrustworthy.

We have also discovered that such messages can break through private walls. Current brain research tells us of the existence of "mirror neurons", little cells that fire off in us when we see another creature involved in an important action. In rhesus monkeys, reaching for food is a trigger; in experiments with humans, a range of signs, from deep emotion to graphic violence, can do it. The mirror cells in us fire off when we feel touched by someone else's feelings, and the process goes the other way. This is why an emphasis on the wider web is so important for a therapist. Not only are we required to understand the threads that link people together, but we also have to become one of the threads. My first supervisor, Harry Aponte, always maintained that there was within him a sort of gyroscope that he always had to be in touch with if he were to be true to the process. If you stay with modernist psychology, you will forever be trying to see your job as a matter of building roads, putting up bridges, and various other engineering projects. If you move to a postmodern psychology, you have to jump, like Alice, into the pool of tears with the other creatures. This position is a great equalizer and carries some dangers, but it is the only source of information with the power to transform.

## *My Three Pillars of Wisdom*

But let me move to what I call my Three Pillars of Wisdom, the three major anchors of the kind of work I and my community do. These are the practices that have signalled the shift from a modernist view that sees emotional problems as within-person phenomena like medical complaints, and the postmodern relational view that sees them as dialogic webs spun from the heart of the interchange itself.

The first pillar is the idea of "not knowing", brought into the field by Harry Goolishian and Harlene Anderson. I once asked Harlene if they took it from the writings of the French philosopher Gaston Bachelard (1964), who speaks of "non-knowing". He said this was not a form of ignorance, "but a difficult transcendence of knowledge". Harlene had not read Bachelard and gave me a much simpler reason. She and Harry began to use the phrase when their students would ask them questions about the family, such as what they thought the family's problem "really" was. They would always say they "didn't know", saying that students should ask the family members themselves, as their hypotheses and understandings were more important and relevant than those of the therapists. In this rather off-the-cuff way, the principle of "not knowing" evolved—unforunately, to the scorn and derision of much of the field. But this simple shift in terms made a difference in basic stance that was powerful, and liberated many therapists like myself from the awful position of "knowing it all".

My second pillar is the practice called the "reflecting team", contributed by Tom Andersen (1987) and his colleagues in Tromsø, Norway. This format challenged many of the methods sacred to early family therapists. It undermined the one-way screen and other devices that walled the family off from the professionals dealing with them. Asking a family to comment on the opinions of the professionals was even more unheard of. Before he died, Goolishian suggested to Andersen that he broaden "reflecting team" to "reflecting process", feeling that to link this idea to a specific format was to limit it.

My third pillar is "witnessing", a practice that leapt out at me when I first became involved in the reflecting team. There is some internal history of the field to report here. Soon after Tom Andersen went public with his reflecting format, Michael White adopted it too. In line with his preference for anthropological rather than psychological language, White (1995) took up anthropologist Barbara Meyerhoff's term "definitional ceremony" to describe it. He saw that adding an audience to his kind of inspirational interview strongly reinforced people's experience of a more valuable identity. Experimenting with this idea led him to create what he called an Outsider Witness Registry, where persons he had already worked with could be invited back to help others in similar situations.

And he saw witnessing as one method of linking up individual transformation with community action. However, I had a Harry Goolishian moment here. As with the reflecting team, I felt we needed a term that didn't belong to any one person or school. "Witnessing process" was a suitably large tent under which most of us could fit, regardless of our therapeutic allegiances. That said, let me go on to some of the novel ideas and language games that are once again enlivening our field.

### *John Shotter and embodied knowing*

A primary source of these first rays that I am talking about comes from John Shotter (1993), an innovative social thinker whose writings on the nature of dialogical communication have become increasingly relevant to the relational therapies as I am describing them. Shotter has been creating a little intellectual whirlpool around the ideas of two philosophers in particular—Mikhail Bakhtin and Ludwig Wittgenstein—and, with colleague Arlene Katz, applying them to clinical practice. In addition, he and Tom Andersen have been sharing ideas and giving workshops together, and this has been a happy development.

For my part, I felt that Shotter was our in-house philosopher. He was leading us away from the belief that we could change social reality by mainly linguistic means. In its place was a picture of communication as a more bustling, jostling enterprise. Shotter (2005) speaks of "embodied knowing" versus "language-based knowing" and describes it as "the sense that addresses itself to feelings of 'standing', of 'insiderness or outsiderness' in any social group". He says it is not a skill or a theoretical knowing, but has to do with the anticipations we bring to a conversation, and the influence these impressions have on us and others.

This realization seems to have led Shotter (2005) to move away from social constructionism, which was the theory the postmodern thinkers among us had given most space to. Shotter formerly very strong on this theory began to feel that it was lacking in any description of the constraints inherent in social exchange. In his view, communication is like a social weather. It fills our sails, becalms, or sometimes wrecks us. Sensing what is called for in a particular context, responding correctly to gestures like an extended hand, feeling a black cloud settling over a discussion, are all responses to a weather system that can impact on us in concrete and material ways. The truth is that the famous "linguistic turn" of postmodernism implies greater flexibility in what is or is not possible than old-fashioned modernism allows. This is the reason many people have accused it of being relativistic, if not morally delinquent. But there are particular reasons why therapists can feel liberated by giving it up. The move to a sublingual vocabulary, like pills that melt under the tongue, often brings us to the heart of the matters that therapy tries to address.

Shotter points out that people with emotional problems do a lot of gesture talk, and often the problem itself is gesture talk. For this reason, he is very keen on Wittgenstein's appreciation of this more hidden realm. He quotes Wittgenstein as saying: "The origin and primitive form of the language game is a reaction; only from this can more complicated forms develop." Wittgenstein explains that by primitive, he means that "this sort of behavior is *prelinguistic:* that a language game is based *on it,* that it is the prototype of a way of thinking and not the result of thought". In this respect, Wittgenstein's intimations were very similar to those of Bateson.

Shotter also feels that the move towards embodied knowing also takes us away from the rationalism of the Western tradition. Where the Enlightenment valued the objective eye of the observer, dialogical reality is based on the shared subjectivity of the participants. Instead of a "representational" understanding, Shotter offers a "relational" one. Instead of seeking to be a master and possessor of nature, as Descartes favoured, Shotter wants us to respect its "shaped and vectored" qualities. He further observes that in matters that concern the world of the living, many important things occur in *meetings*. All the more reason that we should scrutinize the kind of talking that goes on in them. And since not all meetings make the special kind of difference psychotherapists are looking for, it behoves us to examine what is the special nature of those that do.

One of Shotter's biggest contributions from this point of view has been to translate the lofty abstractions that Bakhtin and his colleagues have given us into more ordinary terms. I like particularly his turning the concepts of "Dialogical" vs. "Monological" thinking into "Withness" vs. "Aboutness" thinking. Shotter (2004) says: "'Withness Thinking' is a dynamic form of reflective interaction that involves coming into contact with another's living being, with their utterances, with their bodily expressions, with their words, their works." In describing Monological or "Aboutness Thinking", he goes along with Bakhtin who says that "monologue is finalized and deaf to the other's response, does not expect it, and does not acknowledge it in any decisive force".

The beauty of the notion of "dialogicality" or "withness" is that it addresses the criss-cross of merging and overlapping voices, and their silences, too, in normal, ordinary exchange. Instead of the "expert" individual being assigned the most influence in this activity, as usually happens in psychotherapy, a "withness" conversation allows voices to emerge that have often been stifled or withheld. Attempts to manage meaning may be the norm in our societies, and many psychotherapy models have been built on such attempts, but in these circumstances "withness" does not automatically occur. In fact, there are some who say it is more apt *not* to occur. In thinking back on an interview, the best outcome is that people would feel the conversation itself was the author of what was said.

### *Tom Andersen and "withness" practices*

These ideas fed into my own belief that our theory had to take the mysterious world of the senses more into account. I had been using the idea of "underground rivers" to depict the channels that flow between people when they seem to be connecting. I also looked back at my own journey, from an emphasis on sight in "Constructing Realities: An Art of Lenses" (1990), to an emphasis on hearing in *Exchanging Voices* (1993), to the current move towards touch and feeling. Andersen, of course, had always been persuaded of this emphasis and has always placed the body at the centre of his work. As a result, he is attentive to breathing; to posture; to tone of voice; as well as to his own inner and outer voices and what is going on within himself. He says:

> The listener (the therapist) who follows the talker (the client) not only hearing the words but also seeing how the words are

> uttered, will notice that every word is part of the moving of the body. Spoken words and bodily activity come together in a unity and cannot be separated ... the listener who sees as much as he or she hears will notice that the various spoken words "touch" the speaker differently. ... Some words touch the speaker in such a way that the listener can see him or her moved. [Andersen, 1996, p. 121]

In another article, Andersen (2005) follows the action of an interview he did in Finland step by step. He first describes his talk with the host team, who tell him about a mother with two daughters, one of whom, age 19, was "hearing voices".

> The team said they were worried because so many other persons in that family had been hospitalized for psychosis. Andersen said he could always meet with the team alone, if that was what they wanted to consult him about, but asked if it would not be better to find out from the mother and daughter directly what their own concerns might be. The team agreed.
>
> After noting his exchange with the translator about her preferred method of working, Andersen turned to the body language of the mother and daughter as they came into the room. The mother seemed very preoccupied, the daughter withdrawn. After hearing about various concerns from the team—the daughter's refusal to go to school, the history of family members' hospitalizations for psychosis, the mother's divorce from the father ten years before—Andersen asked the mother if she had any other children. She said yes, from a former husband, whose parents raised this daughter and kept her from her mother. The daughter had become a street person, taking drugs, but now she had written to her mother, asking to come and live with her. Andersen asked the mother if she thought the daughter had missed her, and was told yes. Did she in turn miss her? Yes. The sister nodded yes too.
>
> Andersen then said, "It sounds like your daughter is lonely." When the mother confirmed this, he asked her if she, too, were lonely. At this point she said, "I have so much pain." Andersen asked where in her body was the pain: "In the heart and in the thoughts." "If the pain found a voice, what would it say?" "It

would scream." "With words or without words?" The mother only looked at him. Andersen asked, "Who would you like to receive your scream?" She said, "God." "How should God respond to your scream?" She said she hoped God could take care of her three daughters. A long pause followed, and a long silence. The audience seemed very moved, as was Andersen himself.

In the next part of the interview, Andersen found out that this mother had no adults in her life that she could talk to; in fact, she had no one else but her daughters. She had been close to her father's parents, but they were both dead. If they had been here, might they have helped her? Might she have been able to scream to them instead of God? She began to weep, saying yes. Andersen asked, "If your grandmother had been here, what would she have said?" The mother answered: "Little girl, you have been so good to your daughters." Andersen: "What would you say back?" "Grandmother, I love you so much." "And what would Grandmother then do?" "She would put her arms around me and I could smell her. She smells so good." Many people in the audience were now openly weeping. Andersen asked the daughter what her thoughts were. She said she knew her mother was in pain, but did not know much about her grandparents. She said that she would rather hear about the pain than not hear anything.

Andersen closed the interview with a suggestion that the mother take her two daughters to the grandparents' graves and talk to the girls about them. Andersen then asked the team and the audience to share their thoughts with him, while the mother and daughter listened. The team said they had been very moved by the mother's feelings for her daughters. Andersen asked if there was a grandmother's voice in the audience, and found one; then he asked for a grandfather's voice. These persons said that they had also been moved, and the grandmother said how important it was for a granddaughter to have a grandmother and for a mother to have a mother. Mother and daughter left the meeting "with firm handshakes and firm looks", and Andersen was told by a team member three months later that the daughter had no more fears or voices and was going to school in the autumn.

Andersen describes his work as a communal enterprise rather than an individual-oriented one (Hoffman, 2005), and he currently speaks of networks talking to networks. He also makes this very interesting point about language:

> Language is here defined as all expressions, which are regarded to be of great significance in the above-mentioned communal perspective. They are of many kinds, f.i. to talk, write, paint, dance, sing, point, cry, laugh, scream, hit, etc., are all bodily activities. When these expressions, which are bodily, take place in the presence of others, language becomes a social activity. Our expressions are social offerings for participating in the bonds of others. [Andersen, 2006]

This is the basis for what Anderson calls, following Shotter (2004, "withness practices". These practices operate on a felt-sense level, rather than following codified rules for change. And here we go back to Lowe's distinction between approaches that use "structured questions" as an operational method, and the more serendipitous and collaborative approaches that I have talked about here

In his article, Lowe also refers to the appearance of a radical and extremely effective approach to psychosis called Open Dialogue that has been pioneered by a number of research teams in Finland (Seikkula et al., 1995). News of Open Dialogue, or Dialogical Network Therapy, the term Seikkula uses, is spreading widely (Hoffman, 2005; Seikkula & Arnkil, 2006; Seikkula & Olson, 2004), but I shall not speak of it here because Seikkula himself addresses this innovation later in the book. I shall, however, mention the fact that in practice this development owes an enormous debt to Tom Andersen's reflecting process and, seen on a larger scale, has links to Andersen's creation of a "Northern Network" (Andersen, 2005)—a project that for the past two decades has been introducing "open reflecting talks", as Andersen calls them, to acute psychosis teams in hospitals all across the rim of Northern Europe.

To get back to the question of naming this new, incoming style while still keeping in touch with its ancestors, the term "conversational", or, alternatively, "conversational networks", sounds spacious enough to fit. It suggests a quality of spontaneity together with an emphasis on the social field. I am aware that whenever there is a Big New Thing in our field, everybody seems to rush to that side of the boat where it is, as if it is the only event we should pay attention to. I prefer to hold on to this dialogical community idea until it, in turn, no longer holds up. At the same time, the hope is to keep those terms that describe ways of working like "collaborative" or "reflective" or "dialogical" because they have an integrity in themselves.

Whatever we call this new big tent, it seems obvious to me that we have gone beyond social constructionism's "linguistic system" idea with its emphasis on the malleability of meaning. Instead, we are looking for the aforesaid "withness practices". These entail a special kind of exchange. Being "without rank", they bypass the hierarchy implicit in most social interaction. They do not lead to some predetermined goal or depend on a prearranged format. If a sense of having "got there" occurs, it must come spontaneously, much as Wittgenstein suggests when he says that the aim of philosophy is to help us know "how to go on". Above all, they operate on a feeling level, which is the field where goods are struggled for and contests go on, and where a sense of justice is a constant living thing.

## *The Gee's Bend quilts*

Let me end with the story of the Gee's Bend quilts, made from scraps of old clothes by the African-American country women of Gee's Bend, Alabama, and now hailed as triumphant examples of unexpected folk-art (see Conan, 2003). The family therapy field is also made of scraps and patches. Just as the Gee's Bend quilters used worn-out pieces of material, with their accumulations of history, to create bed quilts, so our movement is made up of pieces of practice from many stages: structural, strategic, interactional, solution-focused, possibility-oriented, systemic, narrative, reflecting, collaborative, to name just a few. Now comes a new term, dialogical, or as I prefer, conversational. This title suggests that elusive quality called "withness" and is represented by those special kinds of conversation or "language games" that give us our bearings in the matter of the art of social bonds. There is no end point towards which this movement of ours is trending. It is only a folk quilt, and its only purpose is to keep us warm at night. However, much of this warmth comes from the fact that it is made of various patches of family therapy's history, memories, and lore.

CHAPTER 2

# "Reflecting talk", "inner talk", and "outer talk": Tom Andersen's way of being

*John Shotter & Arlene Katz*

> "The listener (the therapist) who follows the talker (the client), not only hearing the words but also seeing how the words are uttered, will notice that every word is part of the moving of the body. Spoken words and bodily activity come together in a unity and cannot be separated."
>
> Tom Andersen (1996, pp. 120–121)

> "The listener who sees as much as he or she hears will notice that various spoken words 'touch' the speaker differently. The speaker is touched by the words as they reach his or her own ears. Some words touch the speaker in such a way that the listener can see him or her being moved."
>
> Tom Andersen (1996, p. 121)

> "Sometimes a sentence can be understood only if it is read at the *right tempo*."
>
> Ludwig Wittgenstein (1980, p. 57)

A paper dedicated on his 70th birthday to Tom Andersen, who first pioneered the idea of responsive "reflecting talk" in psychotherapy in March 1985, twenty-one years ago.

We feel honoured to have been asked by Per Jensen and Harlene Anderson to contribute to this Festschrift for Tom Andersen on his 70th birthday. Tom's work has not only been extremely influential out in the world of psychotherapy in general, but also on and in our individual lives. Over the past twelve years or so, as we have struggled to understand and to articulate in more explicit detail the living micro-dynamics of therapeutic processes, it is Tom's way of talking and listening—his very way of being with the people he cares for in a therapeutic setting—that has been *there* for us as a working exemplar of what seem to us to be at least some of the crucial features of a therapeutic way of being with those in need of such care.

## *The centrality of bodily events in Tom Andersen's practice*

Tom is most well known, of course, for his introduction of the "reflecting team" into psychotherapy (Andersen, 1992), and we will have quite a lot to say about the "reflecting process" and "reflecting talk" below. But crucial and distinctive to Tom's way of being with his clients is his sensitivity to what we will call the "livingness" of things, to living, bodily events, both his own and those of his clients. For him, the important events of life do not simply occur inside the person's head, in his or her mind, but in the person's whole body, his or her whole being. "When life comes to me", he says,

> it touches my skin, my eyes, my ears, the bulbs of my tongue, the nostrils of my nose. As I am open and sensitive to what I see, hear, feel, taste, and smell I can also notice "answers" to those touches from myself, as my body, "from inside," lets me know in various ways how it thinks about what the outside touches; what should be concentrated on and what not. This state of being open and sensitive to the touches from the "outside life" and at the same time being open and sensitive to the answers from the "inside life" is what I prefer to call "intuition." At this point in time my intuition seems to be what I rely on the most. In re-walking my professional tracks, my intuition tells me that I shall take part first, and then sit down and think

> about the taking part; not sit down and think first and thereafter take part. As I am sure that my thinking is with me as I take part, I have felt comfortable following what my intuition has suggested to me. [Andersen, 1992, p. 55]

In saying this, as we shall make it clearer in a moment, Tom is emphasizing his attention to events that are not easily observable, as they occur not so much in space as in time; they as are invisibly present, so to speak, in the unfolding temporal contours of people's living bodily expressions. And it is this concern with life and the livingness of things that we wish to emphasize in our celebration here of Tom's work.

Tom attributes the beginning of his emphasis on bodily events to his meeting with physiotherapist Gudrun Øvreberg, who introduced him to her teacher Aadel Bülow-Hansen. About Bülow-Hansen, Tom writes that she had

> noticed that patients who are tense tend to flex their bodies towards a "creeping together" position. As they do so they tend to restrict their breathing. In order to be helpful to them, Bülow-Hansen stimulated them to stretch out and "open up" their bodies. One way to do so was by inducing pain in the patient. She had noticed that if a muscle, for example, on the back side of the calf, is held with a painful grip, the pain will stimulate the person to stretch the body. When the body stretches, deeper inhalation is stimulated. . . . [But next] when the air is exhaled, some tension in the body disappears. [Andersen, 1992, pp. 58–59]

And sometimes when this happened, when after an extra strong inhalation an extra strong relaxation was experienced, Bülow-Hansen's clients would respond emotionally—for a body-memory of a long-forgotten, much happier, more relaxed time in their lives would return.

As Tom saw it, what Bülow-Hansen was doing on these occasions "was a variation on Gregory Bateson's famous sentence, 'the elementary unit of information—is a difference that makes a difference' (Bateson, 1972, p. 453)". She was making a sufficiently unusual difference in the bodily experience of her patients for them to notice a change in their inner experience of their feeling of themselves. Indeed, we might go so far as to suggest that we can describe our dialogically structured exchanges with each other, metaphorically, as "a breathing exercise between people"; as exhalation followed by inhalation; "let go" and "let come"; now listening, now talking (Andersen, personal communication 1987).

Tom carried this in–out, tension–relaxation over into his psychotherapeutic relations with his clients/patients. "Those who do not know what to do [in their lives]", he says,

> need something different (unusual), but this something must not be too different (unusual). . . . How can we know when our contributions are too unusual? The answer is found by noticing the client's way of participating in the conversation. . . . We are thereby challenged to be acquainted with and sensitive to those particular signs that the various individuals send us. We must rely on our intuition in noticing those signs. Andersen, 1992, p. 59]

We have tried in this collection of brief remarks from a number of Tom's past articles to outline what we see as one of the major and distinctive aspects of Tom Andersen's way of being with his client's—his focus on and responsiveness to people's spontaneously occurring bodily reactions to events. But not just the reactions of his clients, but to his own as well: "Sometimes", he says, "these movements are small, sometimes big. The listener might see a shift in the face, a change in the eyes, a moving on the chair, a cough. The words that prompt these movements are the ones that attract my interest" (Andersen, 1996, p. 121). And as we noted above, sometimes we can notice that "various spoken words 'touch' the speaker differently . . . some words touch the speaker in such a way that the listener can see him or her being moved" (Andersen, 1996, p. 121).

It is in the context of these remarks that we would like to offer our contribution to his work. We want to show how with a certain style of talk—what we can call "responsive reflective talk", the sensitive, responsive responding to people's utterances, to their bodily voicing of words in the course of their speaking them, rather than waiting to hear what they have to say and then responding to what we take their meaning to be—we can, we feel, create a certain "intimate" style of talk, a way of talking "without rank", as Bakhtin (1986, p. 97) terms it. In such a style of talk, not only do people become more intimate with each other, more familiar with each other, they also become more able to anticipate how the others will react (respond) to them, more sure of a response in which they feel "recognized" as who they are—in short, just as they come to trust the speaker's responsive talk (and listening), so they also come to trust their own talk in the same way (and that of others around them also, if present). They come to feel "safe" with each other in their talk: "Intimate speech is imbued with a deep confidence in the addressee, in his sympathy, in the sensitivity and goodwill of his responsive understanding. In this atmosphere of profound trust, the speaker reveals his internal depths" (Bakhtin, 1986, p. 97)—this, we feel, is the atmosphere Tom is able to engender in his responsive reflective talk.

Thus, central in what we are emphasizing is not the logical meaning of a person's speech, its content, what is represented in a pattern (a record or transcript) of already spoken words, but something that occurs in a person's words in their speaking, as the person responsively "shapes" the utterance of his or her words with respect to his or her own intentions: "The word in language", says Bakhtin, "is half-someone else's. It becomes 'one's own' only when the speaker populates it with his [or her] own intention, his [or her] own accent, when he [or she] appropriates the word, adapting it to his [or her] own semantic and expressive intention" (1981, p. 293). It is in the invisible, temporal shape of the word, its intonation, that, we feel, Tom comes to express his deep confidence in and his sympathy with his addressee and comes to create that atmosphere of profound trust in which a speaker feels enabled to reveal his or her internal depths.

## *Denys and his bodily expressed distress and disquiet*

The fragments of dialogue we recount below occurred between one of us [AMK] and Denys, a young Englishman, 22 years of age, who had come to Boston from England to pursue his studies in music. For quite a while, a year and a half or so, he had been a victim of sudden uncontrollable movements and of urges to strike himself with his fist on his chest. The movements began, in his words, " . . . during a meditation retreat—suddenly, out of the blue". They were a source of alarm to both him and his meditation teacher, as well as to others present at the retreat. Seeking to "understand" or to "know" what was going on, he sought, in his words, an "explanation".

As he describes below, this initial experience of not knowing what was happening to him was "alarming". Those from whom he first sought help (i.e., "explanations")—a past-lives regression specialist, a Jungian analyst, and a psychic—had inadvertently created a "community of alarm" (to echo Harry Goolishian), which had further exacerbated his disquiet. To Denys, the words they spoke "were all dark, talk of death . . .". He was finally referred to AMK, and in our meetings I began to pursue a much more dialogical, relational way of talking with him.

The interview reported here took place in Cambridge, Massachusetts, two months after his last therapy session. It was an interview in a series, some of which were written up in the "Afterwords" chapter in Tom Andersen's (1991) book, *The Reflecting Team*. Its character manifests a sensibility engendered by Tom's introduction of the reflecting team and the style of "responsive reflecting talk" to which it gave rise. But in this variation of reflecting talk, the therapist goes back to learn from and with a client of his or her experience, before, during, and after therapy. In other words, it is a form of re-search that, perhaps, allows both client and therapist to move on, yet further by further reflecting on crucial aspects of their experiences in relevant therapy meetings (Katz, 1991, p. 102).

It is important to note that although what follows below is my description, my written expression of Denys' expressions, it is important that I include myself, my own experiences in it—for example, my inner dialogue (Tom Andersen, personal communication). In the meeting, Denys reflected back on what initially had brought him in, recalling his initial bodily sense of alarm. Just prior to the exchange reported below, following some of Denys' comments about him still feeling to an extent disturbed, I had wondered, "You'd said that the movements stopped?" And Denys replied, "Yeah". When I asked whether they had stopped completely, he replied, "Yeah . . . they had died away", but originally, he had been "completely out of control". Indeed, after having spoken to "a lot of people" and got "a lot of different opinions", he came to have a "lot of weird images in my head". But, by contrast with his meetings with previous therapist, he had experienced our meetings differently.

> Denys: I guess, when I came here, it was different because we just talked, you know, [*pause*] we had . . . we could like bite off what we could chew or something, you know. And so we just focused, like, on my . . . on my family and things like that mostly, which was, you know, which was really helpful, and sort of stabilizing in a way, you know. And so gradually the movements just died, died away.
>
> AMK: Do you have any ideas what got the movements to die away?

At this point, there was a long pause. I was struck by it. We could perhaps call it a "space of reflection", almost a sigh, a space, a moment, that seemed to draw him in, or back into a feeling or trying to re-feel back into what had got the movements to die away. In so doing, a space was created between us that also drew me in—a space of responsive pause, a space that "called" on me to pause, to respectfully wait for/with him. When he began to smile again, I felt he was ready to go on:

> D: [*smiles, long pause*] . . . I'm not sure, but maybe . . . I mean, this is just a thought, maybe it was something that was trying to draw my attention to certain things like my relationships with my family. And that once I started paying attention, although, like, there's a lot more work but a lot's been done, you know, that maybe . . . that was, um, you know, that it was kind of like a message, although . . . I don't know, to tell you the truth, and I'm not sure how important it is to know as well, I mean . . .

Clearly, his search to "know" had met with explanations that did not fit, that had not helped. Indeed, they had, in his words, increased his sense of alarm, increasing his "pressure to know". But "when I came here", he said, reflecting back, "we just talked". But how was the "just talking" with me, AMK, different from the talking that had occurred elsewhere?

There is, we want to suggest, something very special about the nature of Denys's talk in this "Afterwords"-style interview. But we also want to suggest that this arose out of the special way of listening—influenced by Tom Andersen's spontaneously responsive way of listening described above—employed by AMK in this interview: It is a way of listening that not so much "slows down" the process of communication, as leads it to "dwell on" or to "go into" the experiential detail of what is being voiced. And Denys is able to "get into" his experience then and now sufficiently to make a comparison:

> AMK: It sounds like there was one kind of "not knowing" that was alarming, like at the beginning it was alarming.
>
> D: Yeah. That was alarming, yeah, and now it's [*shrugs, smiles*], it was, it was just one of those things. And now it's, I guess, because now I don't feel this tension [*gestures to heart, twisting*], you know, so much, y'know—like then I was under a real pressure to know—it was like sitting in a pressure cooker, and I had to know what was . . . what was going on. And everyone was talking about, like, execution and all this, and, like, it was heavy and stuff.

What Denys, looking back, had experienced as "alarming movements" are now seen as a way of "drawing his attention to certain things". In the same way, AMK had allowed, and now allows, Denys' words and expressions to draw her attention, to guide her responsive listening. But more than this: besides guiding her responsive listening, she was also responsive in her speaking *as a result of her responsive listening*. In other words, she is listening *dialogically* rather than *monologically*—that is, rather that listening in wait for an opportunity to insert an already theoretically predetermined intervention, an interpretation, or an explanation, she is listening in order to sense the unfolding direction of Denys's thoughts, and speaking in such a way as to relate her talk to his.

In this, I [AMK] am responding to an intrinsic aspect of everyone's living, everyday speech. As Bakhtin outlines it:

> The word in living conversation is directly, blatantly, oriented towards a future answer-word; it provokes an answer, anticipates it and structures itself in the answer's direction. Forming

> itself in an atmosphere of the already spoken, the word is at the same time determined by that *which has not yet been said but which is needed and in fact anticipated by the answering word*. Such is the situation of any living dialogue. [1981, p. 280, emphasis added]

Thus, following Bakhtin (1981, 1986), we can call this kind of understanding—which is, in fact, a kind of action guiding—anticipatory understanding, a *relationally responsive* form of understanding. For, from within it, we find ourselves spontaneously responding to another's expressions in anticipation of what we or they might do or say next.

As such, it contrasts with the *representational-referential* form of understanding that is much more well known to us in our more conscious reflections as intellectual and academic individuals. Understanding representational-referential talk is thought of, usually, as a matter of "getting the picture", of speakers as using talk to transmit a mental representation hidden inside their heads into a listener's head. And sometimes we do indeed talk with this aim in mind. But not in fact very often, for it is a form of talk that leaves us asking, "So what? I get the picture, but what does it mean for my action?" Most of our everyday talk works, in fact, in Bakhtin's terms: questions call for answers, greetings for a return greeting, a request calls for a compliance with it, and so on. Indeed, it is precisely that which has not yet been said, but which is, in fact, anticipated as a response to what has been said, that can, if one is sensitive in one's responsive listening to such an anticipation, guide us in the moment in making an appropriate response to it.

Thus here, with Denys, instead of responding back to him with answers in my own terms, I [AMK] sought to pause, to dwell on, and to reflect back to him his own words and movements. This allowed both him and me the time and the space to respond to his own sense of the "disquiet" he felt—and to some extent (but now in a non-panic provoking way) still feels—and to articulate its nature further. It was as if, in effect, the situation between us "called" him to now reflect in such a way as to draw yet more meaning from his experiences in, and in relation to, his therapy sessions with me.

A comment from Tom, on the importance of speed, rhythm, and pauses in talk, is very apposite here:

> I often notice that the person who is given the opportunity to talk undisturbed quite often stops and starts over again, as if the first attempt was not good enough. The client searches for the best way to express him/herself; the best words to tell what he/she wants to tell, the best rhythm, the best tempo, and so on. The expressions that come (of which the words are a part) and the simultaneous activity (the way the words are expressed) have attracted my interest. Therefore, it has been natural to discuss not only the utterances themselves but also the way they are uttered. [Andersen, 1996, p. 24]

Why is being sensitive to the rhythm, tempo, pacing, and pausing in other people's talk so important in the way we respond to it?

Above, we noted that it is in the invisible, temporal shape of the word, its intonation, that, we feel, Tom helps to create that atmosphere of profound trust in which a speaker feels enabled to reveal his or her internal depths. But here we must add that in a *relationally responsive* form of understanding, more than a person responding cognitively—that is, by getting a general thought or idea "in their mind"—they are responsively "moved to action" in an emotional, moral, feelingful way by the *particularities* expressed in a person's *intoning* of his or her words. And as Mishka Lysack (2004) has pointed out, Bakhtin's (1984) discussion of how one person's words can *penetrate* another's is of crucial importance here, for the "penetrative" word is "capable of actively and confidently interfering in the interior dialogue of the other person, helping that person to find his own voice" (p. 242). Thus, to hear one's own destructive, isolating, and condemnatory words reflected back to one in a caring, relational tone can, in itself, be transforming.

## *Moments of togetherness in reflecting talk*

Above, then, we have emphasized the power of talk, of talk*ing*, to make differences. But on occasions, *moments of common reference* (Shotter, 1993) are needed, moments in which two or more people, with regard both to each other *and* to their common situation, "know from each other's 'attunements', as I shall call them, that they are each sensing it in the same way" (Shotter, 1993, p. 146). Or to put it in other words, in responsively listening to another's words, there are moments when we sense ourselves as being "moved" by them in the same way as the speaker him/herself is being moved—just as when shaking another person's hand or dancing with the person we can sense him or her as being "in tune" with us or not. These moments of "being in tune", these moments of "moving together", we suggest, are crucial to our coming to sense that not only do our words have a relevance for them, but to what that relevance is.

Hence, I begin the section of the interview I want to highlight here by reflecting to Denys: "It sounds like there was one kind of 'not knowing' that was alarming, like at the beginning it was alarming."

AMK: So, I'm sort of struck by now, when you say, "I don't know, it has a very different feel to it".

D: Yeah, um [*pause*] Well, one thing is that it's over, you know, so it doesn't really matter. And the other thing is that, um . . . [*As he gets very quiet, there is a different sense as he says, "it doesn't seem so important to know now", and as I pause, waiting for him, he continues*] I guess I don't know, somehow it doesn't seem so important to know now.

AMK: Uh-huh

D: I mean, I would like to know, but it's not, like, a burning question, y'know. It's not like arresting my life, kind of like it was before. I mean, I was managing: I was getting up every day, I was doing things and stuff but it was really, like, y'know [*gestures*], choking, so it was hard to do things. And maybe that's something changed in me, that I don't have to—like there's so many mysteries—just—I mean, life is a big . . . [*smiles*] . . . who's to know anything. I don't know, y'know.

AMK: So, mystery somehow has a very different meaning than the panic, the alarm of the first "not knowing".

D: Yeah, right. It's like, yeah, it's kind of [*pause*], you don't have to feel threatened by a mystery, by a mystery, you know. Like before, maybe, before I did feel threatened. It was like a big—I actually imagined, sitting, I remember sitting in my

> bed, just sensing this sort of darkness or something, but . . . there was something there, y'know, like a big something and I couldn't . . . and I was really trying to see it and at the same time I was almost petrified of it, you know, really frightened, just—I sensed this presence. But, um, now I don't really [*gestures to throat as he previously did when describing choking*] . . . I sense a lot of [*gestures movements in middle, up to heart*] kind of depth or something in, um,—a lot of stuff in me [*continues gesture*]. But somehow it's not so threatening or something. And I also think that in my case, and I know this isn't true for everyone, but in my case there's some sort of pressure valve or something, I think, that doesn't allow me to go over the top or something . . . although it can give me a rough time, a rough ride at times. And that's how I feel about my sort of own person.

First, let us note in this section, after Denys says that his alarm is now "just one of those things", I reflect out loud to him: "So, I'm sort of struck by now, when you say, 'I don't know, it has a very different feel to it'." And in the course of the exchange, I also reflect to myself, in my own "inner dialogues" (in the parts of the transcript in italics), on the sense of his bodily gestures and expressions—although, as Tom Andersen makes clear, I never draw Denys's own attention to them.

We draw attention to this initial reflection of AMK's above as we want to ask: What does it mean to be "struck" in this way? What is going on when one is being attentive, being responsive to another's breathing, pauses, and rhythms of speech? What is happening when one is, so to speak, groping around within one's own inner dialogues to sense and to ponder what words are also "in" the words a client is currently forming?

I [AMK], listening to Denys, was especially struck or moved by his involvement with the words "alarm" and "mystery". One is not only "called" or "moved" by another's words;. one can also be "arrested", and such moments can also be "resting moments", moments in which one can gain a transitory understanding of "where" one has got to, thus to gain a sense of where one might possibly go next in the conversation. Without these moments of togetherness, one's attempt to make a difference would lack a fulcrum, a resting point, a moment in common with another in relation to which to act. Thus, one cannot underestimate the importance of "the pause", which allows the other fully to express him/herself. We may be moved, but in being moved, rather than moving on immediately without answering words, we must sometimes choose to dwell on the words the person offers. Intimate listening is closely connected with this capacity to pause.

AMK's reflections above are uttered in response to Denys saying that, what had previously been "tension", "pressure", and "heavy", and had (as he displayed in a gesture) been *twisting his heart*, had become now (in an expression uttered while shrugging and smiling) "just one of those things"! AMK's response draws his attention back to what he had just said—about the change being a change of inner feeling—and invites him to go into and to explore this feeling further. In doing so, Denys begins to bring out into the open, to give witnessable expression to, his own initial, and now changed, relation to his own "inner" movements—the movements, one could say, he had found then, and still finds now, as a kind of unwelcome otherness spontaneously occurring within him. In response to it, he embarks on an extremely *poetic* but *struggling* or *groping* account of his feelings and of the changes that have occurred in them.

As we can see, his talk is full of pauses, shifts of rhythm, variations of expression, as well as other looks and gestures. While difficult to articulate in any definite terms—just as the motions of a dance are similarly difficult to describe in a definitive notation—we want to suggest that it is precisely a shared responsiveness to shared events that can give rise to the possibility of giving such events a shared significance. This is expressed in Denys's groping towards a shared linguistic formulation, along with all his other gestures. But it also speaks to what is also invisibly present in the visible, what is hearable but not actually said in what is said. Indeed, it is in such a way that what is better left unsaid is nonetheless communicated—we gain an intimate contact with the inner movements of another's living experience.

What is special, then, in the unfolding temporal contours of a person's speech and their other bodily expressions, is that everyone who is involved in them and is responsive to them—speaker and listeners alike—can "move" in responsive unison with their unfolding. So, although each word in its use may create, semantically, a difference and works progressively to specify a particular region in a shared conversational space, each utterance in the temporal contours of its bodily expression works to express a speaker's living relation to his or her circumstances and thus can also unite everyone in enabling them to orient or to relate themselves towards those circumstances in the same way.

It is only too easy, given its invisibility, to ignore the relational work done within this essentially "musical" dimension of our speech communication. But what is special about a hearable unfolding time-order of events, as we have already intimated, is that all involved—both the utterer and his or her addressees—can all be "moved" by the unfolding movement of the expression in *the same way*. A shared moment of common reference becomes available, against the background of which differences that makes a difference can be shared with others as the *same* differences. What is invisible to the fixed eye alone, the ear (and the embodied eye in its movements) can directly sense.

## *Conclusions*

This, of necessity, has to be a brief chapter (we were severely restricted in our word length by the editors wishing to allow for many other contributors). Thus, of the many dimensions of Tom Andersen's work, we have chosen to emphasize just one of them—his focus on spontaneously occurring bodily activity as manifested in the special intonation of words, in pauses, in the timing and rhythms in and of people's speech—and to explore what this focus means for him in his practice.

We have chosen to emphasize this aspect of his work as we feel that there is something very special about living movement, about what we can call *expression*, something that makes it very different from the mere physical or locomotive movement of things and objects in space, that has not been emphasized sufficiently in the past. Indeed, it is not going too far, we feel, to suggest that our "inner movements" are, quite literally, expressive of the nature of our lives as we live them out in relation to our surrounding circumstances. Hence, they are not simply the movements of our inner lives alone, but are expressive of the movements of our unfolding relations both to the others and also to the othernesses around us.

Thus, when Wittgenstein (1953) remarks that "Understanding a sentence is much more akin to understanding a theme in music than one may think" (No. 527), we wish to agree. The musicality of language, in being expressive of our being "in motion together" with the others and othernesses in our surroundings, has been too-long neglected. But to repeat, it is not simply the inner world of another person's self that we can sense as being hearably expressed in the "music" of their utterances (i.e., the inner life of a separate subject set over against the objects in his or her surrounding world), but the inner life of a subject's relations to the things of his or her world—we can hear (and see) the ease and difficulty, the delight or anger or sadness with which the person deals with the events confronting him or her. We can hear how they matter in his or her life. Clearly, it is the felt sense of this *relational* aspect of an utterance that can all too easily be lost in our records, our transcripts, of people's speech.

But it need not be lost completely. Elsewhere (Katz & Shotter, 1996, 1998, 2004), we have tried to capture the general style of such approaches as Tom Andersen's in terms of a focus on "arresting, moving, striking, etc., moments" and the idea of a set of "social poetic" methods—methods derived very much from Wittgenstein's (1953) later philosophy—in which they might be exemplified. We call it a "poetic" or "formative" style of writing, in that exerts its influence on us not by depicting a true state of affairs to us in our thought, but by "moving" or "striking" us in such a way that we come to "grasp" or "see" something in our surroundings that we have not seen before, not cognitively but perceptually, not because it has been hidden from us but because we have lacked the sensibility to be responsive to what has always lain unhidden before us. Under its influence, we can achieve that kind of "understanding which consists in 'seeing connections'", says Wittgenstein (1953, No. 122). It is a kind of writing that works—through the use of concrete details, the quoting of actually voiced utterances, the use of metaphors, making comparisons—by juxtaposing familiar words in unfamiliar ways, thus creating occasions in which readers must creatively complete, not logically but dialogically, the process of understanding.

Geertz (1983) calls this move in "social science" writing a turning towards the use of "blurred genres". Instead of an array of "fixed types [of writing] divided by sharp qualitative differences, we more and more see ourselves surrounded by a vast, almost continuous field of variously intended and diversely constructed works we can order only practically, relationally, and as our purposes prompt us" (pp. 20–21).

Following Geertz (1983), our writing works by the use of *creative juxtapositions,* occurring in a hermeneutical back and forth between "experience-near" accounts from the field and "experience-distant" insights from certain writers that can be used to "arrest" or "interrupt" our everyday thinking about human events. It is an account of AMK's encounter with Denys which in its telling—as we "tack back and forth" (Geertz, 1983) between understandings derived from our everyday understandings of our own concrete experiences and those derived from academic language games (and especially from those outlined by such writers as Wittgenstein, Bakhtin, and so on)—can "move" us, this way and that, over or through the "landscape" (or better, the "seascape") of connected paths and movements relevant to Denys' disorientation and his becoming, seeming, again reoriented. In our narration of the encounter, we have tried to gain a conceptual grasp of the whole, even though we lack a vantage point from which to view it. It is a view "from the inside", much as we can get to know the street-plan of a city by living within it and walking around in it, rather than from seeing it all at once from an external standpoint, a bird's-eye view. It is an overview, a "survey", that we hope enables us to "see connections" between events not previous seen. And as authors, we have added our own voices in this chapter also, each shifting between the domain of the conceptual and the domain of practice; from internal dialog to open dialogue; from words on the printed page to living exchanges between us and our "dialogue partners" (who, along with Tom, include Harry Goolishian, Peggy Penn, Lynn Hoffman, and many others, all present in the creative space between us).

Thus, instead of reading what we write as an academic argument to be challenged for in its correctness, we invite readers to read our writing dialogically—*with* particular experience-distant concepts in mind as *reminders* (Wittgenstein, 1953)—that when juxtaposed with concrete events can, perhaps, stimulate readers to create within themselves the appropriate *transitional understandings* and *action-guiding anticipations* that might enable them to sense how to "go on" in similar such difficult situations to those described here.

As depicted here, then, our approach is primarily "practice-rooted", not "theory-rooted", and all the questions of concern to us, and to which we seek answers in our juxtaposing of concrete events occurring in a particular practice with pieces of academic literature that might illuminate them, are also particular and detailed questions and not general ones. But the results of our work are presented in terms of suggestions, offers, possibilities, and other first parts of a dialogical exchange to which second-part replies are invited. And it is through a reader's own response that (possibly) transitional understandings and action-guiding anticipations relevant to the reader's own difficulties and struggles (but not his or her problems) might be created—suggestions and so forth that cannot be put into a recipe or checklist, but can be of use, possibly, in a moment of disorientation when one needs a suggestion as to "how to go on".

> "... there's a special providence in the fall of a sparrow. If it be now, 'tis not to come; if it be not to come, it will be now; if it be not now, yet it will come: the readiness is all."
>
> Shakespeare, *Hamlet*, V, ii

CHAPTER 3

# Creating a space for a generative community

*Harlene Anderson*

Meeting Tom Andersen and the Scandinavian community that he introduced me to has been a life privilege. The first time that I remember seeing Tom was when he walked into the hotel ballroom where we (my colleagues at the Houston Galveston Institute) were convening the Epistemology, Psychopathology and Psychotherapy Conference in 1981. Eagerly watching to see who was joining us, Tom stood out from the crowd entering across the room. With his tallness, abundant brown curly hair, and stripped sack-like shirt, he had the look of a "foreigner". It would be a few years later before I had the chance to really "meet" him, when immediately Harry Goolishian and I felt an affinity and felt that we had found a kindred soul. The colleagueship and friendship that grew over the years was so welcoming in those days, when Tom's ideas and those that Harry and I were talking and writing about were often rejected and discounted by others. We were on similar paths, sometimes paralleling and sometimes meeting. The views and interests that served as the beginning common bond have evolved and over time have inspired and linked therapists around the world who form a generative learning community. Though I have known of Tom's global influence, it was not until I read the chapters in this book that I realized how it had spread creatively far beyond the therapy room.

My work is based in the philosophical perspectives of postmodernism, an umbrella term I use that includes contributions from social construction, hermeneutics, and similar perspectives of language and dialogue (Anderson, 1997b). Central in each of these and a common thread that links them is a view of knowledge and language as relational and generative, and therefore transforming. From this view flows what I call a philosophical stance: a way of being with, talking with, acting with, thinking with, and responding with another person. It is a way of being with that expresses an attitude of respect, appreciation, and consideration for what the other brings to the encounter (e.g., story, reality, agenda, etc.) that invites collaborative relationships and dialogical conversations. The important word here is "with": doing with and within, rather than for or to from outside ( for a full description of the philosophical stance, see Anderson, 1997b, 2003).

I am often asked, "How do you teach a therapist to be collaborative?" I do not think that I can teach, train, or instruct a therapist how to be a collaborative/conversational therapist or to have the philosophical stance. I can, however, provide a dialogic space and process for being in relationship and conversation with each other in which learning occurs for all. I think of this as inviting and facilitating a collaborative and generative learning community. In my experience, the space and process must be multifaceted and flexible, providing various opportunities for learners to immerse in the philosophy and practice. Towards this aim, I sometimes suggest formats that give students the opportunity to experience collaborative relationships and generative conversations. Here I shall describe and discuss one such opportunity.

## *The challenge: learning and experiencing a philosophical perspective*

We live in a multi-voiced world in which the voice of the dominant culture often overshadows the provincial voice. This happens, wittingly and unwittingly, in our psychotherapy culture when the voice and knowledge of the therapist take centre stage. In the growing body of dialogical/conversational/collaborative approaches to therapy, the client's voice (reality, knowledge, expertise, etc.) comes forward. Making room for, encouraging, respecting, and benefiting from the client's polyphonic voices (inner and outer) is at the heart of my approach. Letting go of "thinking and acting like a therapist" is at the heart as well.

## *History of "as if"*

I began experimenting with an "as-if" process in 1982–83 at the Houston Galveston Institute with groups of students who presented "stuck cases" for consultation (Anderson & Rambo, 1988). I was frustrated by students who, in their graduate programmes, had been well indoctrinated that the therapist was the expert. From my sustained interest in exploring the characteristics of successful and unsuccessful therapy, I was developing some ideas about "stuckness" in therapy being related to what I called "duelling realities" or monologues (Anderson, 1987): when the therapist's reality dominates and overshadows the client's or when one reality turns a deaf ear to an other. Typically, in consultation/supervision groups, members are eager to share their expertise (whether in the form of questions, suggestions, etc.) with the presenter; when this is done too enthusiastically, the presenting therapist may, like a client, feel overwhelmed as well as judged, incompetent, and so forth

At the time, my intent was to help students learn to think more "systemically";[1] to develop an awareness of the influence of the reality they bring and their role as a member of an observing system; and to learn to provide respectful room for each family member's reality (e.g., their hypothesis about the problem). Towards this, I created two kinds of experiences to give students an opportunity to experience being more interested in learning about the other's reality than in promoting or proving theirs: "if" questions, and "as-if" listening.

"If" questions were questions that the students would really like, or felt they needed, to ask to obtain necessary and sufficient information for formulating the client's problem or for verifying an already formed view of it (e.g., a diagnosis, a hypothesis, or a clinical judgement). Because therapists sometimes think that more information or certain kinds of information is better, an aim of the "if"-questions process was to encourage students to think about why additional or particular information was needed and towards what purpose. In other words, I wanted them to reflect on their thinking, their assumed knowing and expertise. Additionally, I hoped that they would learn to appreciate, stay with, and learn more about the story that the presenter wanted to tell rather than the story (information, facts) that they thought should be told. Students were requested to pose "if" questions for discussion rather than ask the presenter the questions. They posed the "if" questions after the presenter's presentation while the presenter listened and did not engage in the discussion. Afterwards, the presenters shared their inner thoughts—reflected—about the "if"-questions discussion, and a discussion among all of us about the process followed.

Regarding the "as-if" experience, I asked students to listen to the presentation "as if" they were a member of the client's system or as the therapist. Again, my intent was to help students entertain, appreciate, and learn the value of multiple realities. Soon I began using some form of the "as-if" process in all of my teaching, supervising, and consulting. The shape that the "as if" takes depends on the group and the presenter, and their agendas. I offer it as an option and discuss it with the presenter. In the following, I describe a generic "as-if" format that has never-ending variations and then offer an illustration of an "as-if" consultation in a workshop.

## *The generic "as if"*

In "as-if" clinical consultations I invite the presenter to tell *us* (the consultation/seminar/workshop group, and me) four things: (1) What is the reason that *you* chose the particular clinical situation to talk about? For instance, does it represent a "familiar" clinical dilemma, or is the presenter feeling "stuck"? (2) Who are the characters in *your* story? For instance, who will *you* talk about? (3) What are *your* expectations (agendas, wishes) about the consultation? For instance, do you have a question that you want to pose to us, or do you want fresh ideas and so forth? And, (4) please tell *us* what *you* think is important for *us* to know about the clinical situation that would help us regarding *your* expectation of the consultation. For instance, what does the presenter think the listeners need to know to be helpful (see www.harleneanderson.org). I underline the pronouns for emphasis: I want to communicate that *we* (collective language—the participants and me) want to hear the story that *the presenter* wants to tell.

I then ask the other members of the group to divide into silent reflecting-listening "as-if" clusters, and to listen to the presentation from that "as-if" position.[2] After the presenting therapist finishes his or her story, I ask each designated "as-if" cluster to share their reflections with each other as if they were a multi-voiced person expressing their inner voices. I ask them to speak in the first-person, "as-if" voice and to keep the presenter's expectation in mind. I give the presenter the option to visit each cluster, requesting that he or she silently listens to the voices and does not provide additional information or answer questions. I offer this listening option because I want the presenter to have access to as much of the reflecting talk as possible. It is impossible to recreate a conversation, and it is also impossible for the speaker to not privilege some voices over others or for their interpretations to contaminate their colleagues' reflections.

Next, representatives from each "as-if" voice cluster offer the reflections while the presenter and I listen.[3] After the reflections, I talk with the presenter about his or her experience of the reflections. I want to give room to the presenter to respond in the manner he or she prefers and ask his or her permission to pose curiosities or ideas that I may have: I am sometimes interested in learning what the presenter heard that appealed to him or her, what he or she might like to talk about more, and what new thoughts are bubbling, if any. I then include all members of the group in a discussion of the process of the experience that we have just had together. I do not invite discussion on the content of the presenter's story. I want to avoid the likelihood that participants will lapse into being experts who want more content or want to instruct the presenter. For those participants who remain eager to help, I suggest that they write their comments, suggestions, and the like on paper and give them to the presenter at the end of the event. I do not want to interfere with the presenter's new inner talk, whether it remains private or he or she puts it into spoken words. I want to focus on the process and the learning. That is, I am more interested in the generative process for the presenters and the participants. Interestingly, I find that if I am in a country where I do not speak or understand the language, it does not seem to matter if the reflections are offered in the native tongue. I do not need translation or to know what is said. That is, I do not need to know the content. The presenter is the important person. I can still talk with the presenter about his or her experience of the process without having access to the content. I am always aware and careful, however, that others might interpret the lack of translation as being uninterested and disrespectful.

### *Key premise*

The key premise of the "as-if" consultation is that the opportunity for inner and outer dialogue with self and other is enhanced when there is space for speaking *and* listening: (1) the teller can choose the story to tell and how to tell it and has an unrestricted and protected space to tell it; (2) the listener has an uninterrupted space to listen and time to form his or her responses; (3) there is room for a multiplicity of voices; (4) all hear each voice, none is hidden from the teller; and (5) the teller chooses what invites curiosity and what he or she might like to think or talk about more. Feedback, over the years, from participants in the "as-if" process highlights the multiple value for the listening reflectors and for the speaking presenter:

- Uninterrupted speaking: The speaker has the opportunity to talk about what he or she prefers to talk about, rather than what the listener believes is important or have his or her story derailed by listener's interruptions. Language such as "What do you want us to know?" helps to emphasize this distinction.
- On-hold listening: The "on-hold" listening position allows participants to listen differently from the way they would if they were involved in speaking and responding. It is difficult to fully focus on another if you are occupied with asking questions, making comments, sharing ideas, or offering suggestions. Being on-hold also provides listeners an opportunity to experience the difference between listening to what they want and think they

need to hear versus what the presenter wants them to hear. Participants may experience how premature knowing can close off access to the richness of the other's experience. There is also the value of the space and time to listen, to access/form inner thoughts into speech.

- Polyvocality and multi-perspectives: There is room for multiple voices and perspectives in story-telling and in reflecting-listening. Participants experience that there are many versions of a story to tell and many ways to hear it as well. There is also the opportunity for participants to experience the richness of different voices and that any one voice may hold multiple, simultaneous, and even contradictory perspectives. Inviting polyphony lessens the dictatorship of a single voice.
- Public: Participants experience the value of making private thoughts visible.
- Opening: Since the reflecting "as-if" voices are public, the presenter has the opportunity to choose how to respond to what is said and the manner of the response. Both the presenter and the "as-if" listeners are able to experience that anything can be talked about and any question can be asked. Important, however, is the manner, the tone, the attitude, and the intent with which it is presented, as these influence how the words are received and heard.
- Transformation: Participants experience that it is not necessary to strive for an end-product or a solution. They are part of a living, generative process—possibilities (e.g., new meanings, perspectives, actions, feelings, futures, etc.) emerge within the spoken and silent conversations.
- Relational newness: As the presenter hears the reflecting voices and the participants hear each other's reflections, they experience their own ideas shifting. They also experience that ideas are not given or exported to another or imported or taken in by the other as fixed discrete pieces. Instead, each person responds into and interacts with the other's offerings. The newness comes from the fluidity and the back-and-forthness of the interaction. It is, as Shotter suggests, a joint activity: the newness is relational.

I have been asked if the "as-if" exercise is out of sync with my philosophy because it is "instructive". I do not think of it as instructive, as telling a person what to think, say, or do. The "as if" is a forum for a learning experience. I do not need to control the format or have a particular outcome in mind. The form and shape that any one "as if" takes and where it will pause is not predictable. I have found that what each participant takes from it varies, depending on the context, the agenda, and what each brings to the experience. I am always humbled and kept on my toes by the surprises. Learning and therapy conversational/dialogical processes require the ability to do what the occasion calls for, to improvise, and to respond into the situation. If I suggest an "as-if" process, I do not expect—nor require—that the other(s) will agree; I must remain open to others' preferences.

### *Pavel's "as-if" story: "The problem has somehow lost"*

I had the opportunity to share my postmodern collaborative perspective with the Czech Family Therapy Association. During the workshop, I offered a consultation to give participants an opportunity to experience the ideas that I had been talking about. I favour "live" consultations, so that the participants and I can experience something together, instead of showing a videotaped therapy/consultation session and retrospectively talking about it. I mentioned the possibility of a consultation at the beginning of the day and again as we paused for lunch. I specifically requested a team or a group of people who worked in the same setting to volunteer for the consultation. Though I am certainly willing to consult with a "solo" therapist, I like to include as many as possible in the consultation experience.

After lunch I reiterated the consultation possibility and gave participants a moment to talk with each other about volunteering. After a long pause, a young man named Pavel raised his hand. I asked him to join me in the centre of the room and inquired if any of his work colleagues were present. There were none. So, I asked if there was anyone in the room who was familiar with his work. He pointed to the woman who had been sitting next to him; she (Jitka) was a member of a family therapy training programme that

Pavel was in. I had noticed earlier that the two of them seemed to know each other, so I asked him if I could invite Jitka to join us. Looking very puzzled and somewhat wary, he agreed. I asked Jitka if she would mind joining Pavel and me—perhaps we could use her help. She also looked puzzled and wary, but agreed and joined us. I appreciated that there was at least one other person who knew Pavel; Jitka might add to the story and, having her at his side, might be supportive in the uncertainty of the situation.

I reiterated my appreciation for their "volunteering" and hoped that the experience would be useful for them. I also told them that I would not do anything to make them feel on-the-spot or embarrass them. I then spent a few minutes learning a little about them, asking about the training programme they were in and about Pavel's work setting. I then asked Pavel to identify the people in his story, what he expected of us, and what he thought we should know to be helpful with his expectations. I asked Jitka if she would mind listening and that I was sure that I might have some questions for her.

Pavel told us about a miserable situation concerning his relationship with the guards in the prison system where he worked. Briefly, with heaviness he said that the guards did not talk with him and often sabotaged his work by either bringing the prisoners late to their therapy sessions or not bringing them at all. They never included him in their conversations or at coffee-breaks or lunch and often made fun of him within earshot. In fact, Pavel was sure "they don't like me but I don't know why". He gave several examples of painful and frustrating encounters. He desperately wanted to improve his relationships with the guards. I participated in Pavel's story-telling, as I tried to understand it by occasionally making a comment, asking for clarification or expansion, and wondering aloud. When Pavel indicated that he had finished, I thanked him, and then I asked Jitka two questions: was there something that she would like to add, and what were her thoughts while Pavel was telling his story? She knew he worked in a prison but had not heard about the situation before, and she expressed concern for Pavel.

I asked Pavel if he would like to hear from the workshop participants. He quickly said yes. I then told him about the "as-if" process, and he liked the idea. So I asked the participants to divide into three "as-if" listening clusters—the prison guards, the prisoners, and Pavel—and to reflect with each other within their cluster about Pavel's story, keeping in mind what he had requested of the consultation. I gave Pavel and Jitka the option of listening to the three multi-headed voices. They eagerly accepted and went together to listen, in turn, to each voice cluster. Following this, Pavel, Jitka, and I listened to the "as-if" representatives. I watched Pavel as the voices came forward; I felt fairly sure that some of them—particularly the guards' comments that were quite strong—were not easy for Pavel to hear. I next asked Pavel and Jitka to talk with each other, to share their inner talk as they listened to the voices. Pavel was amazed at how the voices expressed the others so well, including his own anguish, frustration, self-doubt, and hopelessness. I then talked briefly with Pavel, learning more about his response to the voices, giving him additional opportunity to form his silent thoughts into spoken words, and sharing with him my inner conversation about the situation. When we paused, there were no solutions, no firm ideas about actions that Pavel might take or how he might think differently about the situation and the people involved, including himself. Pavel said at that time that he was very appreciative for the consultation experience and that it was a very strong and useful experience.

A month later I was delighted to receive an email from Pavel.

> I am not sure if you remember me. I consulted you during your seminar in Prague in September this year. The consultation was a public presentation of your work; we were addressing the issue of my relationship with prison guards. To start with, I would like to thank you again for the conversation. I felt really good and free during it even though the context could have been quite stressful (with all of the people around). Also, the "problem" has stopped to appear as a problem since our conversation even if I have not made any radical changes in my behavior. I am able to see my relationships with prison guards from many different positions now, and the problem has somehow lost.

I thanked Pavel for his email and asked him if he would mind telling me more about his experience of the consultation and afterwards. He promptly replied.

I am not sure if I am able to remember the most important things from the consultation that was held more than a month ago. Anyway, let's consider all the things that I kept in my head . . . to be important.

I decided to volunteer for the consultation for these reasons: first, I consider the direct experience to be the most effective way to learn new things, and second, it seemed a good opportunity to talk about my relationships with the prison guards and about my role in the prison system. I had not discussed this topic with anyone before. I was not sure if my topic would be useful for others, because I was the only one at the workshop from my organization. So I decided to wait and if no group volunteered, I would raise my hand.

I was quite surprised when you chose my training colleague to be the second client—I could not imagine which role she could have [in the consultation]. But I remember that it was very soothing to me when you promised me that you would not hurt me in any way.

When I was talking about the situation in the prison it was very important for me. You were asking about the relationships and about the roles which other people play in the system. So I started to perceive it as a "plastic" and live story, and not so rigid and definite a situation. Maybe this [conversational] process would itself make some change, but I still wanted more from you. Thus, I appreciated the task [the "as-if" listening reflecting positions] that you gave the others. When Jitka and I were listening to the conversations [the "as-if" clusters], it was very interesting. It was a totally new role for me. I was the one who just observes and who knows the most about the context: I could say to myself: "yes, this is possible" and "no, they [the guards] do not speak like this." To tell the truth, I do not remember much of the content of the conversations or the final speech of the representatives. But it was very interesting to realize that they (the guards, the clients) may really have similar conversations to what I heard—and that there are so many different conversations. And I also realized that other people talk about me and my relationships to others, and so at once my perspective was very broad.

I must say that I do not remember much of the final phase. I know that you were telling me something, but my head was so full of my own un-definitive thoughts that I did not give my whole attention to your words (I am sorry). But it was important for me: your voice was very calming and I felt support and appreciation from you. I felt that I could say whatever I want, but my thoughts were so incomplete that I wanted to think about it after I had some time to be alone. The final phase was also important because I felt the consultation was "real" and "complete." It was consultation as it should be—with a beginning, a "technique" and a conclusion. So, it made me feel that "I passed the consultation and now I can make a change".

A funny situation was when the consultation was finished, I was sitting back in my seat and I asked Jitka if she knew who all the other participants were. And she started to name the most famous therapists from the Czech Republic! And I talked to myself: All these great people were dealing with my situation, all these people played roles of people who only I know, including me. All these people tried to help me; isn't that funny? And this was the first shift; I started to see my situation as one of many other similar situations and many more serious ones. And on the other side, I started to see myself as a man who is worth being cared for by the most famous therapists in the Czech Republic (and in the world).

So, when I went to the prison the following days, something had changed. When the guards made some funny comments about me it did not hurt me; I just did not mind. I started to be more interested in the guards, in their view on some things and some clients. And now I do not perceive the situation to be problem. I did not make big and radical changes, I just started to look at the situation and to think about it in a different way.

Well, it was interesting to think about it again!

I sent this article to Pavel and asked his permission to use his story and name. I also asked him to tell me if there was any part of my telling of the consultation that he would like to change. Again, he quickly replied.

I appreciate that you used my own words instead of interpreting my reflections. I also liked to read your own perspective of the consultation

I realized that I perceived my relationships with the guards very personally before the consultation. As I told you, "they do no like me and I don't know why, etc." Now, I'd rather try to understand their perspective and I do not regard their com-

> ments as aimed against me, but rather as their own way of coping with the frustrating and stereotype work. Interestingly, this change in my view started to change my relationships and ways of conversations with the guards."

Pavel's afterwords vividly illustrate a generative process and the critical nature of the conversation and the relationship in which it is embedded. His eyes and ears moved beyond the constraints of his inner voice and the familiar and he opened himself to unimagined possibilities.

Through the "as-if" experience—a polyphonic plurality of the imagined, unspoken voices—therapists encounter the openness, invitation, and respect for, and of, the other as well as the closedness, prejudices, and judgement of the other. They encounter feeling heard and understood as well as unheard and misunderstood. They experience the richness of different and counter-voices, and they experience what is lost when only the expert's voice is heard and when voices are moved towards consensus or synthesis. Importantly, therapists have the opportunity to experience *a way of being* as a different way of looking at and experiencing the world with others, not as a technique. Therapists and clients experience an invention of dialogic interaction: unexpected newness, endless possibilities, and dis-solution of the problem—or in Pavel's words: "the problem has somehow lost."

## *Notes*

1. Systemic was the language that I used at that time.
2. Sometimes at the beginning of a consultation, it has not been determined that we will use an "as-if" process. If this is decided later, then listeners assume an "as-if" position afterwards. I have found that it is more helpful for participants to take an "as-if" position before the consultation story begins rather than afterwards.
3. A variation is that the presenter may listen to the reflections "as if" he or she was a character in the story—for example, as the mother, the son, the grandfather, the supervisor, etc. I have found that this helps therapists develop awareness that the client is having his or her special inner conversation as the therapist or others speak. The challenge is how to invite another's inner conversation into the spoken one.

CHAPTER 4

# Flashbacks in war: a consultation with reflections

*Peggy Penn*

There are things we love and preserve out of simple familiarity; sometime it is beauty or an idea like the ethics of entitlements. In my case, I love a meadow. My daily walks take my husband and me to the top of a hill where a particular meadow stretches out in front of us. I know it's been there long before we knew it. I heard that someone had leased it and cut down a magnificent grey beech; I felt bereft. Walking by, I see how it resembles an elephant's graveyard, with huge severed trunks and branches big as legs, lying in a heap, their raw, yellow ends, splintering. It was as though poachers had done this and, to diminish the tree even more, would readily turn this pile of limbs into ashtrays. However, I seem to have many discontents: this is only one, Israel is another.

I am never simultaneously so happy and so sad as when I am in Israel; I never cry so much or laugh so much. It is the people who move me to such extremes of feeling, the people who exist in this state of war. I am moved by the sweetness of their green land and how they formed it out of every handful of dry earth, and the justice they constructed after the Holocaust. A land of their own not to run from; but, paradoxically, the terror of death remains.

Coexisting has become harder and harder for both Israel and the Palestinians, who are also a moving, beautiful people. They are caught in an endless repetition where they hope for peace negotiations as both sides are confronted with terrible, bloody failures. I was in Israel shortly after the assassination of Rabin and before the suicide bombers had begun. We talked about nothing else.

When in Israel I am surrounded by some former, beloved students who have become my friends and colleagues. And I have discovered a few little-known family members from my husband's side. On this particular occasion, November 1999, I was invited along with two colleague, Tom Andersen and Gianfranco Cecchin, to give a conference. My particular task was to present my work on the use of language and writing in the treatment of chronic illness and also to do a consultation—that is, to meet with another therapist who wanted to discuss a particularly difficult case.

The conference had a large turnout, and at the beginning of my afternoon session I asked who wished to consult with me. The first to raise his hand was Aram, a young man in his thirties, tall, slightly greying, dressed in beige and grey clothes, with an intelligent and modest air. He moved to the centre of a circle and sat facing me. He said he was struggling with the feeling that he had completely run out of ideas. He was treating a young man, a former soldier, and hoped this consultation would help him generate some new ideas and get back to work.

I asked if he could tell me the story and, please, would he include every detail he remembered as relevant. When he first spoke, I could hear the walls in his mind coming down. He was clearly a knowledgeable therapist who had tried hard to help this man who was experiencing a great deal of pain. Though he had tried many things, he felt they had all failed. I hoped he'd have the resilience to try again.

He told me that the young man he was seeing was a 22-year-old new soldier who, with his squad of about fifty other soldiers, investigated a rumour of aggressive activity that was being caused by a group of Palestinian youths. The rumour turned out to be a false alarm. In the course of the investigation, he had killed a young Palestinian boy. This is how the story unfolded: the Israeli soldiers arrived at the designated spot and found everything more or less quiet. However, fifty Israeli soldiers are not unnoticed wherever they go, and some young Palestinian boys had gathered closer to look. One boy, aged about 14, raised his arm, holding a rock in his hand, but did not throw it; he backed off. Aram's client said to his commanding officer, "I'll shoot him!" He had never before shot anyone; in fact, he had never even been on such a foray. Later he told Aram that he felt a soldier should shoot people to be a real soldier, but the Palestinian boy hovered at the front of his group, possibly checking out the next moves of the soldiers. My understanding of the story is that the Israeli soldiers were first armed with rubber bullets, but since they hung around the area and did not leave, the group of boys called Palestinian soldiers; and when they appeared, the soldier shot the boy. The boy's body fell to the ground, and there was an outbreak of real fighting. So the rumour, in being checked out, turned into a full skirmish in which both Israeli and Palestinian soldiers were killed for reasons not available to anyone's understanding—at least not in enough time to prevent it from happening.

It is important to understand that in a consultation, I rely on the participation of the entire group. We join together in order to generate ideas. The participation must take place in a collaborative manner, each idea adding to the one before, foregoing competition but making room for the tapestry of ideas to weave tightly together in rich and different colours. As the ideas draw together, everyone is allowed to feel he/she has felt these feelings, understands this narrative deeply, and has something to offer to its outcome. I am never the primary idea person. I do the interview and, following that, we generate ideas together; that is our collaboration.

There were fifty people sitting around Aram and myself in a big circle to listen to our conversation. We were the listeners, the witnesses, to Aram's story so we could help him develop new possibilities to think about. When the interview was over, all of us who listened broke into six groups and reflected on what had been said. Reflections are a special process that I describe to the group after I hear the story. I added one more complication. I thought we could divide the group into several groups: the first would listen to Aram's story as though they were the soldier's family; another group would listen as though they were his wife and child; another would listen as though they were his wife's family; the final designated group would listen as though they were the family of the Palestinian boy. Those who had not volunteered to be in these groups would make up groups with about six people in each and could reflect on what they wished or thought was relevant. Since this killing took place in the Israeli–Palestinian war, I felt it would help us more deeply understand to hear from inside both families and from other observers, the additional reflecting groups.

Let me speak again and review these reflections. They grow out of the conversation of the interview, particularly the questions. However, there is one important caveat: we never comment on anything that has not been said. In my case, strong feelings about clients often come to me right in the middle of the conversation, and they guide or influence my next question. The poet Rainer Marie Rilke wrote "Learn to love the question", and I have found that loving the question has never let me down. The questions raised position the questioner for discovery; a new thought may emerge that compares, reveals, or sets a direction. Questions also have strong performative value, and unexpected things happen. When a particularly fitting question is asked, I can almost see an idea light up for someone in the family, an idea that was not present before the question was asked.

In the act of reflecting, questions are not declarative; rather, they ask for reflections, considerations, and possibilities. Without literally putting a period down, they resist the "advice-giving" impulse that tempts us all. In contrast, these reflecting questions of Andersen's (Andersen, 1987, 1991) invite the family to be a full participant in the considerations of their own future possible actions.

In a very short period of time after the shooting, Aram's client, Saul, came to see him, saying he could not sleep; he was having terrible nightmares. The worst of these nightmares was the *memory* of his shooting the boy and seeing, over and over, the young boy's body continuously falling to the ground but *never hitting it.* These flashbacks woke him during the night and made it impossible for him to go back to sleep. Then the same flashbacks began to appear during the day. He felt hounded, tormented by the flashbacks. His wife complained he was very bad-tempered with her, was late for work, and acted too harshly with the baby. He couldn't stand to see his parents or his wife's parents. His situation became so oppressive that he felt no longer able to work. His commanding officer had asked him to take a leave from the army "until he felt better". He felt humiliated and degraded. Finally, he moved out of his apartment and lived in a room by himself, tormented by the flashbacks and sleep-deprived. The only thing he could manage to do for himself was to see Aram, his therapist. He felt that he was the one man who could save him. And Aram felt he was failing. Aram got him medication for sleeping, but it didn't work. Nothing seemed to work. Aram was afraid things would get worse and Saul would become psychotic; this was in his mind when he volunteered to ask for a consultation.

Seven years ago I wrote a paper on the treatment of rape flashbacks, which consisted of finding a new way towards their dissolution (Penn, 1998). I thought of it when listening to Aram's story about the soldier who continued to have flashbacks after he killed a boy. On occasion, one can build a new story with a client where the client chooses a protective figure to be alongside him and interjects that figure into the flashback scenario, just as Saul had chosen Aram. This has the effect of interrupting the old scenario *so that it cannot take place in the same way again.* This way he is always accompanied and protected. This approach relies on the client finding a new or freed voice in the treatment conversations in order to be able to tell her or his story differently. The new, *repopulated* story eventually has the effect of altering the client's memory and renewing not only her or his life direction but her or his belief in her/himself. I wondered to myself if the conversation between Aram and me could find such a protective figure to offer to Saul and whether Aram could be that protective figure.

I asked Aram if this might be a good point for me to ask some questions or whether he needed to continue his story a while longer. He looked exhausted from the feelings of impotence he had been describing. I said I admired him for telling this story here at a conference, and I thought we all understood how much it meant to him to find a different way to think about it. "Yes", he assured me, "now would be a good time for you to ask questions." But he added that the conference was the only chance he had to see someone outside his context. That struck me as an intelligent wish: to go outside his context to think with me.

By now Saul had stopped talking to his wife and both their families; he relied only on Aram. But the flashbacks remained stubbornly unchanged. I also knew that as an Israeli therapist, Aram was experienced at handling trauma—it was part of his daily life—but even this special knowledge did not help him help Saul. I had a strong feeling that Aram could be that protective figure.

I was curious about the beliefs in the soldier's family: what it meant in this family to be in the army. Was he obliged to do it? Was it considered an act of bravery? For instance, were his siblings in the army? Did the family share a belief about the possibility of another war? And had anyone in his family ever been lost in a war? Aram answered each question as well as he could, except for their belief about the possibility of war and whether a family member had been lost in a previous war. From what I could understand, Saul's family was proud that he was a soldier and thought he should fight.

Aram knew Saul felt humiliated by the disapproval of his commanding officer. He had disobeyed him and was chastised in front of the other fifty soldiers. It shamed him.

I was also curious about what his wife and parents felt about the shooting and the disapproval of his commanding officer. Aram said he thought they approved of the shooting. Though this idea of their approval was a speculation based on the parents' conservative beliefs, Aram thought it possible that Saul's family would have objected to the officer's disapproval of their son. The shooting had allied him with his parents' beliefs and he had acted, guided by those beliefs. And if that idea was correct, it could explain his burning wish to kill a Palestinian, no matter what the cost. He had never killed anyone before.

His commanding officer saw this shooting as an error; Saul disobeyed a command and was chastised in front of all the other soldiers. Aram and I wondered together if suddenly he was not so sure that what he had done was right. In contrast, he had been very sure before. Suddenly the issue of ethics loomed. This could prove to be a dangerous contradiction since, if true, it would challenge a belief he'd held about himself, one that allied him with his family and their support and with Israel. It would also explain why Saul felt so much pain.

I though it might be important for us to review together the kind of options this man may have had after he had been sent home: he could say his commanding officer was wrong to criticize him. In fact, he had been right to take no chances and kill the boy if there was the slightest chance he might throw a rock.

He could say (though it was unlikely) that his parents were wrong and the Palestinians didn't deserve to die. Saying his parents were wrong, however, would involve a break of some size with them.

To say he himself was wrong also would involve a break with his parents and perhaps with his wife's parents. How would he find a place to be where he could forgive himself and embrace the *rightness* of his act as he wished it to be? I wondered out loud to Aram how Saul's dilemma was a moral one, one that had to do with not justifying what had happened but, in fact, forgiving himself and possibly being forgiven by others. He would need compassion for that. Additionally, he had to understand and possibly forgive his parents for holding beliefs that needed more careful consideration. His feelings of having nowhere to turn became understandable.

Somewhere in the images of the client's flashback, where the Palestinian boy is falling and falling through space, his own different ideas for salvation were locked. It seemed very important to know what his therapist, Aram, thought; should this client be saved and forgiven? Or was the therapist also in a moral dilemma?

Looking carefully at the options present in Saul's moral dilemma helped Aram understand how all roads felt closed to Saul. Aram offered this idea: perhaps Saul feels as though everyone is against him—he was doing what he thought a soldier is supposed to do. Why should he be so isolated and punished? That idea could be some part of his confusion. I asked Aram if he had ever mentioned any different political ideas other than those held by his parents. Did he have a different, perhaps hidden, other political belief that he was uneasy even thinking about? Aram said lately he had mentioned some criticism of right-wing beliefs, so it was possible he was thinking differently from his family. That could mean a possible break with them, but at the moment he couldn't afford to break with anybody.

Perhaps, I wondered, it was not just the boy in the flashback who was adrift but Saul himself, also a man with no firm ground under his feet: not the army, his parents, his job, or his wife and child. We wondered if that could be one meaning held in the image of the boy caught in midair. That seemed a possibility to both Aram and to me. In an odd way, maybe this flashback spoke for both of them, Saul and the Palestinian boy, since both had lost ground. Stubbornly I remained curious to understand why in the flashback the boy never *hit* the ground but remained suspended in midair, his arms held out, so I asked again: was the image a metaphor, a way of undoing what had been done by postponing the inevitable and literal *dead stop* that hitting the ground would entail? I asked if it were possible that the flashback contained a hidden idea? Saul might have wished *not* to shoot the boy but to spare him, but caught himself too late. More, could there have been a kind of grieving wish to reinstate the boy, roll the film backwards, so to speak, and put his gun down? I was suddenly very moved by the idea of the boy's body falling through the air and wanted to raise my own arms to catch him softly in my lap and arms, like the figure of a Pietà. I told this to Aram, and he listened carefully. Once in a while, his eyes looked down and then back up at me again. Watching his body carefully, I had the feeling he was struggling with large emotions.

I asked Aram to talk about what happened in the sessions between himself and Saul. After all, they were both young men, close to the same age. Was there something in particular, a special knowledge, that Aram had used from his own life to help him understand Saul? Could something similar ever have happened to him, something that had been hard to get rid of, something that stubbornly stayed with him? At the moment he was Saul's only witness, and that was very difficult. Perhaps he could find a similar time, not when anyone was killed but when a loss had occurred that one couldn't forget or maybe even forgive. What if this is what he was feeling? I could read something taking place in his face. I wondered out loud if it might release him to feel compassion for Saul. Suddenly Aram began to weep, tears streamed down his cheeks. However, he said nothing. I said: "It must feel as though Saul had fallen overboard and it's hard to save him without diving into the water yourself, diving into those terrible waters of moral confusion." Finally he said he knew this event had exacted a terrible price from Saul, bitter as well as confusing. He said he felt Saul was experiencing a dead end. Aram said he had felt that in his life and was feeling some of it now. Underneath his role as a therapist, he felt deeply for him. I asked, "Does Saul know that you do? Have you told him?"

"No, I couldn't."

"You haven't found a way to tell him?

"No, I have not."

I asked, "Do you think it would make a difference to him if he knew your feelings?"

Aram, still with tears in his eyes, began nodding "yes" and then said, "Yes, I think if I told him it would make a difference. He might feel that someone in the world cared about him and knew how he felt." In my heart I was pleased he had used this consultation to find something new to do for Saul.

I said, "That feeling which has been generated by your relationship is such a good thing! Could it be a new place for the two of you to start? To trust that something new might come from it?" Aram nodded "yes".

We sat quietly for a few moments in each other's presence. I asked, "Are you feeling ready to stop?"

"Yes, I feel I can stop now." He looked up at me and smiled. We slowly turned our chairs back to the group; it had been stone quiet in the room, but now we were ready for their thoughts. We sat side by side.

### *Reflections*

There were four groups, with ten in each group—colleagues listening as Saul's parents, as the parents of his wife, as his own wife and child, as the family of the Palestinian boy who had been killed. Two other groups listened as working colleagues. I asked someone to take notes for Aram because it might prove hard for him to remember everything that was said. In this way he was free to respond emotionally, but he also took a few notes of his own.

As the members of the reflecting groups speak, it is important to remember that they are therapists taking part in a conference but, because of their unusual sensitivities, they are able to identify with Aram's client and by extension with all the families involved. The reflections are not meant to be accurate, but they are true personal responses, often emotional expressions about what has been said or observed. As each one of the reflections is given, it affects the others.

The first reflecting group took us by surprise. The woman speaking as Saul's mother said, "I am so happy my son is alive that I can endure anything, forgive anything! I wish it hadn't happened and I feel for the other family, but if only my son will recover, I will be so happy". Saul's father in this reflection nodded and then bent his head. He did say, "My son did right, he is a soldier!" Another member of this family, a grandmother, just wept.

The family of Saul's wife consisted of two younger daughters, a mother, and a father—four people reflecting. One daughter said she hoped her sister would take her baby and get out of this situation, divorce this crazy man, and come home. She felt that her sister's baby was in danger, and until Saul was much better he should not be allowed near the baby. The second sister remained silent, as though her older sister had spoken for her. The mother wanted her daughter and grandchild home, at least until Saul felt better again. But she offered that she would be the one to keep in touch with him and go to visit him. The father said that no one knows what it's like to be in the army—there are so many pressures, it's hard to know what to do.

The third group was Saul's wife and baby. She said this was a great shock, but she didn't want to give up her marriage; she wanted him to come home. She said she loved Saul. The small girl put her head in her hands and said she was frightened to grow up without her father. Who would protect her and her mother?

The fourth group was the Palestinian family. There was a mother whose hands reached up through emptiness, trying hard to breathe, looking up as though she, too, could see him falling, falling, as Saul did. She stood, turning around, holding her head up. She had no words, but her body presence was very moving to the whole group, especially to Aram. He reddened again. There were two brothers, quiet. The father of the boy turned his chair away from the group, so we could not see his face. This was a silent sorrow, a sense of the oblivion of their loss. The room we were in was still, no one moved.

Finally, a woman from one of the non-family groups spoke. Her name was Sasha and she said, "This is how we felt when my brother was killed in the war. He was in a tank and tried to crawl out of the lid holding on to a white flag to surrender. They shot him instantly." She wept and said she had never spoken about this until today.

We felt along with the group representing the Palestinian family as this weeping young woman was speaking. "I think we never recovered from my brother's death and that death is under every loss I encounter, even in this role play. So many of us have our sons and daughters falling through the sky in our minds and we can't catch them, they fall through our hands like water. They fall onto dead earth."

I asked her, "Do you think Saul may have wanted to undo what he did, literally to reverse the fact of this boy's death, so his obsession takes up every waking minute, is constant, every second must be filled by it so this Palestinian boy doesn't touch the ground, finally?"

I asked, "Do you think Saul will need help in his grieving?"

"Oh yes," she said, "much help."

"Where will this help come from?" I asked.

"From all the families who can reach out to each other, just as we are doing now."

Aram wrote in his notebook. I suspect its meaning was around parts of different families involved to meet together. I wrote in my mental notebook how much I would like to be there!

I believe the question in everyone's mind was this: is it possible to forgive this man? I think in our detailed consideration of the flashback and the possible meanings it carries, we had slowly begun to do so. Years ago I was working with expressions of violence in families and thought at length about forgiveness. To forgive someone, the person in question would need to know that your story was understood and therefore the extent of your hurt was perceived. This is an act of empathy; you must feel it.

At the beginning of the consultation some people were confused by the soldier's story and experienced a mix of anger, some disgust, even limited sympathy. I expected that those who had lost someone in a war or due to war activities felt that we were wasting valuable time on a man who had clearly disobeyed orders and was not hurt himself in the process. Were we dealing with a psychiatric symptom? But as the consultation ended and the reflections began, some shifts began to take place. The change in Aram and his expression of empathy towards Saul moved us. Reading his face, we could see he was in a much different place and saw Saul as someone he could help. We, too, were able then to think differently about Saul and his suffering, his "loss of place". (I would add that these rolling reflections, where one group spoke after another, has the capacity to bring many voices forward to be heard. These many voices hold subtle differences and considerations for those who hear them. We were obliged to find a place in ourselves to tolerate or be swayed empathetically by the presence of so many voices.) I reminded myself that this was a group of therapists, people trained to feel for others and to see parts of themselves in others. Every voice was invited to speak, and the feelings of the group began to change, first towards Aram and then slowly towards Saul.

When we felt we had come to the end of the afternoon and this incredible time we had spent together, a young woman came up to me and said, "I hope you don't leave Israel; in fact, I hope you stay here, right here in this room with us!"

These rolling reflection are characterized by many ideas and emotions that are spoken and offered. They are highly co-influential, one on another, and eventually affect the whole group. Many of these reflections evidenced a sense of empathy for this confused young soldier, growing up and living in a war context, where bravery and self-esteem were reflected in one's ability to kill.

The big question we were circling was: Can we forgive this soldier or anyone who does senseless mortal harm to another? It is a formidable task when lines between groups, like the Palestinians and the Israelis, continue to be drawn so black and white. It is harder to either seek tolerance or even to hold on to the determination to understand another; it seems to disappear into thin air. Can healing take place without it? Perhaps that is a bigger question.

CHAPTER 5

# Voicing voices

*Adela G. García & Lino Guevara*

We would like to share a story about encounters and conversations, about a journey we embarked upon together, first in the field of clinical family therapy and training, and more recently in social contexts that include larger systems. We have been working together in Buenos Aires, Argentina, since 1997. Our paths first crossed after our own individual journeys in the world of psychiatry, psychology, and psychotherapy, including immigration as well as emigration. From the beginning, there were coincidences in our clinical work as well as a common interest in society as a whole. We went from modern persuasion to postmodern uncertainty, from emphasis on interventions to an approach that favours open conversations and reflecting processes in which questions and listening are honoured. It is the way one speaks that affects conversations.

This is where Tom Andersen's voice, through his writings as well as his personal yearly visits to Buenos Aires, comes in and has since been accompanying us on our journey. The fashion in which reflecting teams and reflecting processes promote more equity in client–therapist, supervisor–supervisee, teacher–student relationships is essential to us, as is the inclusion of multiple perspectives and voices. We share with Tom the idea that open and reflecting conversations promote a language of solidarity and, therefore, also a language of democracy. We would like to use this opportunity to relate some of our experiences in the larger social contexts where these concepts and practices have been of great help to us.

## *Cultural background*

Argentina is located in the southern part of South America. It is inhabited by thirty-six million people, some of whom are descendants—those who were able to dodge the *harquebuses* and epidemics—of native peoples who were invaded and colonized by envoys of the kings of Europe, seekers of gold, silver, and spices in exchange for God's word and collared mirrors. Others also disembarked from the ships to find the Promised Land and to escape the wars and poverty of the old continent.

During the nineteenth century, Argentina started to get organized as a nation. Significant agro-export and industrial development followed in the twentieth century, generating educational and economic conditions that facilitated socio-economic growth, the generation of a significant middle class, and a desire for more solidarity in society. Frequent shifts between democratic governments and military coups characterized Argentine political life during the twentieth century, making living in uncertainty a constant feature.

Between 1976 and 1983, a military dictatorship opened the doors for neo-liberal economies, resulting in the destruction of the local industry, loss of employment opportunities, increase in unemployment and poverty, marginalization, and social exclusion. State terrorism abolished the rights of the people; kidnappings, torture, and assassination of thousands of citizens were carried out on a regular basis.[1] These practices of "eliminating" the "enemy" on behalf of governmental forces and the intimidation of the population created a "culture of silence". When democracy was reinstated in 1983, expectations of justice and human rights were reinforced by the Military *Juntas* Trials, meant to sentence all those who had been involved in human rights violations. But the laws of Due

Obedience, Full Stop, and Pardon legitimized and institutionalized impunity[2] and corruption in Argentine society. Hope was regained in 2005, when these laws were abolished.

With the consolidation of neo-liberal practices and the shift from Argentina as a transit country to a country of drug consumption and drug trafficking in the 1990s, the ideology of individualism started to dominate over family, community, and solidarity values, characteristic of our society in the past. This cultural change was so abrupt that many of us felt like immigrants in our own homes. A strong economic crisis[3] generated a citizen's participative response in 2001, which helped them regain their agency and influence. This response was manifested through actions such as neighbourhood assemblies, *"comedores"* [community soup kitchens], *"piquetes"* [road blocks], barter systems, and solidarity movements. In 2003 a democratic government displaying greater concern for justice and human rights took over.

## *Clinical practice as political practice*

South America has been subject to different types of colonization (*"the richness of our soil is the disgrace of our people"*: Galeano, 1981). Colonization implies transferring customs, habits, explanations, and deities from one culture to another, thereby establishing a hierarchy between the colonizing culture and the colonized culture, one being considered the "superior" and the other the "subordinate".

According to Wittgenstein, we are *in* the language that takes place in a community and in a given culture and history, which can provide possibilities but also limitations as to what is to be expressed (Andersen, 1995b). What are the effects of our macro-context on our professional practices? And conversely, in which ways do we contribute to its permanence or even its transformation? Moreover, how does our context influence our ways of thinking and operating? Our culture could be characterized as "unstably stable" and "certainly uncertain", its rules changing all the time. The institutions are constantly being judged, and corruption can be seen throughout society to a greater or a lesser extent.

What is our stance as professionals in the larger contexts? Psychotherapy is not a neutral practice, in that a therapist is never a theoretician in the sense of using *teoros*[4] but, rather, an actor as well as a vehicle for transmitting values from one culture to another, from one social class to another, and so on. Could it therefore be possible for us to become agents of colonization? What effects do our ideas of "normalcy"—often based on family organization in a given class or culture—have on our work with people from different contexts (e.g., exclusion, marginalization) or different cultures? What implications do our ideas with respect to autonomy and independence have on the social fabric? Do they prioritize individuation or individualism? How necessary is it to reflect upon our actions so as not to naturalize authoritarian practices? Or, rather, how naturalized do authoritarian practices have to be before we stop noticing them?

In therapeutic dialogues, the client and consultant mutually collaborate in the construction of reality (McNamee & Gergen, 1996). How can we maintain a professional practice where our experience as psychotherapists is construed on a practice of freedom? How can we contribute to the generation of further acceptance and inclusion when faced with these differences? It is in this sense that we propose our therapeutic practice as being a political one.

We understand politics to mean the exercise of responsibility as participants of social acts, based on its consequences. Deeming language as meaning-making and constituting our world views and as generating our reality, and conceiving words as formative, increases our responsibility as we use it (Shotter, 2001). Changing language, therefore, is changing the world. The language–thought–world relationship is a dialectic one (Freire, 1997).

A stance of curiosity, inquiry, and humility, which prioritizes learning as opposed to teaching, leads to equity among the participants in a conversation and facilitates a meaning-making process, in a respectful and hopeful way. Our own reflections, as well as those of our clients, promote ownership, responsibility, and therefore a practice of freedom.

Lastly, we believe that by being members of a culture of "knowledge" (White, 1990), we also occupy a position of power granted to us by society, in that we are listened to and are role models. That is why we feel that our professional practice becomes a political act, because we try to contribute to the generation of new, more democratic ways in which all the voices and perspectives can be expressed and heard.

Paulo Freire's words with respect to education can also be of use to psychotherapists: "One of the beauties of this practice is that it is impossible to conceive it without risks: the risk of being not being coherent, of saying one thing and doing another. And, it is [precisely] its political character, its impossibility of neutrality, which calls for ethics from the educator" (Freire, 1985; translated for this edition)

## Our work

Most of our work takes place at the Centro de Estudios Sistémicos [Centre for Systemic Studies/CES], an institution devoted to the treatment of families, training of therapists, and research in family therapy. In 2001 we began to expand our vision beyond the office setting and started looking at the larger social contexts. We expand some of these experiences in this chapter.

### Therapeutic conversations based on peace and equity

In the midst of the aforementioned economic crisis in 2002, some of the members of the CES[5] decided to create a space to reflect upon present and future professional actions. We organized a meeting called "Therapeutic Conversations Based on Peace and Equity: A Contribution to the Promotion of Hope and Defence of Life". The invitation said the following:

> "In the face of the grave current circumstances which lead to intense feelings of fear, hopelessness and impotence, we invite you to participate in an interactive encounter for professionals from the mental health, social science, educational, and other related fields, with the aim of construing and implementing collaborative practices and developing technical and human resources to value and defend life."

At the beginning of the meeting, the participants were asked to find commonalities in the problems they were encountering in their practices and then talk about the ways they were resolving them. These discussions took place in groups. Afterwards, we used a reflecting format and "rules" (Andersen, 1994) in which each group took turns sharing their dilemmas while the rest of the group listened and then reflected on these discussions. This experience not only gave rise to new conversations in which experiences were shared and reflected upon, but also generated new responses. The first echoes revealed that the event had been like a *Travún*, which means "encounter" in the Mapuche[6] language, or, rather, "the start of a conjoint journey". The spirit was connected to the greeting *Ouatlá*, which in the Wichi[7] language means "loving and needing one another at the same time". Words such as connection, cooperation, solidarity, trust, peace, and responsibility came up in the evaluation of the encounter.

A second event, in which the networks were consolidated, took place two months later. The number of participants increased and included the involvement of professionals from other areas, such as lawyers, teachers, physical therapists, and so forth. Some volunteer projects in the community evolved as an active response to the economic crisis—for example, the development of guidelines for surviving social crises, provisions of volunteer psychological assistance in different barrios, and so forth. The application of reflecting processes in these meetings favoured the establishment of networks, groups, and relationships. The participants stressed how important it had been for them to express themselves freely and be listened to. They were relieved that they were not "alone" any more—an experience of connection, recovery of hope, and motivation for continued work in networks.

Argentina thereafter continued to suffer further institutional turmoil, in addition to the debacle of the financial system. Society responded with new and creative forms of protest and self-organization, and the professionals found new ways of social insertion in the new social context.

## *Conversations with adolescents*

On 28 September 2004, in a small southern city of thirty thousand inhabitants in Carmen de Patagones, a Province of Buenos Aires, a high-school student shot several of his classmates, killing three of them. The unusual incident shocked the population, leading to intervention programmes by school authorities all over the country in order to prevent further violent incidents. These interventive programmes led us to ask ourselves just how efficient they had been—that is, how the messages of the adults, elaborated by experts, had been received by the adolescents.

On 4 December 2004 we[8] organized an encounter with a group of teenagers from Buenos Aires, ranging from 14 to 17 years of age, to get to know their views on adult actions in school settings in response to violence and on other subjects of their interest. We used a format in which one of us led the conversations with the teenagers in the presence of professionals from the mental health and educational fields as well as some of their parents of these youngsters. Following the conversation with the teens, the adults reflected on it. Then the teens reflected on the adults' reflections. The teens had the "final" word, including an evaluation of their experience.

### *Some excerpts from the conversations with teenagers*

Adela G. García: With respect to the incidents in Carmen de Patagones . . . we were interested in listening to your opinions and finding out what you think we should be considering.

N: There was some violence at my school, but the school authorities weren't able to deal with it. . . . They talked about Carmen de Patagones with us, and they blamed the teachers for not being able to give emotional support to the students. The teachers said if they had had to support the students, they wouldn't have had the time to do the rest of their job.

Adela: And what your schoolmates think?

N: The kids in my grade aren't very united, and the teacher said she would make us unite if we didn't get along; but we didn't get along. We all belonged to our own little cliques. . . . They held some meetings for us to get to know each other, to talk things over, but that was it. The group didn't integrate, because we just didn't want to. Had we been interested we would have done so ourselves.

Adela: Did the adults want things of you that you didn't want?

N: Yes, until we said "we don't want to". But it was too late by then; we just weren't listening to the tutor any more.

Adela: Which teachers do you like best?

M: Some of the teachers are warm, but the higher authorities prevent us from having freedom or doing things in school. Now they've appointed new authorities. I don't know why. . . . And they chose a teacher who the children as well as the other teachers hate. Some of the teachers who come to us don't relate to us genuinely; they just do it out of a sense of duty.

N: What we need when they come and talk to us is for them to help us talk about our problems, so that we can feel comfortable enough with the teachers.

F: In my grade there are five girls who do everything by the book, and we, on the other hand, were the ones who did everything wrong. Yet we were very united, we got along well, and in addition to creating havoc, we would flunk exams and some of us even had to repeat the year. We were a disaster, but we were really close and we all hated all the teachers and directors. We didn't like the way they talked to us. The only teacher who was able to reach the students was the psychologist, and she was the only one who could get us to sit down and be quiet. With her, I had a 9 average. The other teachers would only sit down with those five girls and let us do whatever we wanted to. I like a teacher who can make the class interesting. . . . It's important for them to ask things respectfully.

*Some excerpts from the adults' reflections*

V: I admired the way they expressed themselves, and it got me thinking about the importance of a passion for teaching in a teacher.

L: I was wondering whether conversations like these in schools between groups of teens and groups of teachers would facilitate the relationship between them. The adults talk to the kids they way they think the kids should be without asking them what it is they really need or want. It's great for them to have the possibility to talk about what they want, and that there are adults willing to listen.

M: Adults tend to homogenize; it's great to see so many differences. In addition, the members of the team manifested their interest in find out the about the ideas the kids have on sexuality, drugs, communication with adults (parents, teachers, etc.).

During the meeting they were also asked whether they wanted to share their ideas on other topics, so they also chose to talk about sexuality, teenage pregnancy, safe sex, violence in society and in schools, and communication with parents and peers.

*The teens' reflections on reflections*

L: You can talk freely when you're allowed to at home.

M: There's no point in homogenizing. We all belong to a world of our own . . . Sometimes we can resolve problems with our peers. . . . Sanctions don't work either. . . . You shouldn't have to run out of resources [as adults]. You should always be able to come up with new ones.

T: I am the daughter of "*padres del miedo*" [parents of fear].[9] There were times when they had no choice. Nowadays parents try to give us more options than they had.

F: I think when you're a teacher you should enjoy teaching, draw the line when you have to, and keep a positive attitude towards the children. I went to a school where you had to think like them. I'm not interested in that, but you fall outside the system. I personally prefer falling outside the system instead of being coerced into a way of thinking or a personality type. Everyone has their opinions and personality. And with the way things are nowadays, with all the violence and all, getting into fist fights, things are just getting worse, but it's up to you if you want to get into a fist fight or use drugs. Yet society is also responsible for making these [drugs] available, otherwise I would have never used them. I see 13-, 14-year-olds throwing up at night, so society is responsible for making them available. So that's when you start to wonder . . . what should I do? Some accept them, others don't. The decision is up to you.

T: We've all had access to them. They're everywhere. I personally don't need them. Why? Because I have a choice.

Adela: What makes it possible for some of you to have a choice? What does it depend on?

N: They go with the flow. Maybe they think they will be rejected if they say no. . . . I talk to my parents, but they also let me make up my own mind, let me decide for myself and draw my own conclusions.

M: We live in a consumer society, and they make us consume drugs and things like that. And it's also easier to follow the crowd than to be different, since being different implies many things. When you are different you become more vulnerable and they'll discriminate you.

P: Drugs allow you to escape that part of reality you don't like. You'll be happy for a little while, and find refuge in those different states, but the truth is that you'll then start wanting to escape all the time, or wind up dead or get hooked.

F: There's a rock group who claim that when you're high you live life differently. You live in your own little world and you're happy in that world, and it either destroys you or you decide to live in the real world and enjoy the little things in life, and stop living a fictitious life where you think you're happy but you're really escaping.

*The teens' evaluation of the experience*

One of the most important consequences of the experience was that the adolescents felt they had been listened to. It was surprising to see how they talked to each other as if the adults were not even there. The conversations took place in a safe and trusting environment. Some of the teenager's comments regarding the evaluation of the activity include the following:

> "It's really nice to actually be able to talk with teenagers after what happened; we're the ones who are actually going through this. Adults sometimes experience it a little from a distance . . . to be able to talk so as to prevent this from happening again."
>
> "It's nice that adults can learn something from us."
>
> "I generally don't get along well with adults."
>
> "It was cool how they listened to us in a context which gives you more freedom and power to express ourselves."

The evaluation showed the importance of these types of conversations in that they promote listening, respect, expression, curiosity, and democracy. The generation of open dialogues (Seikkula et al., 1995; Seikkula & Olson, 2003) promotes a feeling of trust, in which its actors participate in a mutual process of uttering and responding, from which the not-yet-said emerges among those who talk and those who listen (Anderson, 2005). Understanding takes place when all those involved have the opportunity to talk and be listened to.

This encounter with the teens led to the implementation, in schools, of important guidelines and courses of action for parents and for teenagers in finding alternatives in a context of mutual respect towards each other, regardless of their differences. In other words, it generated democratic practices.

### *Generation of networks and collaborative relationships*

Tom Andersen has been coming to Argentina and other South American countries on a yearly basis for the last fifteen years. He has become both familiar with many of our social problems and acquainted with many of the human rights organizations. In Northern Europe, he is currently involved in a relational and network postgraduate programme, which is a continuation and formalization of a two-year educational programme in systemic family therapy that was started in 1987. It is a part of the Northern Scandinavian Development Programme in Systemic Work developed in the mid-1970s at the School of Social Psychiatry, which is a part of the Department of Social Medicine of the University of Tromsø. The educational programme developed into a cooperative project between the three Northern Norwegian counties and the School of Social Psychiatry of the University of Tromsø, joined in 1996 by Norbotten County, Sweden. The programme is inspired mainly by the notions of problem-created systems, conversations, language, and the philosophy of language. It is an interdisciplinary programme and is open to everyone who works with individuals, families, and/or larger systems and for those who have been trained in the health, social, educational, and/or police services or any other relevant areas, for at least three years. Moreover, it is aimed at those who work with situations involving many parties with different opinions. The trainees use their own workplace for their training experience.

Tom's experiences in his part of the world, Nord Calotte,[10] and our interest in them led him to ask himself if it would be useful for us in this part of the world to develop such a training programme. He originally shared his thoughts with us in Buenos Aires in October 2003 at the Systemic Family Therapy International Meeting—attended by colleagues from different Latin American countries—and these were received with great enthusiasm. After several conversations, a group was formed by representatives from Asunción (Paraguay), Buenos Aires (Argentina), and São Paulo (Brazil),[11] which was afterwards called the "*Triangulo Austral*" [Southern Triangle].

A two-year training programme for those who work with high-risk populations (individuals, families, and social sectors) was created. It is sponsored by Tromsø University and is hosted by the Universidad Nacional de Lanús [National University of Lanús] in Argentina. Created in1997, located in the suburbs of Buenos Aires ("Greater Buenos Aires"), the institution is in a former industrial zone, where a very large portion of the local community had been employed for many years. The factories were closed and the state railroad had been privatized and dismantled, thereby generating poverty, unemployment, and marginalization in the population. The university was built on the site of the old railway station with its buildings. This made it possible to rehire people, creating new employment opportunities. A large proportion of the students also belong to the same social community.

The programme, Generation of Networks and Collaborative Relationships, is based on autonomy, trust, and responsibility. The selected candidates for this programme come from diverse educational and professional backgrounds: anthropology, law, minority work, psychology, social work, and so forth. They work with issues such as teenage pregnancy or children and adolescents who live on the streets or in shelters, and they provide help for students who come from extremely poor families who cannot pay for their university studies.

Seventy-five per cent of the training programme is carried out by the candidates themselves. They typically work in groups, during which they share their difficulties and skills related to their professional activities and discuss the suggested literature. The *colaboradores* [supervisors] participate in the remaining twenty-five per cent of the training programme. This part of the training is reserved for clinical consultations, experiential exercises, reflecting on specific issues or the readings, and other training tasks.

Twice a year, the three groups of participants with their corresponding *colaboradores* meet during one week, alternating among the cities of the three countries. These meetings are also attended by collaborators from Northern European countries. The collaborators of the Southern Triangle also meet once a year in Tromsø, Norway.

The programme was initiated in March 2005 in Buenos Aires. Here we include some of the feedback from the participants, in their voices, in response to some of our questions one year later:

*"What has it meant to you so far to participate in the Triángulo Austral project?"*

"In addition to having the opportunity to be involved with different peoples and to get acquainted with new ways of working, I think that as I learn to see by looking at and hear by listening to, I also become a better human being."

"It has allowed me to open my mind and recognize a diversity of experiences and realize how many possible ways you can work with people. Every life story enriches me, and it would have been impossible to discover this had it not been for this experience and this way of living through it.

"To me, the experience of the *Triángulo Austral* is a great opportunity to carry out the new paradigms; the chance to create new group relationships, to become aware of [the importance of] co-construction and respect in every sense; the opportunity to participate in a network in which the core is a culture of peace, far-reaching ecology, and spirituality."

*How have reflecting processes influenced your practice and ideas, professionally as well as personally?*

"Since I started the course, my personal as well as professional relationships have changed for the better. On a personal level, I have become less narrow-minded, I tend to challenge my beliefs more, and my questions are more open and useful. On a professional level, I adopt the same stance in an attempt to silence my voice and open my eyes, trying to be more useful for the people I work for, legitimizing all the voices."

"I have been able to see changes in my daily life, the way I look at things; I now incorporate new possibilities. The concept of "useful truths" became important in my life, questions that facilitate connection. I was able to apply new institutional intervention methods in the interdisciplinary team, including in my work with different "players" (educators, managers, families, etc.). What was novel and amazing for me is to see how networks are organized."

> "I was able to apply attentive listening. I listen to what they are really saying and not to what I want to hear, clearing the 'phantoms' that interfere with conversations."
>
> "To take the word of somebody who consults us seriously. Although that may seem obvious, we always forget to do that."
>
> "The interpersonal relationships and the connection with [people from] different countries had a strong personal and professional impact on me. For the very first time, I felt roots and a common identity [which I had] denied for years. I was able to reflect upon personal, social, and macro-contextual reasons that had prevented me from feeling Latin American in my identity. I provided more autonomy to the families [I attend], getting out of that 'triangle' where I usually used to interview them: the office, their homes, or workplaces. I started to interview them at bars, parks, or just sitting on the sidewalk. I no longer go to these encounters with so many prefixed goals or predetermined results. I value uncertainty as a working tool; ways of asking; more and better listening."

## *Our final reflections*

The different circumstances of our recent history have had a powerful impact on us as well as on the families we attend, and this has been a stimulus for us to go out into the larger contexts so as to generate conversational spaces that facilitate respect and diversity. This exercise of curiosity, based on a dialogical, open, and exploring stance, calls for imagination, intuition, and emotion, thereby facilitating the emergence of creative responses. This also entails encouraging questions and critical reflection. Authoritarianism silences, whereas respectful dialogues make it possible for different voices to be heard, for which it is necessary to allow others to speak and really listen to what is being said. This, in turn, requires us to constantly reflect critically upon the coherence between our purposes and actions, and to continuously revise what we do and what we claim we do.

Many voices have been accompanying us throughout the years. We have been encouraged by the ideas of Paulo Freire regarding education as a practice of freedom, autonomy, and hope. Gianfranco Cecchin (1989) is constantly stimulating our curiosity. Harlene Anderson and Harry Goolishian (1992a) influence us with their collaborative stance (Anderson, 1997a). Reflections on culture and colonized practices, and the need for influencing our institutions when we work with populations in marginal situations as proposed by the Just Therapy group of New Zealand (Waldegrave, 1990), have all helped us look beyond our protected office space.

The development of reflecting processes contributed by Tom Andersen have provided us with essential tools for giving expression to our therapeutic stance, ways of conversing, and emphasis on listening, which makes the therapeutic relationship more horizontal and democratic. We would like to stress that his visits over the past fifteen years have permitted an interchange that has made a significant difference in every respect. The possibility of carrying these conversations into larger contexts is a challenge we face every day, with the expectation of collaborating with democracy, peace, equity, and solidarity.

## *Notes*

1. The victims of the terrorism were known as *desaparecidos*, i.e., "missing" or "disappeared".
2. Exemption or immunity from punishment or penalty.
3. The poverty level increased from 10% at the beginning of the 1980s to 50% in 2002, according to World Bank data.
4. *Teoros* in Greek means spectator in a religious festivity.
5. Alicia Bittón, Constanza López, Florencia Oks, and Marina Vinitsky.
6. Native people of the south of Argentina and Chile. To gather or reunite has a special meaning in a country where social networks had been dismantled.
7. Native people of the Argentine-Paraguayan Chaco.
8. In addition to the authors, the CES team was integrated by Alicia Bittón, Florencia Oks, and Karin Taverniers.
9. "*Padres del miedo*" refers to those parents whose children spent their adolescence during the military regime.
10. Training programmes for professionals who work with families in the north of Norway, Sweden, Finland, and Russia. These have been very successful since 1987.
11. Sofía Calcena, Mirta Mendoza Bassani, and Leticia Rodriguez from Asunción; Marilia das Freitas Pereira and Helena Maffei Cruz from São Paulo; Adela G. García and Lino Guevara from Buenos Aires.

CHAPTER 6

# Open conversations that weave changes in contexts of poverty or wealth

*Roxana Zevallos & Nelly Chong*

Almost eighteen years ago, we initiated the challenge to spread a new way of thinking about the human problems in our environment and created the Instituto Familiar Sistémico de Lima (IFASIL), a postgraduate family therapy study centre. Since then we have been training systemic family therapists, or, as we say, training systemic operators, in different contexts: clinical, communal, educational, and so forth. We have also been working with families in varied contexts in our country. Although IFASIL is a private institution, through our training programmes and our links with the community we offer assistance to families of limited economic resources, who represent the extremes of our society.

One of our most famous writers, Ricardo Palma, author of *Las Tradiciones Peruanas* [Peruvian traditions], described Peru as a "mosaic" of cultures, flavours, and colours, in reference to the mixture of races and customs that characterize our country. Along with this, the economic, social, and cultural differences extend the mosaic to complex dimensions. Peru is a country where old and new customs coexist; where the fight against the poverty is an everyday struggle; and where unscrupulous politicians manipulate the "sense" of lack of opportunities (e.g., work, food, education, etc).

There is no model of "Peruvian" family since diverse family models exist, varying according to the customs and the regions that constitute our country. Nevertheless, it is interesting to think that, due to the coexistence between the sense of lack of opportunities and all the mixtures mentioned above, an interesting "style" of solving problems has survived. There is an ancestral solidarity and a capacity to establish networks that has allowed, and still allows, our families to survive—that is, as opposed to governmental inefficiency, the families solve problems for their members.

It was in this context that we started our work as therapists. Since then, we have met and learned from many systemic therapists. Although we had previously been familiar with Tom Andersen's book *The Reflecting Team* (1991), it was not until the International Family Therapy Association Congress in 1995 that we had the opportunity to meet him personally and listen to his ideas. His question "How would you like to use this meeting?" and the discussion of its significance to conversation opened a very important horizon for our practice. We shall return to Tom's influence on our work later in this chapter.

## *The context: the family is the institution*

In 1988, the year when IFASIL was created, Peru was going through one of the worst crises of its history as a republic. The terrorism and the hyperinflation had the country's population living in a climate of constant worry; no one knew where in the city the next bomb would explode and whether the members of their family would return home safe and sound after their daily routines. In Lima, the capital of Peru, where everything that happens in the country is centralized, therapy—and all related to the "Ψ" world—was focused in the psychoanalytic perspective, a therapy mainly visited by people with a sociocultural and economic level superior to the majority of our population. In Peru, approximately fifty-five per cent of the population live in poverty situations, twenty-five per cent of whom live in extreme poverty. There is a difference between poverty and extreme poverty: poverty means very low income; extreme poverty means no income. Poverty is a big statistical category; extreme poverty is a new category and is a subdivision of poverty. Economic classes are divided into A, B, C, D, E, F . Category C is middle class, and D, E are poverty classes; F is the latest category, which means poverty is growing and people in this category live in the worst conditions ever.

The first families we saw at IFASIL had been referred by our students. Our training groups have always been heterogeneous, with members coming from the private and the public sectors. Therefore, our families came from the different social, cultural, and economic layers of our city and country. Then slowly, as people heard about us, they travelled from the provinces to talk to us about their problems.

Over time, we shifted away from the idea of the therapist as an expert who knew what people should or should not do. Through our work it became clearer that an approach was needed that took into account the diversity of the problems and the different contexts of the families. Some of the families were migrants from remote areas of our country and often had customs and languages unknown to us. Even though some of the circumstances and problems of the families that we met were unfamiliar, we wanted to respect these differences and generate a climate of mutual respect. We found that we knew much more about life in bordering countries, and even more distant countries, than life in the distant provinces of our own country.

In this mosaic of contexts, our "family model" that acknowledges and uses these people's strengths stands out in marked contrast to the traditional governmental institutions that focus on deficiencies and not on resources. Families find their own viable alternatives despite the social system's inappropriate or failed efforts. For instance, since a welfare system does not exist, when someone does not have a job, it is very common for them to rely on immediate or extended family for economic support or for a place to live. Also, because the majority of people do not have health insurance, they turn to the family for help to get the medicines or the money to pay the doctor, the hospital, and so on. We have learned from our families the importance of this kind of "belonging": the family is the only institution that in some way always responds to the needs of its members. As we recognized and appreciated the families' strengths, we learned to stop emphasizing their deficiencies as well as our own. We learned that no matter where we come from or the inadequacy we—clients as well as therapists—may have, we all have resources to generate solutions to our problems.

## *Our work in IFASIL*

IFASIL has survived in a changing and difficult context without external aid. Over the years we have confronted many crises in our work, our country, and our personal lives. During the long years of the terrorism (1983–1992), we had to find creative solutions on how to continue working and offering our classes in the middle of the tension in which we all lived. In the midst of a war climate, daily we would arrived at IFASIL and find that the electric power had been shut down as a result of terrorist attacks. This did not stop us: we lit our candles, and the classes and therapy continued.

In the beginning of IFASIL, we were trained in the structural model of Salvador Minuchin (1999). His model permitted us to introduce an alternative way to approach therapy compared to the predominant psychoanalytic model. Over the years this influenced a change: we have seen a shift from going to therapy being seen as unusual (e.g., only "crazy" people and those in crises go to therapy) to the perspective of therapy as a valuable opportunity for change and mutual growth. Although our work in the initial stages of IFASIL was beneficial and enriching, our encounter with Tom Andersen and his ideas brought questions and answers that embraced our restlessness to meet our families and their challenges better.

## *The influence of Tom Andersen on our work: the reflecting team the Peruvian way*

In our training programme, we work with a team of therapists in training, who in the beginning only observed the work of a colleague. The observers and the supervisor were behind the one-way mirror. Usually only the supervisor made the comments and guided the therapist in conducting the interview. When we heard of Tom Andersen's work, we began to rethink our task and role in the "supervision" of the therapists. Our first change was to have all the observers, not just the supervisor, participate behind the mirror. With this change, we noticed that their comments became more useful; they started to feel co-responsible for the therapy, and on some occasions they would go to the room and talk with the therapist, in front of the family, about the thoughts that they were having about the situation. We also noticed that all team members participated more actively with all the families, not just with those for whom they were the therapist. Second, we invited the family to talk with the therapist about the observers' reflections and determine what was useful and what was not. Some time after introducing this form of reflecting team, we noticed other interesting changes. The families and the team had more options to choose from, and some of the options always led to useful change. The therapist who was conducting the therapy also had more opportunities because he or she could listen to the reflections of more people and not only those of "the supervisor"; also, since the reflections came from the family and from colleagues, the fear of being observed and being criticized was diluted because everybody was working and reflecting with the therapist about what the family proposed in the therapy. And third, for the supervisors, working co-responsibly with the team and getting out of the "expert position" was a rewarding experience.

In this context, we began talking with people in the community, learning and listening to their ideas about what we were doing there and what they thought we should do. As a result of these dialogues and learning the expectations and needs of the people and being better able to meet these, the project grew. Team members now also hold workshops on topics that the community members consider important, including single parents, co-parenting, school problems, adolescents, and peer pressure. These workshops have had special appeal to single mothers who work and who have the responsibility of raising their children in a context where gangs and drugs are part of daily life, as are domestic violence, alcoholism, suicide, suicidal adolescents, and so on.

### *The reflecting team in the parish*

One day a student in our training course told us about a priest whom she described as "a very different priest from any other you have ever met". The priest was Father Víctor Müller, who at the time was in charge of the parish of Nuestra Señora Madre del Redentor, which is in Santa Rosa, an economically deprived zone of Lima. The families who live in the community have many serious problems, and they went to Father Víctor in search of advice and guidance, a task that he fulfilled conscientiously. Nevertheless, he thought that it must be possible to do something more for these people. Our student introduced us to Father Víctor, who thought that we could help him with his parish families. In the beginning, only a few of our students were interested in working with Father Víctor to meet the needs of his parishioners. Enthused by the work of these few students, Father Víctor extended the offer for help to many more families, who in turn passed the message to other families who they thought might need help. The requests for our services grew, so we now have a designated place in the parish where we receive the families who come to us for help. In addition, the students' enthusiasm also spread to other students who then wanted to work with Father Víctor and the parish families.

The therapists who work with the parish families use a reflecting team format. Using this format in this context has generated new knowledge and new ways of being for us as therapists. We realized, more and more, that the idea of the therapist as possessing a secret truth based on his or her scientific knowledge made us the owners of knowledge about the family that is unknown and unfamiliar to them. This "knowledge" created a distance between our consultants and the therapeutic team. This distance also interfered with opportunities for us and them to get to know their resources and their wisdom about their own situation. We therefore became more careful with our hypotheses, trying to remain aware that they arise from our own beliefs and how we use them to classifying facts in order to confirm them.

In this community, the people are used to helping each other. One way in which they do this is to form committee networks that support and address families' needs, such as the "Vaso de Leche" [glass of milk] for the kids, pastoral councils, mothers' clubs, and so forth. Each of these groups asks Father Víctor for help on different things: therapies, lectures, workshops, and so on. Their demands influenced the structure of our therapy services. As a result of our encounter with Tom Andersen and his ideas, the therapy team and the family work together around a common goal: diminish the suffering.

It is mainly in this context of working with such diverse needs and circumstances that we have learned and experienced the value of Tom Andersen's (1991) proposal that "each person has his own rhythm and speed and these must be considered while participating in the conversations". This implies a clear notion of respect and recognition of the other, as Maturana (1992) would say, as a legitimate other in coexistence with oneself.

The people who live in communities such as the one that Father Víctor's parish serves are usually met by specialists who come to dominate their resources and potentialities, and who suggest what to do, what not to do, and when and how to do or not do it—all the while ignoring, or not realizing, that although the people may be economically deprived, they are wealthy in resources, creativity, and survival. In our work in this community, more than in any other, we have come to understand what Tom Andersen (1991) means when he says: "we can only contribute to help if the conversation leads us to feel curiosity . . . the curiosity is the motor of the evolution." Our conversations with these families evolve; we do not take anything for granted, we pose questions, and we avoid give speeches or interpretations of their realities, which are often so completely unfamiliar to us. We only gain access to understanding their realities when "we act from curiosity", as Cecchin (Cecchin, Lane, & Ray, 1993) proposed, while we participate in the conversations. We remember Tom Andersen's (1991) words, "the questions are better tools than opinions and interpretations".

### *Tom Andersen visits Peru*

During the International Family Therapy Association's (IFTA) congress in Porto Alegre, Brazil, in 2001, a committee was founded with the mission to spread family therapy to what was called "under-served areas". Tom Andersen was in charge. As a result of this committee, Helena Maffei and Marília Freitas from Brazil and Adela García from Argentina came to Lima to visit the Santa Rosas project to share their thoughts with the team and the people from the community

In October 2004, Tom Andersen came to Lima; this was a great opportunity not only to see him working in our own context, but to get to know him as a human being. The coherence between his epistemology and his way of thinking about the daily life events was very inspiring. During this time, Tom worked with two families from the parish, who faced serious and complex problems: a 5-year-old girl sexually abused by her cousin, and the family of a 15-year-old adolescent who was suicidal. In spite of not speaking the language and being in a very different context, the family, the team, and Tom created a very respectful atmosphere. Everybody sensed the pain and appreciated Tom's respectful ways of approaching this pain. The special atmosphere shared by the participants in this consultation went clearly beyond the languages, the cultures, and other differences: a space of collaborative conversation was made possible in that moment. All were included as actors whose wisdom was respected and valuable, and the reflections made it possible to see yet-unseen resources.

Tom also participated in a meeting with some of the community network leaders and other members of the community; for example, mothers of the Vaso de Leche committee, men and women from the pastoral family, and the mother's club. In this meeting, the participants talked about the family therapy project and expressed new needs. They wanted the project to grow and to keep helping them grow; they described it as an opportunity to do better things for them and their children; and they described it as an opportunity for families to help other families, not as "experts" but as a solidarity network. They (referring to the therapists) "listen to us", they said.

### *Dialogues about the dialogues*

In the contexts and characteristics of the families that we work with as described above, the reflecting processes have been an invaluable conversational tool, guiding our work with families in specific conversations. This collaborative way of being together with the families fits within the cultural context where ancestral solidarity as a way of solving problems is central. In developed countries, governments face the challenge of providing comfort to their citizens. In doing its job, the government turns into an abstract entity that is distant from the people, giving them pre-designed politics based on experts' opinions and not listening to what is being asked. Tom Andersen's ideas and the collaborative way of being together closes the distance between us and highlights the importance of people listening to each other. Through Tom Andersen's ideas, we were able to use these ancestral solidarity networks, turning them into collaborative networks and helping them function as a transitory support instead of traps with no way out.

## *An example of our work*

Juana, age 70 years, asked at the parish project for help from the reflecting team. She and her five children had been abandoned by her husband. She had worked all her life to raise her children properly. She used to sell sweets in the streets, clean houses, and do other menial chores. She was a survivor in a very difficult context. Her two younger sons (ages 35 and 33 years) lived with her, along with one son's wife and his two little girls. The other son was single but planned to get married soon. It is not unusual, in our context, that family members facing economic difficulties still live with the mother. Juana's questions first emerged at the mothers' club, where the other women also talked about their sons. Some of these sons lived with their mothers, but they were the ones working; the mothers stayed home.

When we met Juana, she complained about being "always alone"—even though so many people lived at her house, she felt lonely. No one talked to her any more, except, of course, if somebody needed help or money. When she came back home from work, she ate alone as her elder son was with the wife and the girls, and the other one was usually at his girlfriend's place. She asked for help because she wanted somebody to tell

> her sons that this was not the way to treat a mother. She said that she would like to keep some of the money she earned for herself, so that she could travel to her homeland, Andahuaylas (a province in the Andes of Peru), which she left when she was a little girl and had never been back to. But she did not dare to stop giving money to the sons; they were young and needed money more than she did. She continued to sell sweets in the streets and clean houses. She said that the only thing she wanted was to have some company with her meals and someone to chat with when she came home back from work.
>
> Juana and her sons came for a session. For the first time the sons really paid attention to the mother's tiredness, and for the first time they made explicit their gratitude for all her efforts. None of them ever thought about the end of the "helping time", including Juana, who had never thought about having the right to a time in her life where she was responsible only for herself and no one else.
>
> Juana and her sons listened to the team reflections. These reflections made it possible to talk about how mother's help and family solidarity was useful, but in the present moment it was turning into a heavy duty for an old lady. She began to talk about how much longer she could live and the way she would like to spend the years left—how she wanted to travel to Andahuaylas, have company for meals, and some conversation after work while the children still lived at her home, but not every day because she understood that the wife, the girls, and the girlfriend also needed their time. Juana and her sons decided to have at least two dinners together during the week. She was saving money for her trip, but she hadn't had the opportunity to go yet.

We always consider the extended family as a natural network and a resource. As with Juana and her sons, family situations can turn into oppressing and limiting for some of the family's members, especially when depending on family members for help is not something transitory but a way of living that perpetuates the elder generation's task and delays the departure of the younger.

## *Summary and conclusions*

Our way of thinking and doing therapy has changed after reading and meeting Dr Tom Andersen. As Gianfranco Cecchin said, we no longer hold to our hypotheses, because we realized they did not let us be curious. They put us in the expert's role and excluded our consultants and their valuable wisdom from the opportunity to share the responsibility in the therapeutic process.

Our consultants and the team learn from this opportunity of sharing valuable wisdom. The consultants have been empowered and feel the right to take care of themselves, to pursue happiness, as Father Víctor says. When the project began, Father Víctor's concerns were about people's self-esteem. He wanted us to help them recognize how valuable their lives and they themselves were. He thought that if this were possible, they would have better opportunities in life. We believe that through these dialogues we are contributing to the empowerment of our consultants—they become the true owners of their resources and are listening to their wisdom, instead following the experts and their imported knowledge.

Considering ancestral solidarity—the main collaborative tool of our consultants—has lead us to think about spreading these collaborative dialogues to the community networks. As therapists and individuals, we share with those who consult us the responsibility of the therapeutic process. We share thoughts and ask questions based in curiosity. We usually have this first question in our minds: How does someone survive in such a difficult context? We are very respectful towards those who possess the skills to survive in these very difficult contexts—contexts that sometimes are completely foreign to us.

Psychotherapy models based on pre-concepts and certainty, which are used all around the world, do not take into consideration the differences between contexts. They are usually born in the Western tradition, and experts try to make them fit into their contexts, even if this could be sometimes very disrespectful of local traditions and ways of living.

Beyond languages and borders, collaborative dialogues make it possible to create a respectful way of listening to others, recognizing and valuing all their wisdom and resources. This presents the opportunity for creating the difference that makes a difference, as Bateson said.

### *Father Víctor Müller's comments*

I am pleased to share my thoughts about my experience of meeting Dr Andersen. I was impressed by his capacity for listening and his emphasis on what the other person wanted listened to as the most important thing. His respect for the others was very strong, from my point of view. No interpretations, no assertions. His task seems to be to help people know something else about themselves and their experiences. In an interview with the family of a 15-year-old who had recently committed suicide, Dr Andersen found himself in a new experience. With total transparency and spontaneity, the family shared with him the pain and the grief. These feelings were so intense that the room was full of them; the team, Tom Andersen, and myself, we were all very touched by what we were witnessing at that moment. It was in those moments that Tom Andersen's ideas, about listening and following the path the people want to follow, helped them face the pain and the grief.

Tom Andersen joined them on this path, and in a very sensible way he helped them to talk about this difficult situation. His approach is about patience, not forcing situations, waiting for people to respond in their own time, about collaboration among people. On his visit to our parish, his religious interest was clear. After meeting him, I have been thinking about what he taught: listening, respect, joining. These have been very useful in my pastoral duties.

CHAPTER 7

# Conversation, language, and the written word

*Judit Wagner*

An abundance of thoughts can be conceived when we dare to be present, listen, and even step into these thoughts, as I aim to show in this chapter. I also show how individuals within the organization think, and how they are affected through an ongoing conversation. Some language expressions and how they influence our thinking are described, and I have chosen texts representing language expressions. I also describe how a written text can be used in different ways: as a way of beginning to talk or to tell a story, as one way to describe the other.

## *A place for conversation is created*

I work in a prison in Kalmar, a city in the southeast of Sweden. The prison has a high security rating and houses sixty inmates who are serving long (twelve-year) or life sentences. Nowadays Kalmar is a drug-free institution, meaning that those placed there are not substance abusers. The prison has a school and a workshop, where the inmates study or work. There is now an apartment within the facility grounds where the inmates can receive visits from their families and spend a few days together with them. A placement in Kalmar is centrally controlled by KVS (The Board of National Prison and Probation Administration), the highest deciding body for correctional facilities in Sweden. Most of the inmates have gone through a risk-assessment at Kumla Prison, a big institution serving the whole country, prior to their transfer to Kalmar. The assessment yields a psychological classification and diagnosis of the inmates' capabilities, or, rather, their lack of capabilities. KVS also make reassessments of the inmates regarding decisions about when parole and relocation to lower-security facilities can take place.

When an inmate arrives at Kalmar, he has been in detention for a long time, sometimes almost a year. The inmate has stayed at Kumla for a shorter time, maybe two or three months, and possibly also at some other facility. The inmates may have chosen to come to Kalmar when they were informed about the different programmes at different facilities. They get assigned to a cell and are given clothing, shoes, and information about the practices of the facility; they are then brought before the director (the KVINSP inspector of criminal care, the leader of the institution) and are registered.

I first meet with inmates either at Kumla prison or on their arrival at Kalmar. I tell them about the conversations, the reflective talks, that we practise at the Kalmar facility. In the reflective talks, we always meet as three parties; one inmate, one orderly officer, and myself; or one inmate and two specially trained orderlies. I also inform them that they can select whom to speak with and that they will have the opportunity to start discussion groups. They can choose some of their co-inmates to join them for a topic of interest to them, and they can choose a staff member as a leader for the discussion. The only limitation regarding the choice of the staff member is that he or she has training in reflective conversations.

## Reflective conversations

### Meetings

> "A good conversation for me is when you answer to what I said, not to what you think of me."

The words above, from one of our inmates, summarize the reflective conversations. The history of reflective talks at Kalmar now is in its fifteenth year (Wagner, 1997, 1998a, 1998b, 2001). Our conversations touch on various issues including leadership, personnel, inmates, as well as the entire way of organizing the work at the facility. We talk, listen, and reflect alternately, taking turns with each other (Andersen, 1991, 1994, 2003).

We found that the reflective talks could be utilized in various ways, such as *individual conversations* between one inmate and two staff members; *group conversations* with up to six inmates and two staff members; *family conversations* with the inmates' families, during their visits, and some staff members; *networking conversations* when authorities come to visit, with relatives and staff members; *mediation conversations* when conflict surfaces between inmates or between inmates and orderlies; and *visual stories* organized as return meetings with former inmates. The return meetings are led by Professors Tom Andersen and Georg Høyer from Tromsø University in Norway and are recorded on video.

### Descriptions that influence

I want to present an interview with Anna, an orderly officer who sometimes substitutes as director and who takes part in the reflecting work. Her story is a testimony to how descriptions can influence us.

> "How I decided on reflecting conversations? I saw other possibilities that I compared with one-to-one conversations. Our reflecting conversations tend to be straighter to the point and more honest. The inmates do not blurt out as many thoughtless things when there are two people listening. They think carefully before they say anything. They say important things; they

> regard the whole talk situation more seriously. The conversation turns out different: clearer, more concise. We know what to do, what to speak about, and how to speak of it. . . . I noticed a clear increase in the quality of the conversation. I did not have to carry all of it myself. It was a relief. When you meet an inmate, you have the files and descriptions of the correctional system in the back of your mind, and they influence you. This makes you think in a certain way during a conversation with the inmate: as an orderly, I am on guard, and only ask such things as the description allows; I do not dare to digress.
>
> "When we are two [professionals] in the conversation-room, I have more freedom and confidence to ask different questions and delve into different conversation areas. I am less afraid to digress, I dare to move away from the guidelines of the system, while still feeling responsible."

Descriptions of people affect our thinking: we start thinking in terms given by the description. Our reflective talks give us space to ask for other descriptions, to dare to touch on other language areas. We also strive to let ourselves express differences. When there is space to listen to multiple descriptions, there is also a freedom of mind to think wider, further, differently. In this realm, one does not have to defend oneself or explain. This is a premise for rehabilitation and democracy in our environment. Furthermore, it is a way to relinquish the professionals' privilege of deciding what we can speak about and how to speak about it. As soon as *we*, the professionals, decide what the proper areas of conversation are, we lose our clients' stories and all the abilities hidden within them. Thus we limit ourselves in our thinking about the other, about us, and about the two of us in relationship (Lévinas, 1993). Anna continues:

> "What you read about an inmate locks you up in a certain way of thinking. Now I can share the discussion with another, allowing me to think along other paths as well. . . .
>
> To be three in reflecting talks allows us to see things from another perspective that can be merged together with the first. We begin to be able to see changes in the inmate and to believe them, not just think that it is manipulation."

Anna expresses simply how the reflective discussions gives her thinking more alternatives; she begins to think in multiple ways. When she sees more nuances, she can describe people within those. The individuals she describes will get an increased chance to be seen in the way that human beings are—as complex. The prison and correctional system are inclined to give simple descriptions and reach linear conclusions about people and their behaviour. The "three-way conversation" gives space for reflections, allowing for the inmates to be listened to. They gain voice. Their own stories can bear witness to this.

> "Sometimes you get completely locked up by information you hear about an inmate in another context—for example, from your colleagues at the morning meeting. The concern can be that the inmate has refused to give a urine sample; this leads you to suspect that he is now abusing substances. These thoughts will steer the conversation, even if you do not wish to ask about them, as they are not expressed there. Now we solve it so that we can reflect about this and speak more openly, and eventually drop the subject altogether. If an opportunity arises during the conversation to mention the suspicion, just that might well mean that something will open up, something happens, an important change takes place.
>
> "Reflective conversations remove some shutters; we speak about essentials—real, important things. We can also express uncomfortable things, those that you may only have a feeling about—for example, if you believe that the discussions no longer fill a purpose. Simply put, we raise the level of the conversation. Of course, you guide the conversation through your questions. Nevertheless, you think more about what to talk about that serves the other. I believe that it is only in reflective conversations that this is a possibility; for repose within the conversation. These conversations give a greater sense of security."

Anna's expression "for repose within the conversation" is an important distinction, as we are situated in the criminal rehabilitation system. We are all allowed the space to listen in a milieu where it is not common to have the opportunity for repose. This opportunity to rest permits time and space to prepare thoughts for the next thought, and the next—thoughts such as how to organize one's life without harming others or oneself. Through the way we speak, the entire institution is influenced; we can notice that in the changing attitudes of the inmates and hear it in the language of our colleagues—they are speaking in other ways. The conversations create a common philosophy at the facility.

> "You become more emotionally engaged in your client and take your work more seriously. Oftentimes my colleagues at the placement facility or other facilities will ask, 'How come you have succeeded in Kalmar? How do you deal with those difficult inmates?' The reason that it works here has to do with respect and trust. This respect and trust comes from both the personnel towards the inmates and vice versa. The staff learn to respect the inmates on a deeper level, under all circumstances. The inmates feel that we give of ourselves as human beings. We are not paid more because of that; we are simply interested in them as people.
>
> "I have three roles at the institution: orderly, director, and conversation partner. There is no difference for me to be in the three roles. You separate them and engage in them. You tell the inmates who you are now, when you search them or when you make decisions, or when you engage in a reflecting talk. These three ways of speaking overlap, and I gain more knowledge. The conversations influence my way of speaking when I am director. Since I pose a variety of questions in my reflecting talks, I also do that when I take on my role as director. I tend to ponder more over decisions I need to make. To say yes or no becomes more nuanced; I become thoughtful.
>
> "For the inmates this can be frustrating—they seem to want to fight with something or someone. That cannot take place if you nuance your decisions; both of us end up in a new situation. Openings become possible; we become interested in finding alternative solutions. Decisions about the inmates become integrated in the treatment, the rehabilitation, the questions why certain decisions are taken are answered.

"The work becomes exciting. I do not make decisions just because there is a rulebook, which of course I follow, but I try to make decisions that become more individual. I ask myself: what is it I want to accomplish with my power, to have the power to decide over others? How you use your power is important; you should use it in such a way as to accomplish something beneficial for others. You should strive to make humane decisions. . . .

"When I am not in a conversation, while working as director or as an orderly, I notice that I have a greater inclination just to see the inmates as inmates. I lose perspective—yes, that they are also people with a history before they arrived here with us in the prison system, in a life prior to that. They have not belonged here all their lives; they had a civilian life as well.

"The system does not encourage us to think about this, but we know that they had lives before the imprisonment. It is up to all of us to create an organization inside the system that allows for these stories and gives them a place. We are contacts for the inmates, but that is a shallow role. It concerns practicalities: contacting social services, lawyers, employment agencies, and so forth. I can give an example: if you carry out an investigation according to ASI-MAPS (ASI: Addiction Severity Index; MAPS: Monitoring Area and Phase System) and run through the questions, you can begin to take an interest in a certain question. It can spark your curiosity, and you want to develop it further. But you can just as well get stuck with something you see as a problem area. If you decide on this, you can direct the inmate towards a programme designed for this specific problem. You sort the inmate according to problems. He can only have one problem at a time and can be sent to various locations according to the evaluation of different problem areas. Should it appear that the first choice is not the main problem for the inmate, the inmate can be moved to the next programme. Sometimes the inmates themselves will select a manualized programme, perhaps because this is what they have the energy for at that specific moment. Perhaps it is a choice in order to push their choices ahead of them. . . .

"I myself have been lulled into certain thinking. Information about the inmates is very limited if it is only based on their lives starting with the crime. They are sorted into a file dividing them into different categories, and you do not see the whole picture. Before, when the prisoners were not divided according to crimes, you could speak to them without prejudice. Now, when we receive a person diagnosed with "difficult personality disturbance", we think that this person is not normal. What is normal, though? What do you judge by? Is it the actions or the circumstances that resulted in a certain act? Do you think that circumstances can lead up to or trigger an act? The question is what these judgements do to us and to our thinking, the interpretation of the other. It is very easy to think in terms of good or bad, normal or abnormal, and so forth. The inmates often say that all of us could end up in a situation when we could kill."

The language we create in our culture shapes us and our views, and our actions against the other. In a prison, a location for expected transformations, it would naturally be highly meaningful to create a language system that generates humanity (Bateson, 1972, 1979, 1998). Anna clearly sees a difference between the usual manual-based programme in a prison system that divides people according to different behaviours, directing them to different programmes based on that, and a way of working that invites humanity.

What Anna talks about becomes important experiences, to see where, in this system of strong oppositions and polarizations, to find an area, to create one, where it is possible for all of us to exist. There, each and every one of us has permission to speak; we can form our voices and expressions and have a privileged right of interpretation. This is easy to talk about, but how do you do it? From the personnel's side, they must be sufficiently interested to find their way there and also willing to analyse their assumptions and question the judicial system's descriptions in the form of evaluations, tests, and manualized programmes. Can these descriptions be combined with, or replaced by, dialogues and reflections? Can the orderlies dare to see, hear, and believe in that which they experience. Can they be in areas where there are no clear answers? The prison system is not constructed with an approach that creates these views, but it does allow for them. It is not only the orderlies who should abandon the traditional, but the inmates also—their view of prisons and orderlies is prejudiced and distant. They carry bitter experiences from society's institutions and do not trust anyone. However, they can agree to stick together against the system, not to speak to the orderlies, not to negotiate or give of themselves, not to meet up, and also constantly to oppose and question laws and rules constructed to control them. To come from behind any of these barricades and begin to meet requires many steps. It requires from the inmates a courage to enter unknown territory, where they will not know what to do or how to behave. It is striking that when an inmate has the courage to step into this territory, we might discover a defenceless, bewildered person.

We meet the inmates with deep reverence and carefulness. The three-way conversations open up the discussion-room; the system outside gets a view of what takes place. The criminal justice system enters into the conversation situations. A side-effect of the conversations and the relationships that evolve from them is increased safety at Kalmar, and the atmosphere in corridors is calmer among the inmates. The usual prison discussion about crime and the poorly functioning prison system changes to other topics: how we speak with one another, how we relate to others.

To be in dialogue is necessary for us human beings to survive. We should not refuse anyone this privilege, and certainly not the inmates. It could be society's mission to support institutions that make good dialogue possible and thereby contribute to a just development for the people involved. This could also contribute to accessing linguistic constructs and shared spaces as identity-builders. (Benhabib, 2004; Fraser, 2003). This should be the ground to shape a life in decency and dignity. To be in conversation should be part of human rights.

## The written word

"Descriptions shape our thinking and our beliefs."

A

> *"DO NOT DISTURB ME!*
>
> *This applies to all.*
> *Even prison guards, pigs, and whores.*
> *If you are going to disturb me,*
> *you better have the SWAT team behind you."*

### B: Risk and need profile

*"From the psychology evaluation carried out during the time in the National reception (see attached statement) it is evident that Larsson is oriented towards all qualities. The formal contact is good, the emotional less so. Affectively Larsson appears partly inadequate with tendencies to exaggerations in acting out. Regarding personality Larsson come across as unquestionably antisocial with an early début in crime and norm-breaking behaviour. Furthermore, he is impulsive, with insufficient ability to show empathy and remorse. Intellectually Larsson is at a level slightly above average. On the neuropsychological part of the evaluation there are no indications hinting at neuropsychiatric dysfunctions. No indications of substance abuse exist. Larsson fulfils the criterion for antisocial personality disturbance and histrionic personality disturbance according to DSM-IV. He also fulfils the criterion for PCL-R. Estimates with HCR-20 (in) and (out) signals high values, meaning that the risk of a violent criminal relapse is judged as clearly increased. . . ."*

### C: Letter

*". . . I have not forgotten the question you posed in your last letter.*

*If I would like to speak about what happened that night?*

*Both yes and no, I would like to talk about it.*

*But I do not know how and with whom.*

*Actually, I have not talked to anyone about it.*

*I know, sooner or later I will speak with Jocke and Anni about it, because we have to.*

*But now I do not know.*

*Am a bit afraid to go back, if you understand what I mean.*

*The sad thing is that it will follow me everywhere, wherever I go or end up in life.*

*In some way I do not feel whole, right now, because of it. It is as if a part of me disappeared that night. Or, rather, I know that I lost a part of me that night.*

*But, not forever. But if I am ever going to find it again, I will have to forgive myself.*

*And I haven't done that yet. If I ever will, I do not know either. I am too tied to the past, which prevents me from moving on. And this is probably because I do not let others in, no matter who they are. To let others in and show them my vulnerable side is much too frightening for me, and because I do not know how to. And once you have opened the door, how do you close it?"*

What descriptions raise what kind of thinking in us? These questions catch our interest in the work with the inmates at the Kalmar facility. How do we think that we understand the person described here by others, or the person who expresses himself in these ways? The texts are written by and about the same person. The first was a message he posted on his door upon arrival in Kalmar. The third we were allowed to read during a session taking place when he had spent eight months at the institution. The theme he raised was: If you talk about difficult things, how and with whom do you speak? Johan spoke of tragic events taking place within his family over a short period of time, closely before committing his crime. In the reflection, the orderly, who was the third person in the room, shared a story with me. She finished her thought by saying: "sometimes, if it seems you do not have time to talk about sad or sensitive experiences, they will stay within you and somehow get in the way." "Yes", I answered, "maybe they linger there and persist in wanting to be mentioned . . . do not want to be ignored . . . Johan did not want to respond then to our talks and reflections but, rather, think about them."

At the next meeting Johan brought along the letter. We were absorbed by it and wondered in our reflections what such a door could look like. My co-worker said: "It is probably an automatic door, which shuts." "Yes", I said: "If you open it just enough. . . ." Now I became curious about the "Risk and Need Profile", the description sent along with Johan, and wondered what it said.

Could the first and second text have become so dominating that the third, the private letter, possibly never would have been written? This letter to Johan's friends needed a linguistic context to develop. Johan shared the letter with us; perhaps it was easier to show a text than to talk openly about something difficult. How would we have viewed him if we had read the official evaluation about him first, before he could share his letter? Would we have been able to create these open conversations so that his letter could take shape?

At Kalmar, we take all descriptions as possible expressions for something that we cannot immediately understand. The interesting aspect for us in working with the inmates is to create the opportunity in dialogue for the different descriptions, to be able to talk about how they influence all of us.

One large word often surfaces in all these stories—the word *responsibility*, or, as I usually call it, borrowing a word from Bakhtin, *answerability*. This we try to practise in our conversations at the institution in Kalmar: we answer with responsible formulations to the story of the other as he answers with responsible thoughts. The French philosopher Emanuel Lévinas says that it is a kind of response face-to-face, when you cannot look away; it requires a responsible answer (Lévinas, 1993). To us it means that the conversations become relational: we always find ourselves in relationships and always speak about relationships. Bakhtin (1993) cites Dostoyevsky, saying that I am always responsible for what I say, I am responsible for your reply, I am always more responsible than you.

There are large demands on us professional conversation partners and on inmates, as well as on the people we are in relationship with. Perhaps this is what Anna means by saying that the conversations become more serious. When we read Johan's text from the door (text A), we asked him if he wanted to hear our thoughts, which were about a very angry man, a man who could be violent, which made us be on our guard. Is that what he wants to communicate? Johan's answer was: No.

## *Descriptions of distinctions*

> "I discovered that I began thinking differently and I thought, this is not me, I have to think as before . . . but I could not . . . "

You would expect that forming a statement about another person could not be done in Kalmar Prison. The inmates ask us for that in order to include it with the reappraisal of their conditions. This is how the criminal rehabilitation system works. I do not know how decision makers receive our different writings, whether these have any influence on their judgements. We write those statements in the same way as our conversations are shaped, as a co-production. When we are asked by an inmate to write a statement, we ask him to write down his own opinion of himself and of the conversations he has participated in. We ask him to describe how he experienced them and thinks of them. Those involved in conversations with him—for example, an orderly and me—each write a part. We write on the same theme, we tell about the process in it. Then all texts are combined into one. These statements are usually descriptions of what one experienced during the conversations, what one was exposed to. My lines tend to be accounts of changes I have noticed and the effort the inmate displayed during the conversations. He can give evidence of those conversations and reflections, as well as respond to those that were of greater weight to me. The orderlies' accounts frequently contain their views of the inmate within and outside the prison, during the supervised paroles, descriptions about noticeable changing viewpoints the inmate displays. They can also tell about colleagues' depictions of the inmate, how changes in attitudes have taken place. The inmates' stories tend to be about what has opened up for them, paths to a different thinking, or the discovery that they act or speak differently. The texts describe differences.

> *"I, the undersigned, was asked by Anders to give a statement of opinion of him, including the conversations he participated in at the*

*Kalmar institution. Anders was in Kalmar during 2003–2004 and participated in the prison's programme based on reflective discussions between three: inmate, therapist, and personnel. Anders came from "hard" institutions to Kalmar with their culture imprinted. This means a segregation of the inmates and personnel on many levels, such that no confidential dialogue between the two groups can be possible. Anders's very self-confident way gave him a natural leadership role at the institution. When we began our dialogues between three, he was on guard, but curious. He stated that he had already gone through a transformation process; he had had time to think and reconsider his values . . .*

*"In my view Anders has intelligence and several gifts that he can make use of in the future. In dialogue he has been courageous enough to choose his own path; to enter into something unknown to him, to open doors for himself and for us. Thus also saying no to other things; leadership among the inmates. To go against the prison system is a strong act for an inmate. To open one's senses for exploring new areas over which one does not have control is very courageous. Anders himself expresses that there are essential parts of his life which mean a lot to him that we did not have time to run through. However, I think that because of his various good abilities Anders has a capacity to deal with those. Anders has participated in evaluation and restructuring work within the criminal rehabilitation system led by Professor T. Andersen, University of Tromsø, Norway."*

*Excerpt from Anders's statement:*

*"The conversations I began by my own free will and only stopped because I was relocated. Today I am sad this happened because the conversations had a positive effect on me. I had just begun reaping the benefits of the conversations. I would like to add that in my opinion I would have needed to partake in more conversations. My nature is such that I have a difficult time to open up and vent my innermost feelings with an outsider. I also had this problem at the beginning of the conversations, but opened up more and more as the conversations progressed . . .*

*"I was able to vent my feelings and apprehensions, ponderings, and so forth. In the answers or feedback I received, I could see things from different viewpoints, which you can say opened my eyes. Describing*

*in words exactly what the discussions meant/mean for me is difficult. But I can say that I miss them . . ."*

*Orderly Karin:*

*"In the role of acting director, on the one hand I was confronted with the documented description that follows with an inmate with a sentence greater than four years; on the other hand, with the situations that surfaced around Anders upon his arrival at the Kalmar institution. There was an attitude in him that partially reflected what he had experienced in the prison environment. Other sides soon appeared and indicated an entirely different picture. As the conversations progressed, the positive image of Anders became clearer and clearer; among other things, through his courage to show compassion for himself, his co-inmates, and staff. It did not take long before our orderly-colleagues noticed this change of attitude in Anders, since he also through his actions showed evidence of what he went through during his conversations. . . ."*

*Kalmar 041115*
*Judit Wagner*
*Licensed Psychotherapist*

When inmates are invited to write their own evaluations, most of them are taken by surprise. This may be the first time they have been asked to write about themselves, make their own observations, a path to discoveries and growth. We merely do not rob them of their own thinking and development. It is not always easy for them to write, and not that common for them to be asked. Writing means that they must face questions and strive to answer them—a process we all go through at some point in our lives. The reflective processes continue, the afterthought, the inner dialogue never ends, it continues even through their writing of their own statements. Writing becomes a natural method for finishing the conversations. We find out more about the inmates' attitude towards the conversations; all three of us get an opportunity to express ourselves, and each voice gets to be heard in a democratic process in which all voices are there and are equally meaningful. Statements are not assessments or tests that give answers according to psychological measurements, which tend to be used in order to "make sure where we have them". The statement belongs to the inmate; he is the one who decides how and for what purpose he uses it. It is time-limited in its validity.

## *Afterword*

When we introduced reflective discussions at the institution, I suspected that it would influence the entire prison system, though how, I could not predict. What I see today is that the dialogues have changed the use of language in the institution (Anderson, 1991, 1997b; Seikkula, 1993, 1996). When the language changed, each person's way of viewing things changed too. Attitudes changed. The staff members taking part in reflective discussions noticed that they were influenced by them and that they used their newly discovered skills in their treatment of the inmates. The written word is a natural continuation of the conversations that precede them. We understand the written text as a reflected meaning. Every word is weighed and appraised by the person writing it. The inmates' stories start a creation, the shaping of an identity of their own, one that they can carry with dignity. What we are allowed to create as language formulations is decisive in our expressions. It is shaped through the linguistic environments in which we are present. We should not deny people this possibility; we should make sure that it is created (Tutu, 2000). The word is not decided and carried out by me for the other. We create thoughts and afterthoughts, images, and stories together and discuss these together (Penn, 1998, 2000; Penn & Frankfurt, 1994). There might be possibilities in them. We acknowledge each other as equals, as an introduction to be able to partake in dialogue.

Writing is a powerful language expression, an important continuation of the work we carry out. Conversations, talks, and reflections, the creation of a linguistic space, and philosophizing around people's conditions influence everything that surrounds us, the system in which we work, in a circular coherent whole. Conversations and reflections are followed by afterthoughts: as partners in conversation, we find ourselves continually reviewing and learning. How do I think? What are my obligations? How do I decide, how do I comprehend the other? To what extent can I allow myself to be influenced by others' descriptions and stories? Tom Andersen often cites Wittgenstein's idea that we should stop explaining people (Wittgenstein, 1995). Instead, we should try to create authentic stories. Each and every one of us needs to decide in every meeting with another person: how do we converse, about what, how do we meet another person, how do we describe these meetings?

In what way is the criminal rehabilitation system going to find out what is a good action, and how can they be able to decide? Perhaps it is not possible to answer this in this chapter. However, one thing we should do: we should offer people the opportunity to have their wounded dignity back. Throughout history, this has been done by offering conversation.

Our work would not have been possible without support from the leadership, attendance of the staff, their openness, and of course, the imprisoned men's engagement. I want to thank all of them.

CHAPTER 8

# Balancing between peripheral/central positions when we're invited to be central

*Helena Maffei Cruz & Marília de Freitas Pereira*

> "How you balance between being significant and central and at the same time stay on the periphery is a challenge. How do you do this? What do you say to yourself? What do you say among yourselves [the team working together]? It is such an important balance and yet so difficult!"

These were the first remarks we heard from Tom Andersen when he visited the SASECOP project[1] in October 2000. We were taking part in a team-building process with seven teachers, one psychologist, one social worker, one art therapist, and the administrator, aiming to offer more than just soup, bath, and bed to homeless people who were attending the shelter. The project's objective was to promote inclusion through socio-educational activities.

Tom's description of our way of being with our clients, in that project and in training courses and family therapy, brought a new understanding to our actions: we remain peripheral in order to allow people autonomous actions, decisions, and solutions in situations they describe as problematic. We should say that we are actively peripheral because our central beliefs include Anderson and Goolishian's ideas that "the client is the expert" (Anderson & Goolishian, 1992a). This chapter describes how we maintain a useful central/peripheral balanced position.

Working together for fifteen years, we brought from our previous experiences—Marilia as a child therapist, Helena as a sociologist—words like "inclusion" and "justice".

Poverty in Brazil is, in itself, violence—a historically constructed exclusion of the majority of the population due to the appropriation of lands and other resources by a very rich minority. Through this process, we understand "exclusion" and "poverty", in our country, as being synonymous.

Tom Andersen's (1995b) statement that "language is not innocent" invited us to reflect on alternative assumptions about human beings: "persons are not in the center but the center of the person is outside him/her, in the collectivity with others" (p. 30). Realizing that individual explanations about poverty assume that poors are poors due to lack of willpower or self-esteem, and that these words generate feelings of powerlessness, both in the excluded and in the helpers, we searched for the socio-historical processes that created our present society. Describing poverty as a social-exclusion process opened up new ways to promote "inclusion", which we understand as "social justice".

## *The construction of poverty*

Brazil is a large country situated in an equatorial–tropical region where the length of daylight hours makes it possible to have two to three annual crops on the majority of its land. Its population: area ratio is twenty-one inhabitants per square kilometre. In such conditions, our main violence is poverty: poverty means exploitative relationships.

Brazil's birth certificate is known as "Pero Vaz de Caminha's Letter"—a diary that relates the day-by-day crossing of the Atlantic and the surprising discovery of our coast, an unexpected land with very different "creatures" who puzzled Pedro Alvares Cabral, the Portuguese fleet's captain. He kept asking himself who those people who responded to the newcomers in such a gentle manner might be. How could another world be so different from the one he knew? Was it possible to have fraternity among men living in a communion of interests? Caminha described the land as having a very beautiful coastline and forests, with many-coloured birds, that spanned towards the interior as far as the eye could see—an immense land with no visible boundaries. The climate was temperate, and the water springs were endless. His prophecy was: "Working well the land, all crops will flourish" (Caminha, 1500). These words remind us of Gregory Bateson's (1991) concern with the effects of conscious purpose on human adaptation and his definition of power as an epistemological error. When the Portuguese found the land, they offered the natives a fair relationship.

Thirty years later, the first general governor was sent to the new land to ensure its possession by Portugal's Crown. He allied himself in tribal wars with one tribe against another, enslaved the losers, and received the first African slaves, who themselves were losers of tribal wars on their continent. Sugar-cane plantations made prosperous with slave labour was the invention of poverty as synonymous with the exclusion of the land's richness. Violence is a process, a relational one. Slavery defines a relationship where some people are the property of others. Slaves could be bought and sold; their family ties and other human rights were not recognized. The violence against slaves was not only one of exclusion, but was also exercised through brutal and constant physical abuse. In repeated violence, when the experience is brutal and collective, the effect is that of being brainwashed, which means living without past or future, dissociating personal feelings, and being in a submissive position—a combination that can turn into identification with the aggressor (Sluzki, 1994). Our main social educator, Paulo Freire (1970), described this effect as "housing the aggressor's conscience". For almost four centuries, captured Indians and black Africans were denied a human identity. The women were systematically raped by white men, generating a fatherless race with no past—no grandparents, no tombs to visit, no traditions to share, no abilities to be proud of. When work is "slave work", the best definition of liberty is not having to work. When slavery ended in 1888, the former slaves were illiterate, jobless, homeless, their families split off, and they had few cultural traits to help them forge a cultural identity. In some areas where African descendants formed the majority of the population, their cultural identity—for example, language, food, music, and religious rituals—was more preserved and was an important cornerstone of a new self-conscience. But these were exceptions.

In the last hundred years, the social exclusion associated with poverty has varied in intensity and frequency. Though racial discrimination is unlawful (e.g., it is no longer forbidden for a black or an Indian person to study, to own property, or to marry white people), the racial discourse had lasted so long, however, that it has simply became a self-fulfilling prophecy.

## *Changing assumptions about poverty in our history*

In Brazil's history, since the beginning of colonization, the Roman Catholic Church has had a strong social voice. Though it was against slavery, its authorities never really questioned this social construction. Saving souls was its main concern. In Catholic countries, poverty through the centuries has been—according to the dominant ideology—the state of those chosen by Christ, the easiest way to Heaven. The first phase of what now would be called community work was then guided by the notion of "charity", a Christian virtue in which the one assisted is not a subject but a sort of object sent to save the soul of the one who does charity. Historically, dealing with child abandonment was almost exclusively a Church charity action, and this is a special example of shameful official neglect. The Church was primarily concerned with the salvation of these children's souls, meaning little more than getting them baptized. The children's overall health and well-being were then neglected, and so the death rate of abandoned children was high, as much as eighty per cent.

In the nineteenth century, two factors changed the focus of poverty in our country: knowledge about hygiene and health led to new ways to care for children and the sick, while at the same time it became clear that the deaths of so many represented a loss of valuable manpower.

As a result, charity or social work began to be ruled by scientifically guided philanthropic ideas—that is, services were based on the knowledge of experts, and the people served were seen as victims of their own ignorance. More recently, there has been a third movement, related to what in Europe is known as the "welfare state". The welfare state, however, has never been fully established in the so-called third-world countries because of a lack of democratic traditions necessary to its origin and survival. Our frail democracy, the progressive impoverishment of the agricultural economies, the massive migration to big cities, as well as other phenomena such as urban violence, abandoned street children, and migrants separated from their families, have continually been in the national and international headlines.

For a short time, between 1958 and 1963, Pope John XXIII's social magisterium in the Encyclicals *Pacem in Terris* and *Mater et Magistra* favoured the birth of Liberation Theology. Though this was condemned and banished from our country, it was quite influential among some Latin American priests, social workers, sociologists, and social psychologists and gave birth to a new "social responsibility conscience" and an understanding of "poverty as a socio-political problem" based in Marxist ideology. In turn, this new conscience influenced the development of an important third sector in Brazil: NGOs (non-governmental organizations). There are currently more than a thousand NGOs offering social work services, either on their own or in partnership with governmental institutions. Our SASECOP project is one such partnership.

Among these voices was Paulo Freire (1998), who was influential in promoting new ways of thinking about education as a "pedagogy of autonomy": through education it is possible to transform the world. "To change is difficult but possible" was his leitmotif. Freire insisted that, "In political–pedagogic relationships with popular groups, their knowledge construed out of experience can not be disconsidered" (p. 90). Freire was dedicated to teaching the subjugated—the peasants—and the rural people to read. He sent his students into peasant communities and had them listen to the words that the peasants used frequently every day. He called these "generative words". When they gathered the peasants together for their lessons, the students would ask the peasants about the words. For instance, they would ask the peasants if the family in the big house would use the same words; what other words in the Portuguese language had the same sounds; and to draw pictures of the words. The students would comment on and ask questions about the generative words to learn the meanings of the words and the reasons that these words were important to them. They taught the phonics of the generative words. The peasants in this learning-to-read process were therefore talking about, reading, and processing their socio-political experiences, changing the idea of learning to read as a technique into learning to read as an instrument for a more effective conception of the world.

Freire was interested in their explanations about the world in which they were included, or what he called "conception of the world"—the reading of their context, which anticipates the reading of the word. To Freire, naïve knowledge and scientific knowledge share the same basis, which he called "epistemological curiosity". It is the critical reflection about the practices that make them different. Eventually, the military government persecuted Freire and forbade him to teach, and he took refuge in Switzerland and travelled the world as a missionary, continuing his "transformation through education".

Freire's assumptions carry some similarities to the "not-knowing approach to therapy" (Anderson, 1997; Anderson & Goolishian, 1988), and practices informed by these assumptions constitute one branch of social psychology in our country: communitarian psychology (Ochoa, Olaizola, Espinosa, & Martinez, 2004).

According to Freire, the theoretical discourse necessary to critical reflection has another fundamental element: emotion. For example, in addition to knowing something about a situation of injustice, it is necessary to rescue the emotion linked to this knowledge. He named it "just anger", which gave strength to the birth of social movements of transformation. Practices inspired by "anger" assumptions turn the word "fight" into a very important one: "fight for rights", "fight for justice". Although our work benefited from communitarian pedagogy and psychology, we felt we lacked a more useful metaphor for our work. "Fight" carries with it military ideas of hierarchy, and our main challenge has been to avoid the "expert" position that the hierarchical institutions with authoritarian traditions have given us. In a not-knowing position, which is a more peripheral position, we begin by learning the population's assumption about their situation.

Reflecting processes developed by Tom Andersen captured our hearts and minds and helped us create opportunities for open conversations and multi-voiced dialogues, an excellent tool for including and searching for justice. In the FAMILIAE Institute,[2] we developed a project that we named "Multiplicadore Reflexivos (Bernardes, Barbas, & Pereira, 2001). The principle of "reflection-action" and the notion of "world conception" correspond: the community's identification of what it thinks is important and its own resources, the legitimization of all different voices, and the promotion of enlarging their net of relationships. Thus we share Anderson and Goolishian's (1988) assumptions that "human systems are language-generating and, simultaneously, meaning-generating systems" (p. 372) and the possibility of problem solutions through open conversations.

The project we developed is used as a resource by multiple groups of caretakers from different contexts and institutions that serve needy people. Its objectives include the development of the reflective capacity of the participants to recognize and give preference to their own abilities and resources. It also generates new useful actions and it favours the emergence of alternative stories that make the construction of more harmonic relationships in the institution possible, developing the participants' capacity to solve situations that are usually considered problematic.

Promoting open dialogues, be it among family members, professionals, and clients of psychiatric institutions[3] or with caretakers of governmental institutions working with youngsters in conflict with the law, we believe that we are helping to strengthen a movement that invites people from these groups to reflect on the practices of health and education, to promote a dialogue among various languages, and consequently to enable collaboration among all involved in the situation. Through group meetings we create a conversational space in which each person can speak and hear about situations and experiences they have gone through, and this speaking and hearing leads to the participants developing alternative proposals for possible actions and future planning.

According to Pearce (1994), the most fundamental human resource is to be engaged in dialogues. To him, conversation is defined as "the substance of social life". Taking part in these conversations gives one the possibility to recognize oneself and the other and, simultaneously, to realize that together we build the reality of which we are part. In these dialogues we pay special attention to the idea that the words we use in our conversations affect our living together. We consider, therefore, that our well-being as well as our suffering are products of how we talk, and, in this way, this living-in-language has a constitutive character. This perspective allows us to approach knowledge and truth as plural. Borrowing Green's words, through these conversations one can learn that "each new way of saying has in itself the potentiality of a new way to relate with different consequences" (Gergen, 1997, p. 17).

## *How we work*

Our work at SASECOP with the shelter participants happens in two phases. We begin, usually with two members of our staff, trying to understand how we are supposed to be as helpers. If it is possible to construct a context where the participants' expectations and our possibilities fit, then we can proceed. We next define our participation according to the requests that emerge from the group, keeping their autonomy in maintaining the conversational resources a priority. Our main concern can be summed up in Tom Andersen's words: "When one person meets another he/she has a great interest in keeping his/her integrity during the whole meeting. What I say and what I do determine a conversation to be open or closed" (Andersen, 1991, p. 35). We want each person to maintain integrity, and we want to invite and facilitate open conversations.

The meetings are organized so that all participants are included and able to exercise their reflective ability. In the first meeting, we propose activities that we consider useful tools to help the participants to enter into reflective conversations with each other, stimulating participation, self-observation, and attention to accompanying body sensations. We use exercises that help participants to develop "listening" and the ability to appreciate the legitimacy of different points of view, to identify the ingredients of a "good conversation", and to have an awareness of the intersection points between personal stories and institutional ones.

The format is of small conversation groups in which each participant tells his or her personal experience related to the theme that emerges during the meeting. These small groups allow people who sometimes feel shy to speak within the whole group to express themselves and for alternative stories to emerge. Telling one's experiences in a collaborative group helps participants to recognize many previously unnoticed features. When the telling that includes the testimony of others is completed, it is possible to assimilate and recognize oneself as the author of these skills and abilities. The telling and testimony, the speaking and the listening, create and improve agency for all. After the small group conversations, all participants share their experiences and reflections on the theme with each other. This is a very special moment: in listening to the shared reflections, the whole group seems to recognize itself and get a grasp of the ideas, capacities, and common desires, and the number of valid voices is enlarged.

When coordinating groups, we try to be aware of the connections between processes described by Tom Andersen as "inner" and "outer" dialogues. In other words, there is always continual movement between inner and outer dialogues. Outer dialogue is a process of exchanges that take place in the relationship. So it is important for us to maintain connecting and relating with the other—sensing, knowing, acting—in such a way that the other's integrity is preserved, as mentioned above. This condition for outer dialogue is critical for the possibility of newness, the expansion of perspectives, in inner dialogue. We are also aware of all emotions present in the conversation and believe that their expression is a fundamental ingredient of each meeting. When the emotion changes, action also changes, and this includes what is thought and what is said

Our focus at SASECOP was the staff's teaching–learning relationships with the shelter users. The staff's request was for us to coordinate "self-esteem workshops". We avoided descriptions of self-esteem as an inner possession of participants and, instead, engaged in conversations about how teaching–learning relationships can promote the possibility of self-descriptions of competence, capacity, creativity, and other descriptions that might be inside the word "self-esteem", instead of deficit descriptions such as incompetence, inability, and so forth. An important part of the work was the feeling of inclusion that slowly developed among all involved.

Since the beginning of SASECOP, our attention to the movements of "inclusion" and "exclusion" within the group made it possible to establish and to maintain the "multiplicadores" work as well as that of the staff.

The group's members developed a high degree of collaboration, solidarity, and co-responsibility, as opposed to an essentialist attitude. They felt that working with our staff had been very beneficial, and they even began using the reflecting processes in other contexts.

For us, an important demonstration of the development of our work has been our use of certain words. At the beginning of the work, when referring to the homeless people in the shelter we used the word "user"—a neutral one, since we are all users of governmental services. But in the informal daily vocabulary, other terms were used to label the people who sought the shelter's services, as "those people", "street people", "they", "the poor ones". Now, we use another word: "student". A student is someone who has an active place in society as one who learns. A student goes to classes, can be promoted, and can have a graduation. A student has rights and obligations that are recognized and encouraged.

## *Final comments*

Our present challenge is to develop similar conversations in a reformatory institution with authorities, staff members, parents, and youngsters who have been in conflict with the law. We are learning from experiences like those of the northern Swedish team's work (Kjellberg, Edwardsson, Niemelä & Öberg, 1995), who say that

> working with reflecting processes is especially valuable in situations in which strong feelings such as anger, fear, anxiety are held by clients, family members and all the professionals. . . . It makes a big difference if we see [ourselves] as professionals who create an atmosphere for conversation and communication among all parties comprising the problem defined system. [p. 61]

We believe that experiences of inclusion and cooperation are at the roots of "social justice".

## *Notes*

1. The SASECOP project (Social Educational Service of Professional Qualification and Counselling) is a partnership between São Paulo Municipal Government and Ligia Jardim, a non-profit night shelter.
2. Instituto FAMILIAE: http://www.familiae.com.br
3. http://www.soesq.org.br

CHAPTER 9

# Celebrating moments of discomfort

*Judy Rankin*

Reflecting upon the influence that Tom Andersen has had on how I think about my life and work and how it has transformed or shifted my practice is a privilege. In this reflection I do not make formal reference to his written words but, rather, to the *words I heard him say* in the various workshops that I have attended and in the conversations that I have had with him. I stress that it is *what I heard* and what I wrote down. The words are not direct quotes (although I wrote down what I thought was verbatim), and they cannot be formally attributed to Tom. As in any dialogue, I cannot be sure that he said this. I heard what I was ready to hear, which is influenced by what I was bringing to the dialogue. His words (or the words I heard), as well as those of others, gave some form to my feelings of discomfort. As my practice involves teaching others, my journey through these moments of discomfort has had to be articulated and consciously reflected upon through the written word and through my teaching. This chapter has given me the opportunity to uncover and read notes from workshops over the years and reflect consciously on the influence of Tom Andersen on the form of my practice. I have used the words I heard Tom say to organize the chapter.

Being a white South African, I frequently experience discomfort in my work as a psychologist. I have no doubt that if I had lived and worked in another context, these feelings of discomfort may have been similar. My practice is in South Africa, and it includes the training of psychologists within a university setting; engaging in community partnerships including the co-development of a peer counselling programme in a rural area of southern Africa; being a consultant and trainer in other diverse community settings; and being a practicing therapist. In this chapter I address one of the above contexts, the Maluti Peer Counselling Project. This project, supported by Tom Andersen, has been the most definitive experience of my working life.

## *"Listen to the uncomfortable feelings the body felt, then a new practice will come from this"*

Like others in this activity of *psychotherapy* and *training,* I am drawn to the *big events* called "international conferences" to learn more. Over the years I have often left disappointed because these are not favourable contexts for learning. The 2001 IFTA Conference in Porto Alegre, Brazil, however, was different. Along with the magical energy of Brazil and its people, the discomfort and disappointment I am usually left with after such events was absent. Though the format of the conference was the same, there were new and different proposals for practice. What was the personal and familiar discomfort that I took to yet another conference, in Brazil in 2001?

I had repeatedly felt that people seemed to speak about things that were not relevant to my life and work. People looking like "experts"—often from the Northern Hemisphere—often spoke with an expertise and certainty that I experienced as a new form of imperialism, a new colonization of ideas about families, lives, and relationships. I would question whether it was because I come from Africa, part of the *developing world,* that contributed to this discomfort. I have since realized, however, that it is more than this particular contextual challenge, as I have met people from many parts of the *developed world* who also struggle with such expertise and certainty, often legitimized by conferences and scientific journals.

I was working in contexts that challenged the relevance of first-world theories and practices of family therapy. Using the metaphor of dance and music (Rankin, 1999), I had searched for relevant and respectful ways of working with families in the South African context. After floundering in my own disequilibrium and feelings of incompetence as a "family therapist" in the contexts where I worked, I wondered whether I was "doing family therapy". I wondered whether I was teaching "family therapy". The actual practice within the contexts where I worked seemed so different from how I was trained, what I read, and what I heard at conferences. I wondered why I was attending an IFTA conference at all. Initially, in the face of darkness and fear of incompetence in my practice, I had relied on the Milan systemic therapy principles to create the circular interview and made attempts at non-directive interventions, which initially exacerbated the paralysis that I experienced as the music played. These skills facilitated the therapeutic conversations and enabled people to tell their story and possibly make new connections as the more inclusive story was developed. But at the end of the sessions, there was always a silence as the team intervention was read. The music stopped, and my clients slowly left the room and went home perplexed and confused. They had told their story and were waiting for the direction, arbitration, mediation, or a prescription that all good doctors give (traditional and medical)! Instead, they received a cleverly worded statement with ambiguous messages and paradoxes. I felt their silence, and my paralysis returned. In the words of an 84-year-old grandmother who had expected a directive from me after a lengthy family session where she sought help in dealing with her troublesome son: " You are learned people and speak caringly but you don't know what kind of person we are dealing with." She went home. We had to change the tune.

I knew that I drew on the skills and practices of the dance I had been taught, but the new context demanded a new dance with new steps if I was to meet meaningfully with the people with whom I worked. It also demanded new steps from them. Once I abandoned my old moves, together we created new dances and steps that led to greater harmony for them and for me. The dance was always changing, and I had learned to stop looking for the ultimate steps.

On one occasion I presented at an international family therapy conference, arriving with a paper that I had written to describe, explain, and share "training ideas". Writing a paper helps you pretend that you know something and enables the university to co-sponsor your search for certainty in the hallowed halls of the wise. Yet as I sit here five years later and read what I had prepared and written, I celebrate the familiar and historical uncertainty:

> I teach. I am aware of the responsibility and power of this position and activities. I therefore teach and train, train and teach, and constantly need to reflect about what we as health professionals are trying to do, what are more or less useful theoretical frames, what are more or less useful skills and techniques. As time goes by, and I watch the grey hair emerging, I seem to "know" less and less and seem less clear and yet more passionate about what I am doing. Is it possible to learn more but know less? To have less knowledge, despite the grey hair?

In the informal contacts at these conferences, I discovered many people who experienced a similar uncertainty and who came to connect. It was in these informal connections and associated conversations that the shifts in my thinking happened. I had my first conversation with Tom Andersen at the IFTA Porto Alegre meeting. I was familiar with his work and ideas, as he had travelled to South Africa and given workshops, and I had taught his work and ideas in my family therapy courses. This meeting, however, was significant because it set in motion the development and support of a project that I describe below.

## *The beginning of a "new fork": the Maluti Peer Counselling Project*

At another IFTA meeting, in Istanbul, Tom spoke of "forks"—significant emotional new directions in our lives and our work. A new fork in my own professional and personal life began to develop at the Port Alegre meeting. In the IFTA executive meeting at that conference, the board of directors resolved "to reach out to areas", and a committee of four was formed to start this work. Tom's voice was influential in this decision. Unlike what so often happens with good intentions, at the conference the committee made personal connections with those attending from South Africa, South America, and Scandinavia. Meetings were held to discuss possibilities, and positive action followed. There were to be three projects that would involve professionals from the North working in local communities in underdeveloped parts of the world. The projects would involve outside local assistants from the South, outside local assistants from the North, and representatives from the local community. I became involved with one of three projects. I was not aware that my decision to participate in the project and the work that evolved from it would have such a profound effect in my life and the lives of others. It will always be a major fork in my professional and personal journey.

The project involved the development of a relationship with Funeke Radebe, a life-skills coordinator within the Maluti Education Department. She invited me to work within the "community" she served: the eighteen secondary schools in the Maluti Township, which is located between the rural towns of Mt Fletcher and Matatielle, Eastern Cape, South Africa. The township has an unemployment rate of over fifty per cent, is very under-resourced, is gripped by poverty, and has a high rate of HIV/AIDS infection: stigma and silence abound, and specific knowledge and counselling support are virtually non-existent. Added to this is the cultural taboo of adults speaking to youth about sex and sexuality. The Maluti Township lies on the outskirts of a former colonial farming town, Matatielle. Those living in the township are generally working-class people, plus rural people who "service" the town, as well as the unemployed. The Maluti area is larger than a usual township; it includes a large area of rural homesteads in the remote foothills of the Maluti Mountains. Setting up the project with Funeke was extremely difficult because communication relied mainly on fax and sporadic telephonic contact. In consultation with Funeke, we agreed that the broad aims of the initial pilot project were to train selected senior students from five high schools in basic counselling skills, to introduce them to the concept of a peer-support programme, and to set up peer-counselling structures within the schools. My responsibility was to develop the programme and select the trainers, and Funeke was responsible for the local arrangements and the selection of trainees. Since 2002 we have "trained" a hundred and fifty peer counsellors from various secondary schools in the area, as well as seventy-five teachers who acted as mentors.

## *See first and then think: "connect with what they bring"*

Towards the end of our first planning meeting, my heart was heavy at the prospect of realizing this project. It had taken an enormous amount of organization and coordination, and I was tired and questioned the value of a venture that involved so much uncertainty and difficult communication. I was trying to communicate with Norway and Maluti, and both seemed just as far away (it takes eight hours to travel by car over dangerous roads to reach Maluti). The weight of the responsibility with outside visitors, as well as the weight of coordinating students and other participants, was heavy. I worked hard and for long hours to be prepared for the training and to create a "knowledgeable structure": a structured programme with "training manuals" and a training programme. I characteristically encourage students to take *themselves* into a process that guards against and assists in diminishing the effects of the "gaze of expertise", but I slipped into over-preparedness, as I had constructed myself to be under watch from the North. I had been told that Per Kristian was an "expert" on HIV and AIDS and on setting up peer counselling structures. I was also a little sceptical about Tom Andersen's idea of people from the North travelling to the South, being very cautious and mistrustful of "first-world expertise in Africa". What could an "expert" from Norway offer our work in Africa! I worked hard to make sense of how I could manage the outsider roles. I shared my scepticism, caution, and mistrust in notes to Per Kristian and to Tom in a positive way: I suggested that a sounding board, an outsider's questions and reflections, would be useful. This is an excerpt from one of my attempts to define (*and contain*) the outsider's role:

> I would personally find outsider insights and questions useful in the process. He would essentially be a witness to the process and would be useful in the reflective questions. I often feel bogged down, invited into despondency, so the newness of ideas, questions, and reflections from outside would add value to the work.

The voices of self-doubt and feelings of being under their gaze still lurked. I know now that I should have trusted Tom's sense in bringing me an *angel* from Norway. Tom had only a vague sense of the work I do, but he managed to bring together two souls who connected strongly from the first long hug of recognition; our connection with each other has grown over the five years of our work in Maluti and through other projects that emerged from it. Our mutual sensing of process, thoughts, perceptions, and questions was uncanny. Beyond this mutual sensing was the security I experienced in Per Kristian's strong presence, which gave me the courage to work beyond the boundaries I sometimes construct. These boundaries are often located within the sensitivity to cultural taboos and a respect for these, and a caution in evoking the voice of the colonizer. I discovered that it is in these boundaries, and the risk in crossing them, that the areas of new possibilities happen. I knew these things in my stomach, but my history continued to contain me. Having someone from outside this history gave me the courage, confidence, and permission to cross into new territory and to work in ways that I had yearned for. I felt "less white" after every visit.

By reifying culture or ethnic identity, we run the risk of minimizing the dynamic nature of cultural and community identity and its ever-changing nature. A South African identity is formed by the meeting of many diverse cultures and the divergent ways of making sense of our world and how we act in it. As therapists we share many more commonalities than differences in our humanness with the people we meet on our journey. Through these commonalities and a mutual respect, we are then able to explore differences and our connectedness as human beings.

## *"Listen to what they say, and see how what they say affects themselves"*

With the focus on HIV and AIDS as a "pandemic in Africa", large amounts of money are allocated for training. There have been hundreds of well-intentioned AIDS prevention/education programmes and trainings for lay counsellors from urban and rural contexts, various educational levels, professionals, and community health workers (many of whom are illiterate).These training programmes disregard the various dissident views of the HIV virus and Africa. The programmes and trainings attempt to change behaviours through fear and by teaching abstinence and the use of condoms. There is never any attention or space given to the realities and thoughts that people have about their own lives and relationships. *"Listen to what they say . . . "* has no space in these programmes.

Historically, the black majority in South Africa was denied an adequate education; participants remained affected by this history and saw any qualification—even a certificate of attendance at a ten-day training course for counsellors—as highly valuable. I have great discomfort with many of these trainings, which are structured around top-down, "talk-and-chalk" delivery of "expertise" by highly paid experts. Participants, eager for this expert knowledge, are largely silent as they acquire these first-world bags of techniques that have little relevance to their own local knowledge and application to their contexts. The re-colonization of people through "universal truths" about relationships and behaviours, as well as principles of traditional counselling, negates the richness of what people bring with them: their own thoughts, experiences, and ideas of healing.

## *"Expressions come first . . . then the meaning. Expressions form ourselves"*

Top-down "doom-and-gloom" lectures, under the guise of AIDS prevention, have become more pronounced in adolescent education and training programmes. The only way sex and sexuality has been approached is in the form of lectures that are predominated by fear and ultimate death. In the Maluti Peer Counselling Project we wanted to bring forth the peoples' expressions of their lives and their relationships. The young people were hungry for these types of conversations. We worked with the peer counsellors to create opportunities for other expressions of life, performances of meaning, and possibilities of relating. We created the scaffolding for the experience, and, through dialogue, reflecting team work, witnessed conversations, music, dance, play, drama and touch, new realities were constructed and new ones performed.

Priority was given to the expressions—with words and beyond words—and the voices of the young people. Discussions about sex and sexuality within small groups brought forth important personal and intimate experiences. The young people expressed that they had never experienced such a safe and welcoming forum for their questions and experiences. There had been no forums with adults to discuss these important questions, nor had there been forums for discussions between males and females. To facilitate the conversations, we used reflecting teams with larger groups. Tom often says "I have *no rules . . .*", and this statement has helped open many possibilities of ways to work with reflecting teams within community sessions and larger groups. Michael White's concept of outsider witness groups has also contributed to some of our practices and ideas. These forums, of others reflecting and witnessing upon what the youths had heard, have a good fit with "African ways of being", where community forums and family meetings remain central to their contextual experience. The experts' alien ideas of "confidentiality" and "self-actualization" assist in the silence and stigma that now abound regarding HIV.

I recall driving from the community centre at the end of one of these days together and witnessing young men and women walking, arm in arm, just talking and being together in a different way. That image is the *gift* I carry with me, and it motivates the continuation of this work.

### *"We are born into bonds with others and depend on someone to receive our screams"*

The more recent work with adolescents in the Maluti Mountains of South Africa has evoked new questions for me as I reflect on my own healing. I speak of the experience that invites me to believe that the connections we made during our short intensive stays in the Maluti Township have been life-giving to us all. I believe that everyone who was involved with these experiences over a period of four years takes sacred moments with them that may make an important difference to their lives and relationships. This includes the professionals (teachers and psychologists) as well as the students.

Yet in the world of professional care, we meet so many who are bondless, whose connections with others are eroded or non-existent. An experience of existential alienation abounds in the lack of satisfying connections. These people seek that connection from professionals whose job it is to care, to connect, and to bond. Yet, Western traditions of professional discourse focus upon ways of developing professional relationships that are punctuated and controlled by "ethics" that limit the connection the person is seeking. The person becomes an object of our care, yet the professionals are cautious about encouraging overdependency and over-involvement, becoming a rescuer, limiting physical touching and holding, and limiting personal sharing by the professional. In essence, the rules or ethics eradicate humanness in the name of professionalism. The sacred moments of different colours and textures we shared while working in this project were, of course, varied and diverse, but they were woven by the experiences of moments of "be-longing." I believe that the experience of "be-longing", for which we ache, is the core of the healing. The "be" in belonging becomes controlled by technical language that dictates the nature of the relationship and, in turn, threatens to destroy the act of "be-ing-in-relationship" with the other. These connections in this project were not primarily forged by the trading of ideas, knowledges, and truths. While some of these activities were and are important, I believe that the healing happened at a different level of coming together in our fragile humanness. In the context of the workshops, these moments were revealed in silences, in touch, in song, in dance, in smiles, in the sharing of pain, and in the sharing of joy.

In leaving Maluti in April 2003, we were invited to visit an AIDS orphanage in the nearby town. As we entered this safe haven filled with children and babies, good food, and compassionate carers, the babies and toddlers crawled towards us with urgency for touch and holding. There were too many to count or hold. Those who were more active and demanding for this contact received the connection, while others remained staring from the outside, only their eyes beckoning for the contact. But the outstretched arms of others clouded our experience of the watchers on the outside. This was also true of our experience with the adolescents. Some watched while others were more persistent and demanding, even in quiet and powerful ways, for connection. Our challenge as "professionals" is to be there, to meet one with the other, and to notice those who are more reticent about making demands!

## *"I am not a teacher. But a walker . . . and a talker"*

This reflective writing has given me the opportunity to write about my walk over the last five years. This walk has involved words that I "heard" Tom Andersen say—words that have helped me listen to my own discomfort as a teacher, a trainer, and a talker. He has walked his talk and helped me talk my walk. The words I heard him say have often given form and shape to those moments of discomfort that recur in my practice as a healer.

CHAPTER 10

# Networks on networks: initiating international cooperation for the treatment of psychosis

*Jaakko Seikkula*

On a visit to Falun in Sweden in June 1995, Tom Andersen, myself, and the local team working with psychotic patients got the idea of proposing a meeting place for psychiatric units that wanted to develop new, more humane practices in treatments for psychosis. Tom had been travelling around in different countries and in different psychiatric contexts and had encountered a shared need for an alternative to mainstream psychiatry. Mainstream psychiatry meant a treatment that focused on controlling psychotic symptoms and psychotic behaviour by heavy medication from the outset and by inpatient treatment for long periods. In Falun, the acute team had received interesting experiences after decommissioning a hospital ward for psychotic patients and organizing a psychosis team instead. In addition to the inspiration of Tom Andersen's reflective processes, they had their inspiration from both psychodynamic individual psychotherapy, having as their supervisor Murray Jackson from the United Kingdom, and the need-adapted approach from Turku in Finland; they had met Professors Yrjö Alanen and Viljo Räkköläinen.

At that time I myself had already been invited to several places for presenting experiences from Finnish Western Lapland of the new family- and social-network-oriented treatment of psychosis. Immediately I agreed with Tom's suggestion of organizing a forum for psychiatric units. This happened for the first time in 1996, and Falun was the obvious host for this very first meeting. When planning the forum, we thought that it should be organized in a different way compared to "traditional" international cooperation. Instead of building up an organization to oversee and organize the meetings, we decided to see if it would be possible arrange it such that different psychiatric units would host the meetings each in their own turn. The other idea was that the meetings should not be planned in detail in advance but, instead, should introduce the possibility for dealing with experiences on three levels:

1. to share experiences in clinical practice;
2. to share experiences on an epistemological level concerning how we understand psychotic problems;
3. to share experiences of how we describe our practice and how we develop research on what we are doing.

Concretely we organized a general frame for each of the five days of a meeting. At each meeting, we would come together on Wednesday night to plan the conference. On Thursday, we would work in small groups on different subjects concerning our clinical practice; we called this the "Clinical Day". On Saturday, the focus would be on research and descriptions of our work; over the years this day has been named "Research Day". For the first meeting in Falun, we proposed that on Friday local people could be invited to listen to our presentations to make our work more known among other professionals, patients, and relatives of the patients; this was named the "Open Day". Because of cheaper air flights, we decided to stay over the Saturday night, and thus Sunday morning was reserved for summarizing the experiences of the previous days and planning for future meetings, should there be a need for it.

The very first meeting was a success. More than twenty units accepted the invitation and came to share their experiences. Many were from Sweden, but there were also two from Finland, some from Norway, and even one unit from Germany. Because we wanted to build bridges across cultural boundaries, we decided to invite some professionals we knew from Estonia and Lithuania. Their invitation required economic support, and this was organized by the Institute for Community Medicine in the University of Tromsø. The Swedish East European Committee subsequently contributed additional economic support to the network to make it possible for units from Latvia and Russia to participate as well.

The content of the meeting was extremely refreshing for us. People eagerly shared their experiences of clinical practice. One specific group focused on treatment where the outcome was not that expected. In annual meetings afterwards, this group became a custom and was named the "failure-case seminar". For us, this spoke of the security of the network: it was possible to share in a safe form all types of experiences, including the most difficult ones. The Open Day aroused enormous interest among local professionals, patients, and relatives. Some presentation were attended by several hundred people.

We had succeeded in opening a forum for describing our clinical practices and talking about research. This had to be approached in a careful way, because research has always been a loaded subject at our meetings. Already in the first meeting some were interested in discussing qualitative analysis of the treatment process. A proposal was made that we had to start to follow up our new way of working to make it more known and acceptable to other professionals and politicians. In the first meeting, some experiences were shared on doing research in Western Lapland on first-episode psychotic patients. Many professionals, however, felt that traditional psychiatric research is based on objectifying the patients and pathologizing psychotic behaviour, and for that reason statistical analysis should be avoided. Quite heavy arguments were used both for and against the idea of follow-up. No decision could be reached at the first meeting.

In concluding the first conference, many of us felt that a new tradition had been established. We decided to meet the following year, and the psychiatric unit in Jorvi Hospital in Espoo, Finland, took responsibility for hosting that meeting. Each year since then, a different unit has accepted the challenge of inviting other units to a meeting. Both the number of units and the numbers of participants have increased. In the tenth meeting in Roskilde, Denmark, about a hundred and seventy participants attended. We have visited Pärnu (Estonia), Vesterålen and Tromsø (Norway), Tornio (Finland),

Falun and Skellefteå (Sweden), and Kaunas (Lithuania). The form of the meetings has stayed much the same, but, of course, with local variations based on how the host unit chooses to organize the meeting. Some indication of the importance of the meetings is that during the Open Day in Tornio about four hundred people from all over Finland attended; in Skellefteå, about five hundred attended, mostly from the province around; and, in the second visit to Falun, about seven hundred attended.

The Clinical Day has maintained its popularity and significance throughout. But a most remarkable success has happened in the Research Day. Professors Anders Lindseth and John Shotter opened an important forum for a qualitative description of the treatment process. In 2001 we finally succeeded in deciding to begin the follow-up of first-episode psychotic patients. This happened after we concluded that it is not feasible to include all the units in the study, and therefore only those units who wished to do so are participating. Of the twelve units that decided to participate, five have succeeded in starting the registration of patients since 2002. Some first statistics have already been presented at two conferences, and this has aroused huge interest, particularly because it produces information about cultural differences in treatment.

### *What is it all about clinically?*

There is no hierarchical structure to plan the annual meetings, nor are there any criteria as to who can attend. The basic idea from the very beginning has been to introduce a meeting place for psychiatric units that take total responsibility for psychiatric services in their catchment area. This is the distinguishing factor from the many academic meetings that focus on psychosis itself or some specified aspects of treatment. We focus on developing treatment systems based on daily clinical practice.

The units that have attended share an interest in developing a social-network-oriented approach with most severe psychiatric problems. The units also seem to agree with focusing on psychological understanding and psychotherapy in different forms with patients who have psychotic experiences. In addition, most units seem interested in finding alternatives to hospitalization in a psychotic crisis by organizing acute teams for taking care of the crisis and thus, together with other professionals, preventing needless hospitalizations. The question of neuroleptic medication has been important throughout. We who initiated this forum had many critical questions about the over-medication of psychotic patients and thus wanted to find possibilities for such treatment processes in which neuroleptic medication is not used, and, if used, only where there is a specified need. In this, the units seem to follow different traditions. Many units share in their practice the tendency to decrease medication. At the same time, though, there are still some units that use neuroleptic medication with almost all psychotic patients, as they have always done. The distinguishing aspect seems to be whether the units have the possibilities and resources for developing alternative approaches for controlling treatment. For instance, some units in the Baltic countries only have the possibility of inpatient treatment for psychosis, and we all know that in a hospital the use of medication is more usual than in an outpatient setting.

Concerning the content of the specific approaches, the staff members in different units have different interests. Network-oriented approaches and a focus on reflective processes and open dialogue in the meetings is aimed at in all places. The main inspiration for the participants comes from variations on the reflective process that Tom Andersen has developed together with different units. But in addition, the network is inspired by the Finnish need-adapted tradition and especially the development that has happened in Finnish Western Lapland since the early 1980s. Starting in the Keropudas Hospital and spreading throughout the service system in the small province, a family- and social-network-centred treatment system has been constructed. This approach has been functioning for about twenty years, and thus a lot of experience exists regarding its effectiveness and specific dilemmas. In 1984, when a patient was hospitalized the hospital staff started to organize open meetings. This meant that all discussions of the actual problem and all planning of the treatment, including the origins of psychotherapeutic meaning-making, started to happen openly, in the presence of the patients. At the same time, a step was taken away from a family therapy orientation in the sense that, in every hospitalization, the families were invited to these open meetings without any specified indication for family therapy. The new practice actually opened up a way in which the entire treatment system became reorganized and—what is perhaps even more important—understanding of psychiatric problems on a whole changed. The new practice caused new descriptions of the practice and new theories of what is important.

Another inspiration has come from Tom Andersen's work in developing reflective processes, first with his team in Tromsø and later in the many different contexts into which Tom has been invited. What is interesting is that the change from a systemic view, and organizing ourselves into family therapy teams as systemic family therapy, into an open reflection of our own observations and work happened about the same time in Tromsø as in Tornio. Tom has described (Andersen, 1991) how, during several years in the early 1980s, their team felt unease at knowing better than families how to define their problems. The change happened in January 1985 when, in one difficult situation with a family, they proposed to the therapist and to the family that the team behind the mirror could reflect openly on their ideas of what they had heard. A new way of collaboration with families was opened. As this is described in other chapters of this book, I do not go into details of the importance of reflective processes, but I think that these two cornerstones of reflective processes and open dialogue are of equal importance for the network. They both deal with openness, but they focus on slightly different aspects of openness. This is important to note, since often these ways of thinking are grouped under the same heading, and thus valuable resources that each offers individually can be missed.

In Western Lapland the approach developed into a comprehensive family- and network-centred treatment. What happened during the 1980s was that many confusing experiences of treatment emerged, because the staff did not have any useable descriptions of an open treatment system. Towards the end of 1980s, the conclusion was reached that what was needed was both a systematic analysis of the new system and systematic training of the entire staff. Several studies were conducted in 1988 on both the new treatment processes and the effectiveness of the open dialogue approach. Starting in 1989, three years' family therapy training for the entire staff was put into practice. All this was done in cooperation between the health district and the Department of Psychology at the University of Jyväskylä. Both the studies and the full-time ongoing training offered a deeper understanding of the system. By the mid-1990s, it had become possible to give a description of the basic principles of the new approach (Seikkula, Alakare, & Aaltonen, 2001).

These principles included seven basic ideas:

1. The crisis treatment should start within twenty-four hours of contact from either the patient, a family member, or a referring authority.
2. The social network of the patient should be invited in all cases as early as possible into the open meetings, and they are invited to stay in the meetings and in the process for as long as the process is ongoing. The social network includes both the private social network of the family and all the professionals with whom the family has been in contact.
3. The staff should be flexible in adapting their treatment response to the specific and varying needs of each patient. There is no ready-made programme from case to case; rather, the best-fitting method of treatment is chosen together with the client(s). This means that different methods are integrated with each other, and thus no sensible way of working should be excluded.
4. The team contacted must take responsibility for organizing the first meetings and for taking into account everything necessary for making decisions regarding the treatment. In this, the training of the staff helps a great deal—it is not always necessary for a doctor to attend meetings to make the decisions.
5. Psychological continuity should be guaranteed by forming case-specific teams that can include staff from different units (e.g., one from social care and one from the psychiatric outpatient clinic) and across the boundary between inpatient and outpatient care. It is advisable that the same team can take

responsibility for as long as needed, not just for the crisis phase of three to five meetings.

6. The uncertainty that the crisis calls forth must be tolerated. In a crisis, no rapid conclusions or decisions are possible, so the process should create sufficient safety to tolerate this. This means that the team and the family should meet often enough—perhaps daily, in a psychotic crisis—and the quality of dialogue should be such that everyone becomes heard.
7. Dialogicity must develop, such that the meetings aim at constructing new words for experiences for which there are no words, or only symptom descriptions. The aim becomes that of focusing on dialogue itself, because in the dialogue the polyphonic resources of the networks become available.

These guiding principles for organizing a treatment system that focus on the social network's own psychological resources have proved to be a major inspiration. In many units, their own local ideas have been applied—for instance, by organizing acute teams to make possible an immediate response after the contact. In different cultures the system becomes specific to the history and the local circumstances. Among the thirty units that have participated in the meetings, there is a lot of experience regarding family and network orientation in cases of the most severe psychiatric problems. The clinical questions of the participants cover a wide variety of important dilemmas in treatment processes. Taking an example from the 2005 network meeting in Roskilde, during the Clinical Day the following subjects in small groups were handled:

- How do we understand psychosis?
- How do we generate dialogue in the best way, and what is the meaning of dialogue in the meetings?
- How do we assist organizations to become more dialogical?
- What is the best way to deal with resistance towards the new treatment coming from fellow professionals, from administration, from families?
- How do we take children's voices into account in the meetings, either as the client or as the child of a psychotic parent?
- What is the best training for open dialogues?

## *What is this all about concerning research?*

In Western Lapland a systematic analysis of the new system became a cornerstone of the new practice. For the most part, the research was based on some ideas of social action research, in the sense that we who were involved in developing the open dialogue practice started to analyse our own work for both a greater understanding of it and for defining the problems of outcomes in the new approach. This was not, of course, fieldwork in the sense that Kurt Lewin and other founders of social action research meant. But it is still a way of making sense to ourselves of our own work with patients in severe crisis. Compared to those studies that most often are referred to in evidence-based medicine (EBM), we are always interested in having information about our practice in order to develop it further. We are not researchers outside the context and making efficacy measurements in order to have information for comparison with other studies.

As an example, the very first research project, conducted between 1988 and 2002, consisted of analysing what happens during the first contact between the patient's family and the hospital in an admission process (Keränen, 1992; Seikkula, 1991). We found out that at the boundary between the hospital and the family, a new type of interaction seems to emerge that makes it possible to use the family's own psychological resources much more than in a situation where the patient is hospitalized. An important factor is the quality of the cooperation that is generated between the family and the team. The team had to take into account a family's earlier experiences of treatment. If the family had previously experienced that hospitalization helped the patient, it was more difficult for them to accept home treatment instead of hospitalization. However, if the family did not have any experience at all from previous treatment, home treatment was easily accepted.

Another large research project, looking at open dialogues in acute psychosis, had an inclusion period of March 1992 to March 1997; there was then a five-year follow-up into the effectiveness of open dialogues. Three outcome reports have been published (Seikkula, 2002; Seikkula, Alakare, & Aaltonen, 2001; Seikkula et al., 2003, 2006) and also one on the differences of dialogues in good- and poor-outcome patients (Seikkula, 2002). Results are promising.

Compared to treatment as usual, the patients were hospitalized less; they used neuroleptic medication in about a third of the cases compared to all cases in traditional treatment; they had relapses in twenty-nine per cent compared to seventy-five per cent in the comparison group; more than eighty per cent had no remaining psychotic symptoms, compared to half of the comparison group; and eighty-one per cent had returned to employment and studies compared to thirty-eight per cent in treatment-as-usual.

The follow-up was done in a natural setting—that is, as a part of daily clinical practice. This is a quasi-experimental design, compared to experimental studies that are designated as randomized trials. In the psychosis network, the same type of follow-up in a natural setting has begun. As stated above, five centres have started to register their first-episode psychotic patients in order to follow how their treatment is taking place and what outcomes are reached after two years. This comparison is taking place in a "real-world" setting; no specific laboratory is constructed. This means that the study design does not introduce a medical pathologizing-minded model for the family and the team, as often happens in randomized trials. In the latter, qualities of the patients or the family are condensed into a few symptom ratings, and symptoms are treated using specific manualized methods.

A total of a hundred and sixty-nine patients have been included from the five centres, and their treatment is being followed. The aim of the follow-up is to obtain information about new psychotic patients in different cultures and to follow up the outcome of their treatment, using simple measurements. This information is of most value to the local units, but it also allows for the possibility of comparing the processes between different units.

## *New practice—new descriptions*

Psychiatric treatment is organized in specific contexts by specific staff working in the units. There are few general rules that can be applied, as such. The contemporary tendency of creating rules for adequate treatment of schizophrenia and other problems seems to rely on the idea of generalized knowledge. What is problematic is that randomized trials often create an artificial reality, and the results of trials are compared to other studies, not with other practices. In our network for the treatment of psychosis, the focus is on the actual practice in each context. This means that description of the praxis happens on its terms, not the opposite. In the annual meetings, each of us in turn has the possibility for deliberating on our own practice around the same subject.

One of the main ideas behind the meetings is that there is no hierarchical structure for taking care of the network; instead, the organization of a meetings is the responsibility of whichever unit has elected to hold the meeting. Every psychiatric unit attending the annual meeting is there from their own choosing and not because of some ready-made plan of tasks. This means that a unit may decide to come some years but not others. A number of units have participated in all meetings, but many have attended most meetings. In the meetings, the professionals share a lot of time within their home unit, which illustrates the balance of a joint meeting and the local need for developing the practice.

Another main idea consists of combining the three elements of clinical practice, epistemology, and research in the same meeting. This network was not initiated for conducting a trial in which every unit participated; instead, units have different interests. Some will participate merely in the clinical discussions. Others will also participate in the qualitative research sessions but without attending the multicentre study, in which only five of the more than thirty units participate. The defining rule is that nothing is prescribed regarding how and what each shall do. This applies to both clinical practice and research issues. For instance, there is no single definition of how each should work with reflective processes; units can have their own orientation in daily clinical work. Of course, attending the annual meetings means having an interest in open dialogues and reflective processes, but these need not be the basic organizing factors in the units.

It is interesting to compare our network to the core ideas in evidence-based medicine. In EBM systems, multicentre cooperation is important. But the thinking behind the aim of the research is to conduct research projects to obtain explanations of changing mechanisms in treatment. This most often means organizing randomized trial to creating generalizable knowledge. The action in each unit is controlled to guarantee that each unit really is working on the same principles. This is not the case in the psychosis network. We do want to increase research, but this is the case mostly because of finding tools for analysing one's own practice in the specific context to define problems, dilemmas, and successes. What is aimed at is not meta-analysis of different research centres, but a comparison of experiences.

CHAPTER 11

# True stories: acts of informing and forming

*Eugene Epstein, Manfred Wiesner, & Margit Epstein*

"Not all I might say and do is acceptable for society."

Tom Andersen (1995b, p. 31)

"The aspects of things that are most important for us are hidden because of their simplicity and familiarity."

Ludwig Wittgenstein #129

Until now, nobody has asked us to tell the truth. So when we were asked to contribute to this book, we thought, truth be known, now is our chance. The three authors have been living and working in exile for more than a decade in a remote corner of northern Germany. Although the weather is abominable there, with cold wind and rain throughout much of the year, the winters are not nearly as dark and cold as they are in northern Norway. This is perhaps but one of the many important reasons why the authors have not been able to develop anything nearly as simple, radical, and aesthetically beautiful as Tom Andersen's idea of "reflecting talks". But what, might the reader ask, have "reflecting talks" to do with the authors? That is the beginning of this mostly true[1] but, in any case, very personal story.

> "But for the purposes of our investigation, we would like to know what really happened."
>
> "What really happened?"
>
> "Yes"
>
> "So you want another story?"
>
> "Uhh ... no. We would like to know what really happened."
>
> "Does the telling of something always become a story?"
>
> "Uhh ... perhaps in English. In Japanese a story would have an element of invention in it. We don't want any invention. We want the 'straight facts', as you say in English."
>
> "Isn't telling about something—using words, English or Japanese—already something of an invention? Isn't just looking upon this world already something of an invention?
>
> "Uhh ..."
>
> "The world isn't just the way it is. It is how we understand it, no? And in understanding something, we bring something to it, no? Doesn't that make life a story?" [Martel, 2002, p. 405]

A first meeting between Tom and one of the authors, Eugene, took place in Orlando in the autumn of 1986 at the national conference of the American Association of Marriage and Family Therapists. Eugene was then a faculty member at the Galveston Family Institute and was sitting at a poolside table along with Harry Goolishian and a small gathering of friends and colleagues. Tom had just presented his workshop at the conference and joined us at the table for a drink. Shortly thereafter, Harry and the others left, leaving Tom, Eugene, and another colleague, Victor Loos, at the table. Taking the opportunity to get to know Tom a little better, they asked how his workshop had gone. His face became ashen and his body grew slack as he then recounted what a failure it was. After three hours of talking together, it was no clearer exactly what Tom thought had gone so wrong with his workshop, but Victor and Eugene were drunk and Tom was no longer depressed. After the conference, Tom and a couple of his colleagues joined Harry and his group at the Galveston Family Institute, where many long evenings were spent debating the various possible explanations for this dramatic turnabout. What could explain the change in

Tom's demeanour if Victor and Eugene had no clear idea of what they had done that was helpful? Could change have occurred non-instrumentally, and, if so, how might one begin to theorize about this? Was it the conversation or something else? Harry and Tom found some possible answers to these interesting questions while raising many more.

## *From the hermeneutic circle to the Arctic Circle*

In Tom Andersen's classic article introducing the field to the idea of "reflecting teams" (Andersen, 1987), he tried to explain his ground-breaking ideas using Gregory Bateson's theories on epistemology and Humberto Maturana's structural determinism. Such language, read today, seems quaint. But one should not miss the subtle but most radical break this article made with the work of the then very popular Milan approach (Selvini-Palazzoli, Boscolo, Cecchin, & Prata, 1980). In Tom's words, "For one thing, we choose to meet people without making any hypotheses beforehand. ... We have also deliberately avoided interventions because family members can so easily believe that our intervention is better than what they themselves have pictured and explained" (Andersen, 1987 p. 428).

What a monster blow to interventionism these rather unassuming suggestions represented! Up until that point, most in the family and systemic therapy field were in love with the idea of "creating change" in families and systems. In this metaphor the therapists were the change agents, and the Milan approach represented a very sophisticated version of this kind of thinking. In 1988, Harry Goolishian in his opening address to the Galveston Conference described this shift away from interventionism as follows: "The narrative vocabulary of the post-modern self promises to permit, a vocabulary of description that will be free of concepts of power and oppression. Isn't this a refreshingly optimistic, if not altogether radical thought for all of us professionals, acculturated to unquestioningly accept and communicate within the very language of pathology, power and oppression, namely the ICD-10?" (Goolishian, 1988).

Thus, by the late 1980s, Tom no longer referred to the language of constructivism and epistemology to explain his work. Instead, he began to use the language of hermeneutic philosophy, narrative theory, and postmodernism, writing: "The reflecting processes can be seen as hermeneutic circles" (Andersen, 1995b, p. 13).

## *Not knowing*

Many have attributed the therapeutic stance of "not knowing" to the pioneering work of Harry Goolishian (e.g., see Andersen & Epstein, 2002). His brilliant, if not also sublimely subversive, idea that therapists do not have to possess some kind of expert knowledge to be helpful to clients did indeed open new doors for systemic therapists to explore and experiment with postmodern ideas. Because this is an article about Tom, we shall not discuss how Harry came to develop these ideas. But one thing that we share with Tom in common is that whenever we write, present, or do therapy, we sense the presence of Harry's ghost nearby. Tom described it recently as this "immediate and intense bond that developed between us, which not only lasted unto his death, . . . but remains to this very day. I always mention Harry when I do presentations, for wherever I am, I want his voice to still be heard" (Andersen & Epstein, 2002, p. 43).

The authors vaguely remember a story about Tom at one of his conferences in Sulitelma in 1988, where he allegedly walked around the whole time in an old trench coat smoking a cigar. At this conference the epistemologists (a group that included Heinz von Foerster, Ernst von Glasersfeld, and Humberto Maturana) debated issues of theoretical and practical import with three teams of therapists (representing the Galveston, the Milan, and the Tromsø styles of therapy conversations). Tom's closest colleagues later came to realize that while there, he had experienced a fundamental and, epistemologically speaking, rather earth-shattering crisis. Tom realized then and there that the less he knew about his conversational partners, the easier it was for him to ask them questions that they in turn could easily answer. Like Harry, Tom had early on discovered that nobody likes to teach an expert anything, since an expert, by definition, if not by arrogance, already knows everything. Everybody has a story to tell about themselves, and most people like to talk about themselves when they have the sense that the listener is listening with sympathy and curiosity.

Later we heard that Tom began to play around with similar ideas during the long, dark, bitterly cold Norwegian winter while watching television reruns of *Columbo*. Columbo, played brilliantly by Peter Falk, only acted naive in order to pump crime-solving information out of witnesses and suspects, and many systemic therapists tried to imitate this style in order to pump "facts" out of their clients. Unfortunately many clients did not like being made fools of and responded with either silence or cancellation of further appointments, so that Columbo-style therapy was tossed into the systemic dustbin of discarded theories and disappointing ideas, while trench coats remained for some time in fashion. Whereas Columbo was always constrained by the modern discourses around truth and justice, Tom transcended this kind of thinking. Tom's manner of questioning leads to further questions rather than towards deeper meaning or enduring truth.

Following in Tom's footsteps, the therapists in our clinic stopped wearing the white coats that were then most fashionable among European medical and psychiatric elites. Instead, they all started wearing trench coats with cigars in the pockets. Independent of our evolving and changing dress codes, it has become our habit (and that of our clinic colleagues) to believe in the expertise of our clients to best determine how to conduct their lives. Thus, as we came together to develop a model for child and adolescent psychiatric services in northern Germany in the early 1990s, we were challenged to weave this respect for and belief in our clients' expertise into the rather traditional and often less-than-respectful structures and thinking of the various systems in which our clinic is embedded.

## *Viking influences along the German North Shore*

In the early days, we struggled to put Tom's ideas into our own form of reflecting practice. Years ago, Gary Larson drew a Far Side cartoon[2] depicting a group of researchers in white coats suddenly realizing that the one-way mirror, through which they had been observing, had been installed backwards! Once we realized that no matter which way we installed the one-way mirror we could not avoid observing ourselves, we began to see the advantages of this arrangement. Whenever we engaged in reflecting about our clients, we were offering our reflections not as interventions or suggestions in the hope that the clients would adopt our ideas, but, rather, that the clients would offer us feedback and correction of our own thinking, language, and ideas. Indeed, in this manner, we actively invite our clients to help us avoid the multiple seductions of (a) thinking we know our clients stories and can tell them better than our clients themselves, (b) trying to be helpful without ascertaining first whether help, and in what form, might be desired and (c) trying to convince or seduce clients to adopt our perspectives instead of exploring theirs.

Ideally, we wanted to develop a large outpatient service without an inpatient unit. But the German health insurance companies and authorities require psychiatric clinics like ours to also provide inpatient services. Therefore, most other clinics here tend to have large inpatient units and only very modest outpatient facilities. Unlike these clinics, we have the smallest inpatient unit, with only twelve beds, but the largest outpatient service, conducting conversations with around two and a half thousand clients and their families each year. In this way we are under no pressure to "fill beds" and can exhaust any and all possible outpatient resources before considering inpatient possibilities. In our clinic we rarely, if ever, suggest to families that inpatient treatment might be helpful for a child or adolescent. Instead, if families or other involved helpers occasionally raise the idea in our conversations, we then engage with them in discussing the pros and cons of such ideas. Often such conversations lead us to explore new ideas and topics in our conversations such that the idea of hospitalization simply disappears or dissolves. Occasionally, our clients help us to see how and why hospitalization might be useful to members of the family, and we then develop a mutual plan for the stay in our hospital unit.

One of our responsibilities is to provide twenty-four-hour crisis-intervention services for children and adolescents in a region with around three hundred thousand inhabitants. Our experience in adapting Tom Andersen's reflecting process within our crisis response services has encouraged us to continue exploring these ideas. In comparison with other crisis services in northern Germany, we have been able to resolve crisis situations with the fewest number of children and adolescents being placed in court-ordered secure hospital units. Indeed, it is our experience that most crises may be resolved without resorting to hospitalization or medication. We believe that our best available tool in therapy is conversation, and our belief has been strengthened time and again. When we take the time to listen carefully, most crises tend to resolve themselves.

Although we are extremely sceptical of the pharmaceutical trend towards "better living through modern chemistry" *à la* Ritalin and SSRI inhibitors, we are not fundamentalist or dogmatic in our approach to the subject. Not surprisingly, given the level of media exposure, we are under a lot of pressure from referring sources as well as parents to medicate children and adolescents who are brought to us. We do not believe that we have any objective criteria with which to decide whether medication is indicated or not. We make it clear to our clients that the decision cannot be made by us alone. Instead, we invite all present to discuss together the idea of medication. What are the various hopes, fears, benefits, and/or possible side-effects of ingesting a particular substance? Questions like these invite us to discuss together the pros and cons of medication on a basis that allows everyone to have an opinion. This approach can be quite challenging for clients who believe that "doctor knows best" or for therapists who are easily seduced by the notion that they know better. Such talks have transformed the act of prescribing (which often engenders a hierarchical discrepancy between the person prescribing and the patient) into a joint experiment in which all persons are actively engaged.

One of the most difficult aspects of our clinic work is the challenge of cooperating with the department of adult psychiatry in our hospital. Here, in the state of Lower Saxony, there are very few locked psychiatric wards for children and adolescents, and an agreement has been reached that adolescents between the ages of 14 and 18 years who are determined to be acutely dangerous to self or others may be placed, under court order, in an adult locked ward. The adult psychiatry staff believe in biological psychiatry (psychopharmacology as the main course of therapy). The staff of the locked unit do not provide any psychotherapy services for patients (allegedly due to "time constraints"), and the staff tend to believe that our department practises irresponsible psychiatry because we prescribe antipsychotic medications only very sparingly. We are often not consulted around the decision to admit adolescents to the locked ward, although determining acute danger to self and others is part of our responsibility as the crisis-intervention team. Often we are asked to consult *after* an adolescent has been admitted. We are frequently requested to coordinate discharge planning with the family and youth authorities and to provide in- and/or outpatient follow-up treatment usually with little or no prior warning.

Because we have a very different understanding of what constitutes ethical treatment, it would be easy to get into disagreements and conflicts around patient care. To the adult psychiatry staff, ethical treatment means providing the treatment *they* as experts believe to be necessary, whether the patients concur or not. We believe that ethical treatment entails actively cooperating with clients around what *they* think might constitute help, even if this requires us to rethink and change our own ideas about help in the process.

## *Four questions*

How Tom came to decide upon four important questions is not clear to us. We suspect that he developed the idea years ago after attending a Passover Seder in New York. Within the Jewish tradition, the youngest child present at the Passover Seder service always asks "the four questions", which then allows for the retelling of the story of the Jewish exodus out of slavery in Egypt. (Personally, we think it is better that he developed four questions rather than expounding upon the ten plagues.)

Tom came up with the following four questions:

> "Is what is going on now appropriately unusual or is it too unusual?"
>
> "The second question is about the history of coming here today. Who had the idea?"
>
> "The third question is simply to ask all present how they would like to use the meeting."

"Who might/can/ought to talk with whom about which issue in which way at which point in time?" [Andersen, 1995, pp. 21–22.]

In our view, all four questions revolve around the theme of cooperation in conversation. The questions invite all persons present to consider how they wish to converse and cooperate with each other. In our clinical work, we originally started out with a catalogue of a hundred and fifty questions we thought to be important to raise with our clients. If the clients provided us with the answers to these questions, then (we thought) we would know how to cooperate and best be helpful. Unfortunately, many of our clients fell asleep before getting beyond the fifth question and we had to answer the rest of the questions by ourselves. So we were very thankful to Tom for helping us cut the list down to four.

## *Slowness in postmodern times*

> "It feels intuitively right that clients should be given the time they need in order to tell me what they want me to know. That means that I, as the listener, must be cautious not to interrupt."
>
> Tom Andersen (1995, p. 23)

Going against all current trends towards speeding up everything (see, for example, Gleick, 1999), Tom's therapeutic style places great emphasis on proceeding very slowly. He is not interested in the quick elucidation of information from clients in order to develop therapeutic plans. Rather, it is his careful and consciously slow-moving attempts to understand what the clients are trying to say that appears to be the catalyser for the therapeutic conversations. Thoughts and descriptions can be better explicated and elaborated upon when the quieter, incomplete, and less certain thoughts and voices are allowed to join in the conversation alongside more dominant thoughts and voices. In this manner, multiple descriptions around particular issues may be developed. Thus new forms of description and self-description have the possibility of becoming "real" in the process.

But Tom did not always work this slowly. Audiotapes of some of Tom's first attempts at making therapeutic conversations (which, unfortunately, have disappeared over the years) conveyed a very different picture of this "early Tom". Some of his colleagues back then called him "fast Tom" or, in a slight modification of the well-known poem "Jack be nimble, Jack be quick", they called him "Tom be quick!" Such nicknames have long been forgotten, but colleagues who have followed his career over the years have pointed to a major transformation from "early Tom" to "late Tom" having taken place after he returned from a consultation in Montana in 1990. With a glint in his eye, he reported having spoken there with executives of a large company, who had turned the hiring of "SLOBBIES" (slow but better working persons) into a successful business philosophy. Following this revelation, one could observe Tom incorporating slowness into his therapeutic stance. His rediscovery of slowness achieved notice and acclaim not only within therapeutic circles—rumour has it that, in 1993, Tom received an honorary degree from the Department of Time Studies, also known as the Department of Procrastination and Delay, at the University of Klagenfurt.

We too, have been very much influenced by these developments and have reassessed not only our conversational behaviours, but also our work methods and routines with respect to these novel ideas. For instance, what for us at first seemed to be relatively simple and straightforward jobs, such as requests for certain kinds of psychological tests (like, say, for dyslexia) or for inpatient treatment of a child or adolescent, were suddenly no longer questions that could be answered with the utmost speed and reaction. Rather, within the framework of our outpatient conversations, we could take our time to discuss the many questions connected with such requests. How these questions are answered may have great relevance for further talk and actions. We might thus avoid having to admit a child or adolescent to our inpatient unit too quickly or even at all, in spite of strong outside pressure to admit applied by teachers, youth services, or paediatricians. Admitting an adolescent for inpatient treatment without exploring whether that adolescent has any interest or motivation for this enterprise is not only a bad starting point for a cooperative venture, it is an invitation for the kind of trouble we generally try hard to avoid.

## *Outer and inner dialogues and reflective processes*

Tom's therapeutic style and theoretical position have become well-known and well recognized throughout the field and, indeed, throughout the world. He has become a role model for many practising therapists as well as therapists in training. Reflecting teams and reflecting processes have been granted an important and honoured place within the history of the field (e.g., see Hoffmann, 2002). But few still remember the insecurities associated with the emergence of these ideas back in the 1980s. The writings and ideas of Voloshinov, Bakhtin, Wittgenstein, and other philosophical heroes of the last century were pointed to as providing the theoretical legitimation for these ideas (see Shotter & Katz, 1998).

But it is only recently that that which has long been one of the systemic fields' best-kept secrets may—and, indeed, must—finally be brought to light and openly discussed. The inspiration for these new ideas about therapeutic process may be found not in philosophy, as was commonly thought, but, rather, in art. It was Woody Allen's popular 1971 film *Play It Again, Sam* that formed the kernel of these ground-breaking ideas. Here, for the first time, inner dialogues were made both audible and visible to the film-going public. The dialogue between Alan (alias Woody Allen) and Humphrey Bogart, in which their inner talks were turned into outer talks, had a major and lasting effect upon Tom. And he was the first to make these early ideas about transforming inner talks to outer talks accessible to systemic therapists.

It was simply unthinkable back in the 1980s that theoretical constructions might be derived from popular cinema. At that time, postmodernism was just emerging within the social sciences and was certainly not well known among psychotherapists. But Tom pointed the way, and so today we can finally openly honour Woody Allen's masterpiece. (As an aside, we must note that a number of Woody Allen's later works—for instance, the film *Zelig*—have also set standards for therapists and therapy that the professional world has not yet begun to grasp and fully appreciate.)

Just how valuable and instructive popular film stars can be for our therapeutic reflections may easily be illustrated through our daily work in the clinic. How often, *à la* Marlon Brando, have we made our clients "an offer they can't refuse" or said to a despairing client, *à la* Lauren Bacall, "If you need me, just whistle. You know how to whistle, don't you?" It is profundity and pithiness that can be found in manifold form within cinematic works and offers us very accessible, as well as richly varied, sources for our reflecting processes. In order to preserve Tom's special ways of conversing for future generations of therapists, we are currently negotiating with Sofia Coppola around a film project with the working title "Constructing Tom Reflecting". Johnny Depp has already indicated interest in playing the role of the "early Tom".

Now that we have arrived at the end of our story, we wish to leave our readers with one very well-known question of Tom's, which we believe to be most fitting at this point, namely: "What do you *see* in the words?" (a question that will certainly find a place in our film!).

## Notes

1. "Rather than a denial of truth, the postmodern temperament allows for attention to a much wider range of truths . . ." (Collins, 1993)

2. Larson & Martin (2003); permission to include this marvellously insightful cartoon was unfortunately not forthcoming from the copyright holders. The ideas of Gary Larson, who had been playing with constructionist ideas long before they became fashionable in therapeutic circles, have proven most helpful in guiding our current thinking and work.

CHAPTER 12

# The June Seminars at the North Calotte

*Magnus Hald, Eva Kjellberg, Anders Lindseth, & Pål Talberg*

## *The background of the June Seminars*

North of the polar circle in Norway, Finland, Sweden, and Russia lies the geographical area called the North Calotte. The area is vast, barren, and sparsely populated: people living there are often long distances from the central communities and hospitals. Tromsø is the capital of North Norway. A mental hospital, Åsgård, was established there in the early 1960s to provide psychiatric services in the Norwegian part of North Calotte. The hospital was planned to have more than four hundred beds to serve a population of two hundred thousand. Humanistic currents in psychiatry in the 1960s, together with the magnitude of the catchment area, contributed to some professionals at the hospital daring to try out new routes in forming the psychiatric treatment that could be offered. They travelled out into the districts and began to work in the local communities together with the ordinary local staff. This "outdoor work" paved the way for family therapy that reached Norway in the early 1970s to gain a good foothold in this part of the country. At first, strategic and structural therapy forms were central, but as time went on the "Milan-model" attracted a growing interest and became the starting point for the further development of the field in North Norway. Ideas about the significance of time and context in our lives became especially important. People change according to circumstances around them, and important parts of these circumstances consist of their family life and life in the local community.

Tom Andersen started his career at the University of Tromsø in 1976, and since then he has been engaged as a professor at the medical faculty in the social psychiatry division. Tom thought very early that psychiatric care should be provided as close as possible to the patients' ordinary local surroundings and that it was the specialists' responsibility to help the primary-care providers provide the psychiatric care. In the late 1970s, along with some colleagues, he launched a project to experiment with this new approach to psychiatric care and together to study "system-oriented family therapy". The outcome was very successful: inpatient care in mental hospitals was reduced by half. Everyone was pleased except the psychiatrist colleagues in the mental hospital, who were sceptical. Most importantly, the scepticism centred around the fact that the practice of the project broke with the more usual individualistic, medical–psychiatric ways of understanding and providing psychiatric care, which eventually was influential in the termination of the project. Tom and his group learned markedly that "systemic thinking and practice" must also include themselves and their relations to the surrounding society—not only the patients' communities, but their own collegial ones as well. In addition, they learned that change grows more easily from within a system; it cannot be pushed in from the outside.

It was, however, hard for those involved in the project to give up the ideas about the great significance of time and interpersonal relationships in working with psychiatric problems, and it was considered important to also let others get the opportunity to be familiar with these new ideas. In 1982 there was a large seminar in Tromsø under the headline of Psychiatry in the Local Community. Much of the attention during the seminar was, however, directed away from local communities and instead focused around the psychiatric hospital in Tromsø. This experience contributed to the recognition that when you meet and talk in a centre, you will easily get preoccupied by what is happening in that centre. That is why meetings concerning "local" work must also be held "out there".

This was the starting point for the June Seminars, which Tom began to arrange and opened to all clinicians in northern Scandinavia interested in systemic theory and practice. The seminars were three-day meetings held in June each year, convened in out-of-the-way small communities situated far out in the mountains or on the North Atlantic coast. The settings were so remote and the facilities so modest that only those guest "lecturers" and participants came who were genuinely interested. The long days and nights under the never-setting sun invited and became the good-fortune containers for never-ending talks and meetings. Refreshed by the seminar, we would return to our widely scattered homes, looking forward to meeting again the following year, as many since have done.

The first seminar, in 1983, was in a small fishing village, Gryllefjord, on the edge of the Arctic Ocean. Lynn Hoffman and Peggy Penn came and enchanted the participants. The next year the seminar was held in another local community, and Luigi Boscolo and Gianfranco Cecchin came. The seminar has been convened at a different remote location with "interesting people"—some new to the seminars, others returning—from the "big world" each year, and attracting more people. Harry Goolishian and Harlene Anderson were two of the guests who later returned a number of times, and many from Scandinavia also travelled to visit them in Galveston and Houston, Texas. (The Appendix contains a list of the June Seminars and the guest speakers and locations.)

After the Swedes joined in 1988, the June Seminars were arranged in northern Sweden several times. In 1994 two Russians were invited, and three years later the seminar was held in Archangelsk, northwest Russia, which was the starting point for the spread of the network there. For many years the seminars constituted the theoretical base for a two-year training programme in systemic family therapy. The programme engaged about five hundred participants and has now, since 2000, moved into the College of Tromsø as a formalized education in relational and network therapy. The June Seminars continue outside this as a meeting place for reflection and development of the ongoing clinical work.

Clinical research as a social practice has been an important area for the seminars to encourage.

The June gatherings have become "meeting places". Some participants have come every year, some now and then, some only once. Those who came and come knew and know what is best for them—to participate either in the seminar discussions during the day or, instead, in the discussions during the sunny nights. Everyone is welcome to participate and all are included: that has been an important first principle. The second principle has been to bring in good speakers. The third has been to hold the seminars at the margins. People from all disciplines and all agencies have come, creating a multiple society with mixed wishes, meanings, and beliefs

### *The significance of the June Seminars*

The June Seminars were popular from the very beginning. Though part of the reason for this success was the participants' experience of taking part in something significant, it not easy to say precisely why or in which way the seminars were so important. One reaction among the participants could be: "This has been exciting, engaging, interesting, but I don't really know what I'm left with." This statement shows the difference between the June Seminars and other seminars and courses. Ordinarily, educational programmes for social workers, therapists, and other professional helpers aim at concrete teaching and information. Although the content of the June Seminars generally was useful and informative, they also cleared the ground for something different, something that was less common: they created room for the participants to interact with the guest "lecturers" and with each other and for their own reflections. Those who took part in the seminars often experienced very concretely how their own questions and skills tied in with the themes that were presented.

The June Seminars represent a different approach: the participants' own experiences, thoughts, assumptions, and ideas are given priority—instead of the presenters' ideas of what the participants might need. In this way, the participants enter a movement in proportion to their own understanding. They have the possibility to consider the foundation of their own understanding. They enter into a movement that also comprises themselves as understanding individuals—with their own particular cultural and geographic belonging. It is very exciting, although it is not easy to describe a concrete source of this excitement: the excitement is just as much the movement in itself as the more specific theoretical content.

Though one might think that all seminars and training programmes for professionals should try to present new information and new theories in such a way that they relate to the participants' own experiences, this, in fact, is often not the case. Even when the participants are invited to bring their own experiences, often information and theories will be given precedence over the materials and experiences that the participants bring. It is generally understood that the most important quality of such participatory education is that those who participate take in—and are able to "take in"—the presented information. In this way it is generally not too difficult for people who have been to a seminar to tell others what they have learned. But this new "knowledge" will seldom be perceived as very exciting because it does not challenge the existing way of understanding.

Today we might say that the June Seminars were ahead of their time. They underlined the importance of the practitioners' own experience, at a time that it was fairly uncommon to do so. For decades, so-called evidence-based knowledge has been given primacy as the basis for action. Confidence in knowledge has been attributed to the kind of science that tries to establish evidence for certain assumptions in a quantitative, positivistic way. Today, however, it is ever more apparent that clinical practice cannot solely base itself on assumptions, hypotheses, explanations, and theories regardless of how good the evidence is. Practical work claims, above all, embodied knowledge that appears in action and that manifests itself as an answer to the challenge that the acting subject experiences in a certain situation. In other words, practical work requires not only that the practitioner is updated in proportion to scientific knowledge, but also that she or he can relate to, and answer to, the different challenges she or he meets in everyday work. This kind of embodied knowledge must also be valued and scrutinized, just as we in the field of science demand evidence for our assumptions. The June Seminars have challenged this bodily anchored basis for action and, in this way, contributed to the development of this kind of knowledge.

It is not enough to spend time in "the practical field" to become a wise practitioner. Time does not prevent the development of unfortunate modes of action. If the practical knowledge is to be developed, it must be challenged and reflected upon. The practitioner must become aware of her or his own way of working and the extent to which theoretical knowledge is utilized, as well as the extent to which traditions and habits determine the way in which practical work is conducted. What kind of familiarity with the context is expressed? How necessary and crucial is this kind of familiarity? Which attitudes among those involved are significant for the course of action? If clinicians can find answers to these kinds of questions, it can contribute to their practical work: a kind of research is needed that is different from research preoccupied with verifying or falsifying assumptions. An exploration of the embodied practical knowledge is required. This kind of research presupposes a "communicative space" in which the practitioner can articulate her or his own experiences and ideas and try them out in open dialogues with other practitioners. In these discussions, theoretical perspectives are needed to help the practitioners consider the meaning and importance of their experiences and thoughts. Rooted in the nature and culture of the North Calotte, the June Seminars have represented such a "communicative space" for many of the participants.

## *Tom's significance for the June Seminars*

The seminar leaders have been invited as Tom's friends, and, with his careful and sweet attendance, he saw to it that all present could feel free to speak in their own words, and thus he brought about a very warm, friendly, and creative atmosphere. He has done this in the same way as he taught us to perform reflective talks: being very careful with the form of the talks, in the sense that the ones who invite persons to a meeting should be responsible to make room for those who come to listen to what is said but also to be free to express themselves in their own way and themselves be listened to with respect. This carefulness and space gives those invited the possibility to create personal understanding by adding something new to what was previously known and understood. Simple and ingenious, this could not have been accomplished by anyone without Tom's firm, never-yielding belief in this "just" way to distribute power and control. Democracy in practice, Tom's work has not been favoured by all in the professional field and has been challenged by many, and he has had to stand steady in the face of many storms to protect it. For all of us in this loosely knit network who also like these ideas, Tom has been, and continues to be, the natural leader and authority by virtue of thinking a bit faster and broader and staying in these thoughts a bit longer than most of us; daring to believe what he has seen and, not least, felt in his body; and trying the new ideas that emerged from practice "out-there". Always together with others and saying he could not have done it without all those around him, Tom very carefully organized the June Seminars in all details to ensure that every participant has a place and feels at ease. He was, and is, also always there ready to talk and listen to whoever wants to discuss what is important for them. In that way, he not only takes seriously the expressions of patients and clients, but also acknowledges the significance of the experiences of colleagues.

In this respect, the June Seminars have always been a "safe place" for expressing yourself, having room for reflection, and receiving impressions. You could also say they are an open, exploring, communicating, and reflecting-room: Rare, valuable—and all in the spirit of Tom!

## *Appendix: The June Seminars*

1983 Gryllefjord, Norway. "Family Therapy". Lynn Hoffman, Peggy Penn (USA)

1984 Kabelvåg, Norway. "The Milan Approach." Luigi Boscolo, Gianfranco Cecchin (Italy), Peggy Penn, Lynn Hoffman (USA)

1985 First, Karasjok, thereafter, Sulitjelma, Norway. "Systemic Family Therapy." Harry Goolishian (USA), Donald Bloch (USA), Peggy Penn, Lynn Hoffman (USA)

1986 Alstadhaug, Norway. "Aadel Bülow-Hansens's Physiotherapy." Gudrun Øvreberg and her physiotherapy colleagues (Norway)

1987 (a): Honningsvåg, Norway. "The Psychiatric Patients and Their Adjustment to the Local Community." Alexander Blount, Raphael ben Dror (USA)

1987 (b): Skogsholmen, Norway."Supervision". Harlene Anderson, Harry Goolishian (USA)

1988 Sulitjelma, Norway. "A Greek Kitchen in the Arctic. Family Conversations Tried to Be Described in a Constructive Perspective." Heinz von Foerster, Ernst von Glasersfeld (USA), Humberto Maturana (Chile), Lynn Hoffman, Fredrick Steier (USA), Stein Bråten (Norway), Luigi Boscolo, Gianfranco Cecchin (Italy), Harlene Anderson, Harry Goolishian (USA), Tromsø group

1989 Skibotn, Norway. "Practical Work with Families." Judith Davidson, Martha Ratheau, Dusty Miller, William Lax, Dario Lussardi (USA)

1990 Melbu, Norway. "Construction, Language and Meaning in Research and Practical Work." Kenneth Gergen (USA), Harry Goolishian, Harlene Anderson (USA), Jan Smedslund (Norway), and the Tromsø group

1991 Alta, Norway. The seminar about the crisis along the coastline of the north of Norway was planned a year and a half ahead, but the crisis declined and so the seminar was cancelled.

1992 Gryllefjord, Norway. Groups from the North present their own work.

1993 Svolvær, Norway. "Constructed Realities: Research, Clinical Work, Theory." Margareth Wetherell, Jonathan Potter (UK), Steinar Kvale (Denmark), Harlene Anderson, Kenneth Gergen, Mary Gergen, Sheila McNamee, Jack Lannaman, John Shotter, Peggy Penn, Donald Polkinghorne, Brent Atkinson, Ron Chenail, Tom Conran (USA), Max Elden, Hanne Haavind, Sissel Reichelt, Åge Wifstad, Anders Lindseth, Magnus Hald, Tom Andersen (Norway)

1994 Björkliden, Sweden. Groups from the North present their own work.

1995 Svanvik, Norway. "Writing as a Part of Psychotherapy." Peggy Penn, Marilyn Frankfurt (USA)

1996 Sulitjelma, Norway. "The Conversations and the Language Influence on Practical Work and Research." Sheila McNamee, John Shotter, Harlene Anderson, Mary Gergen, Kenneth Gergen, Peggy Penn, Marilyn Frankfurt (USA), Jukka Aaltonen (Finland), Viggo Rossvær, Åge Wifstad, Anders Lindseth (Norway)

1997 Arkhangelsk, Russia. Professionals from Northwest Russia, North of Finland, North of Sweden, and North of Norway meet and exchange experiences and questions.

1998 Gällivare, Sweden. "Qualitative and Quantitative Quality-Assurance." Groups from the North

1999 Bodø, Norway. "Working with Children and Adolescents." Child guidance clinic Gällivare, Tumba child guidance clinic (Stockholm), Houston Galveston Institute (USA), Bodø child guidance clinic (Norway)

2000 Cancelled

2001 Sulitjelma, Norway. "The Most Important (in My Life)." Participants in the network

2002 Harstad, Norway. "Expressions in Supervision and Practical Work." Janet Swensson, Eva Kjellberg, Ingegerd Wirtberg, Marianne Wikman (Sweden), Gudrun Øvreberg, Ingeborg Hansen, Eli Rongved, Ingar Kvebæk, Anders Lindseth (Norway)

2004 Tromsø, Norway. "Appreciative, Narrative, and Reflective Language in Consultations." Elspeth McAdam (UK), Michael White (Australia), Tom Andersen, Lynn Hoffman, John Shotter, Harlene Anderson, Hilde Ingebrigtsen (USA)

2005 Björkliden, Sweden. Groups from the North present their own work.

CHAPTER 13

# Crossroads

*Tom Andersen,*
*in conversation with Per Jensen*

Practice comes first, says Tom Andersen. It is not easy to be a hierarchically oriented psychiatrist if one wants to be part of the reflecting team, he believes. Speaking less and listening more became an important crossroad in his practice. We met for a few hours one evening to speak about the important crossroads in Tom's working life. I began by asking whether there are any special experiences that have come to mark important points of departure for him. "Experiences with contexts made a strong impression on me", he says, and he relates two of many such episodes.

"For example, when I was a young regional doctor making house calls, I saw that family and neighbours filled the kitchen. They were there to show their concern and willingness to do something if it was wanted. When I came back to the kitchen after having examined the ill person, my 'reports' produced, as a rule, relief and joy, while sometimes the seriousness of the situation got even more intense. Another example is from the psychiatric hospital in Tromsø where people who were admitted often came from far away. Most became silent and quiet, and that touched me deeply, bordering on being unpleasant, to see how powerfully they longed for home. These are just two of many examples of how important it became to be reminded of and sensitive towards different contexts."

*When you look back, what would you say characterized family therapy's early years?*

"We said to people, 'we think you should think this way', meaning: stop thinking like you do, and think like us. Stop doing what you're doing, and do this instead. It was about telling people how they should live their lives. This got unpleasant after a while, and that lead to us having to give it up.

*Can you give some examples of things you stopped doing?*

"We stopped saying what people should do and think, and then alternatives popped up almost by themselves. It might be, for example, that instead we said, 'In addition to how you are thinking, we have thought . . .' and 'In addition to doing what you've been doing you could also consider this . . .'—in addition to, that is. It became a great relief. And it was a big transition—from 'either–or' to 'this *and* this'. Without really realizing it then, I would now say that 'either–or' belongs in a world one can describe as immoveable and to what one can also call 'the non-living'. So that is to say we worked with living people as though they belonged to 'the non-living'. It felt uncomfortable, and it was a relief to move over to the 'this *and*' perspective. But we were also made to leave the closed room—where it was unpleasant to be."

## *The confrontation with "either–or"*

*It was the choice of a new direction?*

"A crossroads, I call it—because I am very uncertain of to what extent this was choice. It was more having to give something up, really give it up; we couldn't continue any longer in the same way, it wasn't possible. We had to give up."

*Would you say the next crossroad you would mention is the confrontation with the closed room?*

"Yes, that was the next one. The ultimate confrontation with 'either–or' came during the writing of a book about Aadel Bülow-Hansen's physiotherapy. Gudrun Øvreberg and I began to film her, and it became my job to describe everything that happened on the film, all the movements, all the sounds, and all the words—everything. We began to film in 1983, and we were finished with the book in 1986. We called it *Bülow-Hansen's Physiotherapy* (Ianssen, 1997). It was hers. We connected her name with it. Didn't want some general title, but her name. She influenced us all so strongly. We noticed in particular how she saw, but also listened. When one sees and listens, then, of course, one experiences it through the body, and then something happens in the body. Initially you feel it *with* the body, then you feel it *in* the body—and then along come the expressions and with the expressions come the meanings.

"Her influence was great and can't be fully explained. It was no doubt her refined feeling for what is appropriate and what isn't appropriate. It was during the writing of that book that we left 'either –or' for 'this *and*'. And shortly thereafter, we left the closed room, never again to return to it. Away with it!"

*Can you say a little about what you mean by the expression, "the closed room"?*

"Where previously we sat with the family and said, 'Now we'll take a break—so you go and be by yourselves for a while and drink coffee—and we'll think a bit more.' Then we sat there and didn't always speak very nicely about people. 'Imagine being as stubborn as he is', or, 'she is so talkative'. That was the way we talked then. It certainly wasn't particularly pleasant. But the main impetus was that I spoke with Aina Skorpen about what the reason is that we leave them. Couldn't we just sit here and talk, then they can see and experience how we discuss, how we relate to this situation? This was in 1981; it was the autumn of 1981 when this idea came. But we didn't dare do it. We thought we would continue to speak as we had done in the closed room. We thought we might end up hurting and offending people. Therefore, we didn't do it. That's the way I remember it.

"But the idea lay there and gnawed away. Then came one day when I said, 'This is the day!' So we went in to the family and asked, 'Can you join us . . .' and all that. We had been there a whole year, and this particular day—I just said, 'Here is a double set of everything, microphones, speakers—everything'. Then we went and asked, 'Would you like to listen to what we've thought when we've thought about you?' We were probably very nervous—and I thought, what in the world, what have I done now? Then they said yes, and then we turned all the technical equipment around so that they could see and hear us."

## *The reflecting team*

*Are you saying now, Tom, that it's almost as though you can point to a particular day when the reflecting team, as it was to be called, got its name or was born?*

"It was a Thursday, after dinner in March 1985; I haven't made a note of the exact date. I asked Magnus Hald and Eivind Eckhoff, 'Might you be interested in joining us in speaking out loud?' We hadn't talked about this before, but they said yes. So then I went to the door of their room and knocked and asked would you be interested in listening a bit to what we've been thinking and hoped deep down that they would say no, but then they said yes.

"The idea came in 1981, the same year that we were at the first Milan gathering, the first time they got different groups together. It was in Montisola, a little village on an island out in Lago d'Iseo—the Iseo sea. It was the first time they had one of their famous gatherings."

*But the first time you actually did it was in 1985. The idea was there, but you did it first three-and-a-half years later. When you look back now at this idea and the practice that has developed from it—it has certainly become a practice that has had an enormous influence on the field and something I believe you'll find no matter where in the field you go. Can you understand this influence? The breakthrough or gravity of the idea?*

"Yes, I basically can. But different therapists practice it very differently, of course. But if one does it in certain ways—for example, such as I tried to do it—it brings in a similarity of meaning which I believe appeals to many. They do what they do, we do what we do—and it is different, but it is of equal worth in many ways, just as meaningful, even though it has different meaning. And it is striking how therapists in countries with totalitarian regimes—for example, South Americans—are very attracted to it."

*I have often heard people say about you that you were reported to have said, "I will never say anything about a person that the person will not hear". Is that a Tom Andersen quotation?*

"It might be that I said that, possibly not as strongly—*have* said, I think I should say. Because there is much one should keep to oneself—just as in ordinary life. It is purely and simply the case that some things are inappropriate to talk about. Sometimes people can't bear to speak about something—so one doesn't do it. There were many crossroads at that time—for example, the moment I stood in the door and said, 'Would you like to listen to us?' Then the therapist got up in the usual way; he thought he should go along with us, just as we'd always done before. But I said, 'You belong here'. It was almost like having the feeling that we had abandoned him—he was left alone and abandoned. It was very unpleasant as well, but it had to be that way."

## *Meeting Harry Goolishian*

"When Harry Goolishian came to Northern Norway for the first time in June 1985, we talked about the problem-created system—that is, that the system is shaped in the conversation around a theme. So the therapist belonged to another system—he belonged to those who talked about the difficulties. While we talked about their way of talking about difficulties. That was a different system. But when it happened, along came the words, 'No, you belong here', completely by themselves. It was only long after that I understood it. But the spontaneous came from what is felt in the body."

*Someone has said that this has destroyed the possibility of an ordinary treatment conference in psychiatry.*

"Well . . . destroy an ordinary treatment conference? It is, in any case, different. Yes, it is not easy to be a hierarchically oriented psychiatrist if one wishes to be a part of this. And maybe there are those who don't wish to give up their position."

*Is there also an ethical principle you refer to with this?*

"Yes, what I think is that what is unpleasant is to orient oneself away from participation in relationships the whole time. To feel the discomfort and of course think that this is an uncomfortable situation for the others as well. So I believe I would say that it is to dare to take seriously that which one feels—what one feels with the body and in the body. And we were nearing a new crossroads—'should I do this or should I . . .'. At this time we were very rational and sensible, with almost military interventions. We placed rationality before the immediate emotional reaction.

"But when one feels that this is unpleasant, and can't manage to deal with it, then one has to adjust oneself to accommodate it—then one can deal with it afterwards. Don't wait to deal with things rationally first."

## The feeling comes first

*You say it was a crossroads?*

"Yes, to dare to let the feelings come first. All this came at once, and with it the understanding that systems are built up around conversations—that there are different conversations around the same phenomenon. We stopped talking behind a one-way mirror, for example—as we had been doing in the Milan method. While now it got quiet—because, of course, we were supposed to say something afterwards—and then it got instead that we sat by ourselves and thought about one, two, or three things. And then when we talked—then there were many things.

"That was also an important transition. Afterwards we talked less and listened more. We stopped trying to be so active and emphasized ourselves less. Emphasized ourselves less and listened more, and in that way the others were better able to assert themselves more."

*When you talk about daring to put the feeling first, are there some of these places or networks that you are a part of to which you would connect this idea?*

"There are two episodes I remember. The first was a meeting with a family in which a young woman was with her mother, father, and brother, and she flew back and forth between the rooms. She was very restless. And then she began to speak badly to her mother and called her a whore and other ugly words. We stopped this, because we knew it was pointless. But by then it had gone so far that she had been able to say very hurtful things that this mother never got over. Later on I talked with the mother's grandson, and he told me that she had never gotten over it. I wondered whether I could meet with her and ask forgiveness for not stopping it before, but he suggested I not do this.

"The other was an episode with a little boy who was very restless and had concentration difficulties. During the work there was something not quite right. At that time I went hiking a lot in the mountains to think. And this episode got me thinking about how, no matter what, we had to establish who among those present wants to talk and whether there is anyone there who doesn't want to talk. We had in any case to decide what we could talk about and what we weren't going to talk about. These realizations came from these episodes.

"A new form began to assert itself. It became important to discuss with people how we should cooperate before we began the cooperation. With this, we abandoned the idea about having plans beforehand, that it was planned before we met. We had to plan together, if planning was needed at all.

"So there were a good many things that got left behind in a very short space of time. It was concentrated. For several years, two or three, we expressed ourselves with the help of *our* metaphors. We stopped doing this also. It was uncomfortable for us to make our formulations, and therefore ourselves, so central, so there was a stop to that. We began to keep ourselves within the family's expressions—only their expressions. We did not apply our metaphors at all. And then along came this about preoccupation with the expression itself."

## *Practice comes first*

*What do you mean by "the expression itself"?*

"When one only emphasizes words, one can miss out on the fact that people express themselves with the help of more than words.

Where words are concerned, we can *see* that when they themselves hear their own expressions, that they can react strongly to them. For example, a speaker can react by crying, and then the point is to get hold of what they said that led to the reaction. And we don't need to be so concerned with the reaction, but, instead, with what the reaction came along with in what they said. Then we can take hold of what they said and speak a little about that. For example, if one becomes thoughtful when they hear something, we can get hold of those words that made them become thoughtful. In that way we can begin to study expressions and discuss what the expressions contain. Not what lies behind them or under them, but what is *in* the expression itself.

"This came at the beginning of the 1990s, but it lay there actually for the first time in 1988 without my being aware of it. And again it shows that practice comes first. I have seen some old video films and asked this question without being aware of it, and it is strongly connected to getting out of unpleasant situations, to abandon an unpleasant practice."

*A crossroads can also have meaning or influence. Are there other crossroads you would point out as having been important?*

"Crossroads, they have certainly become apparent in encounters with people—encounters with these small networks, families, and helpers. Bülow-Hansen was unbelievably sensitive in relation to identifying contexts—when she did something with her hands, she saw the reaction and she saw how she should continue the work. She is a good example of what Wittgenstein said, 'Don't think, but look!' It is easy to create theories and guesses in situations where we look too quickly and are not explorative enough, and then we don't see what is there. Then we can quickly end up guessing about what something is."

*It is rare to hear you using words such as "theory" and "method". I hear, now and then, maybe, that you say these are words you prefer not to use.*

"Method is often something one has planned to have along for the consultation, something one has made in another context than that in which one is working."

## *To see is to participate*

*But if you were to single out some alternatives to terms such as theory and method?*

"To look and hear, to sense. Sense is to look and hear, taste, smell, feel the strokes on the skin after an impact, an impact on the body. In therapy there is, of course, much to see and hear. This one feels *with* or on the body, and then there is what we feel *in* the body. It is convoluted, but has probably to do with the breath in each expression; the in-breath is extremely sensitive. We can feel this, for example, when we yawn and when we stop breathing, a knot in the stomach, and stop breathing from the stomach. Expression is, to begin with, a bodily thing. Later on we begin to formulate ourselves—and then the point is, the whole time to see what will happen. To notice when a person reacts to their own expression and then to which word it was or which expression was it that this person reacted to in order to go back to it. It is something to work with."

*What is the difference between when you were a 25-year-old therapist and now, as a 69½-year-old therapist?*

"I don't know. In my case, I am not particularly different from how I was as a 25-year-old—it was, and is, the discovery of quite simply to look and to see. To look is a way in which to participate—so a therapist is a participant, I think. To see, that is to participate. If we are to take this even further, we have, with the help of Bülow-Hansen, been able to contribute to describing people who literally *are* in motion the whole time and where the movement of the breath is central. It is from there the expressions come, on the out-breath. And, in addition, I think that one participates in the shadow of the other's movement and notices that something of what they express, which is also a part of the movement, affects them. It is that we should work with. One is actually working with the movement of another by speaking about what they said.

"Harry Goolishian was an important acquaintance. He first came to Norway three months after the first reflecting team. First we were in Karasjok, and then we went down to Sulitjelma—Lynn Hoffman and Peggy Penn were also there. When they got to hear about the reflecting team they were quiet at first, but then they asked, "Why have you done this?" and said: this is something completely new, never done it before. I understood after a short time that it would appeal, and I understood as well that it could be misused by becoming categorizing, instructive, and oppressive. Then I said to myself that if I was to write about this, I would have to be willing to travel around in order to contribute to preventing it from being misused.

"Harry came in March with the expression, the *problem-created system*. The first time he spoke about this was that trip to Norway."

## *Professional network*

*Can you say something more about what Harry and your meeting with him and participation with him has meant?*

"When he was introduced in Karasjok, I saw that he had been invited to Norway because he was such a kind man. He had an unbelievably simple and warm manner with other people. He liked the fact that people liked him; he liked to have an audience. He was so unbelievably generous in his dealings with people.

"He came in June, then we'd practised this new way, and after talking with Harry a bit—this was one year after—I began to realize that we were involved in a completely new way of thinking. We stopped making family maps and everything that concerned structure. We thought about the person in a completely different way connected to the conversation, which is again connected to a topic and a situation. We gave up the word 'structure', and Harry was the first to abandon it in 1988 when we had this 'Greek kitchen' in Sulitjelma, and, after that, all the engineering words were gone."

*You and Harry also shared an understanding of the word "language".*

"Yes he died before he got as far as being able to describe in detail what he thought about that, what he sensed about that—for example, what John Shotter is now doing. In Harry's practice, one could sense that he had this understanding of language. It was he who invited Ken Gergen into the whole thing, and it was he who invited Humberto Maturana and Paul Dell into the family therapy field. It was Harry who discovered them and, later, others; among them John has taken it further. Gergen speaks about language almost as though it should be something one has in a drawer: the person has a drawer, and in there lays language. Then one takes it out and uses it. While John thinks that it lies in every single movement, it is connected to the movements of the body. And I define language as all expression. The artificial division between verbal and nonverbal—this falls away, because everything is language, all expression is language. Expression with sounds, without sounds, blows, dance, of course the spoken word; singing is expression. So thus language becomes all expression and lies in the movements of the body."

*I would like to speak more with you about your participation in professional networks. And not just as a participant, but also as the builder of professional networks. You have, of course, been active over many years both as a participant and as one who invites others to participate.*

"I don't know exactly, but initially it was about creating meeting places. One works better together than alone, and it was certainly to a great extent about finding like minds for this thinking which was rejected by psychiatry. To begin with, it also concerned creating meeting places."

## The June Seminars

*Where did you meet first?*

"It began with the June Seminars, the first was in 1982. The first thing we did was to create a project which was based on seven of us from psychiatry who didn't have our own quarters in Tromsø and who would work in the offices of primary care services and especially the Health Service offices. We had regular hours there, and they could use us for whatever they wanted. If they wanted to, they could join us in working with us. The idea was to meet the task so early on that we could contribute to lowering the admissions to the psychiatric hospital. And there were actually fewer admissions.

"This got to be a battle with the consultants in that they wanted to place this in their own domains. In the meantime, we got support from the Social Department, who said we were to have three positions. And the administration in Troms County couldn't say no to that. But the consultants were not happy. It was an important crossroads when the experimental period was over and it was actually successful. The admissions went down, primary care was satisfied.

"So we asked the authorities whether we should continue. They went to the consultants, who thought it was a bad idea to continue. This was a strong and important blow, a cuff to the ear that got me to understand that one cannot change living systems like individual persons or organizations from outside. They can only be changed from inside themselves. So that was an important crossroads, and that was also a forerunner to the first reflecting conversations. One cannot change people from outside."

*But then you created the first June Seminar in 1982, and then you invited . . .*

"The first one was in Tromsø and then we had been in Italy in 1981. It was there the idea about psychiatry in the community came about. We invited one from Canada, one from Italy, and one from Belgium. But instead of talking about psychiatry in the community, everyone in Tromsø managed to twist it around to talking about psychiatry in *that* psychiatric hospital in Tromsø: too little money, too few positions—and then I thought, no more. No more conferences in the town; we had to move out to the local community.

"Then we ended up out in Gryllefjord. I have always been good at finding practical solutions, and practical problems have never been unsolvable for me. Emotional problems are another thing, but practical . . . Then came Lynn and Peggy, and we lived in fishermen's shacks. It was incredible, just incredible."

*How many have you arranged?*

"With the exception of two years it has been every year—until my last, which was in 2001."

## *International contacts*

*But you have also participated in many other network gatherings.*

"The network is a meeting place, in which things happen by themselves. What I did with the practical aspect was important. I maintained order around the meeting times, food, beds, and travel arrangements, and I invited good people from outside who were non-instructive and who could describe their practice and who were also humanistic. So I've certainly contributed to people being able to meet, and to meet they have to meet about something interesting—we had to find something interesting that they could meet about. And then we had to make it pleasant and enjoyable. It has been important that I have made sure that everyone has been OK. I've learned that that is very important. Give people the opportunity to meet and have a good time—but also that there is a little quality, and then one has to invite some good people. I also assume that people have it in themselves, if only they get the chance, to, in a way, see it themselves. That's what I always believe when I travel around. I'm convinced that they have it. In South America now, for example—they have it in them—that is not something I should have to point out—they have it, of course, if they can just see it themselves. Every person has it in themselves."

*You have participated in South America, you have been repeatedly in many different environments. Are there any among these environments that have come to mean a lot to you?*

"Yes—the prison in Kalmar in Sweden. And the work with the handicapped in Uppsala—that is to say, those who are born with a handicap or develop one after illness or accident, and maybe, in particular, those who are so-called mentally handicapped. That has been very gripping. In addition I would mention the network in the physiotherapy milieu and the network over all the gatherings we've had and South America."

## *Psychosis*

*Psychosis is a phenomenon that has preoccupied you in a special way over the past few years. When did you start these psychosis networks?*

"That was in 1996. Jaakko Seikkula and his colleagues in Finland were already under way. But what they were doing wasn't found anywhere else, so I thought that if they stop or if something happens to Jaakko, it will all fall apart. Then I thought that we had to get a few more posts to stand on and now there are thirty-five posts, thirty-five projects in eight different countries. But it is still going well in Jyväskylä. We move these meetings all the time, and the meetings have been held in all the countries. So, I think, they arrange them under their own conditions, for us and their people, and at the same time it becomes a meeting place. It is purely and simply to let people get the chance to see what they have in themselves and what's there. And we have to move away from this terrible idea that one has to train up or teach people. That is an arrogant position which I cannot be a part of. And this goes back again to this, about not being able to change people from the outside. It is not possible to train people."

## *Working against oppression*

*If I were to say, Tom, after hearing you, that you have often referred to some people you have met—some, I don't know if it is correct to use the word, personal destinies? How would you say such meetings have affected you? Your own practice, own thinking?*

"I don't really know, myself. I certainly get very moved by people. Go along thinking a great deal about it and get filled with a restlessness in my body that won't leave me alone. So I have to often formulate something and formulate something that can be taken into other contexts. I could cite many examples both from Norway and from other countries. I will only give one example.

"It was an episode in Asunción. We were met by the consultant at the mental hospital, a woman, with whom we talked a bit. She was very serious, and it was clear that it wasn't easy for her to show us the conditions there. It was like going a hundred years back in time. Some went without clothes, some had no speech and they screamed. It was overpopulated and—ugh—we went first to the men's ward and then to the women's ward. Pål Talberg came along, and Pål actually couldn't bear to stay there and the female consultant couldn't bear it, she waited outside. It was horrible.

There was a malformed woman who lay on the floor there, and she grasped after my hands. They shouted and screamed, and one held on fast and all of them said, help me get home, help me get home.

"A tiny little woman, she stood behind a wall of iron bars that held her captive. She shouted: 'Help me get home, there are so many who want to kill me here!' A little tiny, thin woman. 'Have you spoken to anyone about this, then?' I asked. 'Yes, I have talked with God', she said. 'And what did he say?' 'Kill them before they kill you', she said. So then I thought: What should I say? I've decided that if I have a good internal discussion, then the others can see it and then I thought that: 'we have to try to do something for you'. So I went out and met with the consultant. She was interested in changing psychiatry in her country. She wanted small units in which people could live, not these big, central hospitals. I said: 'I can understand that you want to change psychiatry in your country', and then she started to cry.

"I assumed I would never see her again, but in cooperation with the University College in Tromsø we began to discuss the possibilities of doing something in South America. So it happened that the college went in for developing an educational project in cooperation between several centres. So then I went down to Buenos Aires again and spoke with the seven who were to be supervisors. The consultant from Asunción was one of them. I asked her later in private whether she remembered my visit and the episode where I said to her that if I can do something, just tell me—and then she started crying again. Now we're under way."

*The fight against oppression? Is it possible to use such big words do you think?*

"I would prefer to call it working against oppression."

## *Afraid of hurting others*

*If you were to point out something you have been especially happy to have participated in, is there anything that stands out as a lighthouse or anything especially important?*

"It has actually been tiring, and the only way to deal with it is just to get to work. I have actually been afraid a lot. Afraid especially of being made a fool of and being laughed at publicly and I've certainly been that. And then, of course, I'm afraid of hurting people, but that is not what I've been most afraid of. I hear that in areas of Norwegian psychiatry I have a so-called non-name. That is not particularly pleasant to hear."

*This is what you answer when I ask if there is something you have been especially happy to participate in?*

"I have, of course, been lucky in that I've been one of many in a growing fellowship who have wanted the same thing. Without all these others, it would never have worked. My responsibility has been to use the position I got at the university for the best."

*After a class where you taught one of the first classes at Diakonhjemmet many years ago, a stalwart and solid Norwegian priest came up to me and said: "Per, you know what? I have been on holy ground." You can almost never get a better compliment after having shared something with someone, I think. But do you say that you haven't heard this properly? I mean, in the sense that you have been able to take it in and be happy about it?*

"Yes, actually there was a lot that was pleasant in the summer. My childhood friends—we are eight, and five of us began school together sixty-three years ago—we gather in our summer place out in the mouth of the fjord, that is to say by the last rocks before Denmark. There I have built some small houses, and having these houses and this place filled by these childhood friends gave an intense joy I cannot describe.

"In any case, there was a meeting in England in the summer with Lynn Hoffman and John Shotter. We seem to be more and more in agreement that language is part of the body's movements and not—as one can sense within other areas of 'social constructionism'—that language is something 'we have in a drawer inside us' and which we take out and use."

## The desire for new meeting places

*If you look forward now, Tom, now that you know you will retire next year from Tromsø, what will you continue with?*

"I'll continue probably to work with relating and relationship and with the network study in Tromsø. That will run over two years, and it may become a Master's programme. I'll continue to participate in Nordkalotten [North Calotte], but everything lives its own life. They manage well without me, but I really want to be included. Then we have this international network, the psychosis network, which also lives its own life, but they want me along there as well. The work in South America, though, that's also living its own life now. I've been in South America for fifteen years. It's almost as though I enjoy working there best.

"Then we have the rehabilitation work in Uppsala and the prison in Kalmar. And, not least, the continuation of the conference in May 2004 on coercion and voluntariness in psychiatry—even the work of preparing the conference was rewarding. These were present, among others: National Association of Relatives and Close Others in Psychiatry, Mental Health, Norwegian Psychiatric Association, Norwegian Psychological Association and the Nurses' Association.

"We got to be such a good gang that we want to continue. The idea is to make new meeting places, for example, every third month, in which we get together around success stories—that is to say, hear what they did, how they came out of the difficult stuff and back to a normal life. Maybe one of us at a time takes along their own personal and professional network and then we others listen to what happened that made it work out well. Then many can come to listen: professionals, politicians, the press, as well as families who are in the middle of their own darkness. As many as possible should be included here.

"It means a lot to me as well to try together with, for example, John Shotter, to come out with an academic proposition. We want to provide alternatives that are in accordance with the practice and the understanding of the person as an *expressive movement*, and then we have to get on with it and actually put the legacy of René Descartes behind us."

# GREETINGS

*Living at 70 in 2006*

Guantanamo

If you look into that word,
what do you see?

If that word had a face,
how would it look like?

If many faces . . .

If those faces could speak,
what sounds could you hear?

Would there be any voices to be heard?

If your body sensed these voices,
what could it tell?

Would it tell any words that you know?

If you look into those words,
what do you see?

Do you see any ways to go on?

*Anna Margrete Flåm*

CHAPTER 14

# "When it starts buzzing in your ears, you must lean forward!"

*Knut Beine Lykken & Trygve Grann-Meyer*

When honouring the birthday of important men and women, it is common practice to look back on their active working life and what they have accomplished. So we, who have known Tom David Andersen the longest, thought that it would be interesting in this short tribute to look at a little of the background of this complete man and person, TOM. Heredity and environment are, after all, the basic influences in life . . .

We who have known Tom since the first day at school soon noticed that there was something special about this boy. He was unique, a boy whom one always listened to. One could not ignore him.

The war years brought problems and sorrows for Tom and his family. Tom's father was one of the teachers who was sent to forced labour in Finnmark by the occupying forces. But the war years meant that we experienced a community that was unique. Perhaps our friendships and our urge to go our own ways grew steadily

---

The words in the title were said by Tom just after he had completed his very first ski jump on a really big hill and was giving advice to an anxious friend who was about to jump.

stronger because of just that. We had no entertainment other than what we found for ourselves. Our play went far beyond that which we today find consistent with basic child safety.

We were inventive, active, and had an unbelievably good time. One wonders whether we had nine lives or whether we had an extra good connection with a higher power. We learned from our experiences, and we got through without injury. What we learned, in addition, was that nothing was utterly impossible.

Whether Tom was the originator of our physical rashness or not is hard to say, but we competed with each other in everything throughout our younger days, and Tom's "fighting face" was always apparent. In free athletics we naturally had a full decathlon programme with our own carefully worked out decathlon tables and home-made hurdles for hurdle-racing. We were real all-rounders: champions in tennis, cross-country running, bike-racing, kayaking, and skiing in the winter.

The ski-jumping at Holmenkollen stimulated us to compete in a triple combination: cross-country skiing, ski-jumping, and slalom. Often we cooked our own ski-wax at home in the kitchen, using our own, secret recipe. The winner of the competition received our diploma, which we had drawn ourselves.

Tom knew well that nothing was impossible. Even with a broken arm, he completed the nearly sixty-kilometre-long Birkerbeiner ski race over the mountains. Then there was the scout hut at Brunkollen he built "almost" on his own. The same applies today when he fights for what he believes in,

Tom chose psychiatry as his mission in life. But when we today see something of what Tom has created with his wealth of ideas and his hands—for example, the cottage of natural stone that he has built in the fascinating nature of Sørlandet—we think that Norway has failed to recognize an architectural accomplishment well beyond the ordinary.

As we became a little older the journeys became longer, and we pressed deeper in over Nordmarka, Jotunheimen, and Rondane. We have seen the pleasure Tom gets from nature and noticed his ability to describe the gifts man experiences when he overcomes very demanding challenges. It was hard on the ascents, often in a headwind, rain, or snow. But when we finally succeeded and reached the summit, we had the finest view in the world and could look at new summits, new opportunities.

Perhaps these experiences are important for Tom to continue his wanderings from his childhood and youth, by constantly going up new paths, always thinking of others, and with his fellow creatures in mind.

Bjørnstjerne Bjørnsson once wrote a poem that perhaps could have been written for and about Tom:

*I en tung stund*

*Vær glad, når faren veier*
*hver evne som du eier:*
*Jo større sak,*
*dess tyngre tak,*
*men desto større seier!*
*Går støttene i stykker,*
*og vennene får nykker,*
*så skjer det blott*
*fordi du godt*
*kan gå foruten krykker.*

*A hard time*

When danger comes, be ready,
with all your power hold steady;
the higher climb, the harder time,
but victory is heady.
And if by friends upbraided
and help and hope have faded,
then pay no heed,
for you'll succeed,
and reach your goal unaided.

Bjørnstjerne Bjørnsson, 1861
(as translated by Mike McArthur for this greeting)

With congratulations and best wishes to an inspiring friend,
from your friends of childhood and youth.

CHAPTER 15

# Of course I knew everything from before, but . . .

*Georg Høyer*

It started with the professionals: a psychiatrist, a psychologist, two nurses, and a police officer. Then came the relatives, and after them the consumers. Small groups of five persons or fewer talking quietly among themselves about their experiences related to the use of coercion in the delivery of mental health services. No analysis, no interpretations, no messages; just stories. Very personal stories. What else? Over three hundred and fifty people in a huge congress hall, listening in silence. Deep silence.

The event took place in Oslo in May 2004. It was a conference called Coercion and Voluntariness in Psychiatry, and invitations were sent to all kinds of people interested in the subject. In the announcement, the conference was promoted as a "different conference". And it was different. Here I try to share some of the experiences from the conference: why it turned out to be different, and why it is hard to forget it.

The idea was born sometime during 2002. Tom Andersen came to me one day and said that he had been thinking of arranging a conference addressing the use of coercion in the field of mental health care. Through his many contacts with consumers, consumers' organizations, and relatives, he felt that the time was right for such a conference. And he particularly insisted on arranging such a conference in cooperation with the relatives' national alliance. As I have known Tom since 1969, I knew I should trust his idea, even if I had some (unexpressed) doubts about the feasibility of such a conference. At the same time, it was a pleasant surprise that there was an interest in discussing the use of coercion; I have myself dedicated my entire academic life to the role of coercion in psychiatry, and for most of the time it has been very lonely. So I agreed to join. At least, I agreed to participate in the planning process and see how the work developed. In retrospect, it was a good decision for me, because the conference turned out to be a success far beyond my expectations.

Inclusion was a key word in the planning process. Representatives from relevant professional associations (psychiatrists, psychologists, and nurses) were invited to join the planning group along with representatives from the consumers' organizations, relatives, and the health authorities (i.e., the directorate for health and social affairs). And all of the invited organizations responded positively and participated in the planning group with great enthusiasm—and with different opinions about the programme and on how the conference should be organized. We spent quite a lot of time discussing the "expert" concept. In the beginning there were many voices in favour of inviting top-notch professional experts in the field as keynote speakers. Others underlined the importance of focusing on the experiences of the consumers and relatives, arguing that they, too, are experts—probably the most important ones, when it comes to experiences related to the use of coercion.

Tom Andersen has always argued that the knowledge and the expertise of patients and relatives are crucial for the understanding of mental disorders. In his work on reflecting dialogues, he always regards the persons defined as "the patients" as his co-researchers. Relatives have the same status when they are involved. It sounds simple and obvious that you should listen to the stories told by your clients, yet it is often difficult to listen on equal terms and to involve the patients as real co-researchers. Again, Tom has been ahead of most other professionals when it comes to recognizing this; many years ago he sought contact with the relatives' national alliance—not to advise them, but to listen and to learn himself.

Little by little, enthusiasm grew for letting patients, relatives, and professionals tell their story. At the same time, we all realized the challenges we would face regarding the conference format if we chose to focus on personal histories and experiences. There is a tremendous difference between the traditional conference format—where professionals present their well-prepared papers supported by amazing PowerPoint illustrations—and having an audience of more than three hundred and fifty people listening to low-voiced conversations between small groups telling their stories, in some sense, unprepared.

Dare we? We obviously did, even if some of us were worried about the risks we might be running and that anything and everything could go wrong. What we all seemed to agree upon was that we (and most likely everyone else regularly attending conferences) were tired of the traditional conference format. When forced to listen to endless lectures given by professionals with little or no room for discussion or questions, fighting drowsiness and struggling to keep your daydreams at bay is often the price conference participants have to pay. This common experience helped us to stick to our decision to try something different.

Tom Andersen met with the group of consumers and the relatives a couple of days before they went on stage, to discuss their expectations and tell them about his (or the planning group's) ideas about how the conversations might proceed.

No formal instructions were given, but the panellists were encouraged to talk among themselves and not to address the audience. And to stay with their personal experiences and perceptions, or to discuss what they had been thinking while listening to the other groups or to members in their own group. The professionals were also invited to a similar discussion, but logistics prevented them from gathering before the conference. They were, however, given the same kind of advice in advance. There was also a fourth group, not yet mentioned. This group consisted of powerful decision-makers from various authorities. This group, who came on at the end of the first day of the conference, was more specifically challenged to comment on what they had heard and witnessed during the day and not to defend policies or promote political plans for improvements. Members of this last group were the Chief Executive Officer of the Norwegian police, one Board member from both the Norwegian Medical Association and the Norwegian Psychology Association, a Board director of one of the five Norwegian public health trusts and a representative from the Ministry of Health. Even if they were extremely busy people, they were told that it was a mandatory requirement that they be present (and listen) the whole day, a condition they all accepted and adhered to.

All groups were attended by two moderators whose task was basically to say as little as possible; they were only to intervene if the conversation within the group stopped or came to a premature end. It was rarely necessary for the moderators to encourage the groups to go on or to guide them.

The professionals started. The members of the planning committee were anxious: would it work? And we were equally relaxed when we all experienced that it did. The professionals were low-voiced and prudent. They reflected on topics like the necessity to sometimes use coercion, the lack of alternatives, of resources—and of ways to try to minimize the use of coercion. Not much talk about what they felt and what their thoughts were when they had to apply coercion or after coercive measures had been used. The silence in the hall was extraordinary. Everybody paid careful attention to the conversation that took place on the stage. Like the other groups, they went on for just under an hour.

Next, the floor was given to the relatives. Their stories were more personal and definitely more heartbreaking. They were stories about being excluded from taking part in all kinds of decisions concerning their family members, about lack of information, and about treatment teams not being interested in their experiences and knowledge. At other times they were left alone with unbearable burdens with no one there to help them. There were stories about not being taken seriously when they asked for help at an early stage, often followed by the degrading experience of police interventions at a later one. Again, the eager attention of the audience was easily sensed.

After the lunch break, it was the consumers' turn. There were four of them. It is hard to believe that their stories could leave anybody untouched. We were told about degrading and unnecessary use of force and violence in the admission process. We learned how unwarranted use of police powers could leave consumers with extremely traumatic experiences that seemed impossible to heal.

One patient told us that she did not dare go outside her apartment for years because she was afraid the police would get her. She still started to sweat and had palpitations at the sight of a police car. Another patient vividly conveyed the panic he felt when he was handcuffed and transported for hours to the hospital, lying on the floor of a van. "I needed someone to hug me and comfort me, not handcuffs", he said. The silence in the hall was such that you could hear a pin drop.

There were also stories of good experiences, like encounters with warm and caring health professionals. Unfortunately such experiences could not make up for the negative events most consumers had perceived when they were subjected to coercive measures. Oh, but these consumers are not representative of the way most patients are treated in the mental health care, many readers will object, and rightly so. They are not. The consumers were recruited by consumers' organizations, and obviously those who stepped forward were those who wanted to tell about their bad experiences. Nevertheless, the stories that were told by the consumers are not unique. An increasing body of scientific literature indicates that coercion leaves patients with a lack of confidence in psychiatric treatment, and many of them feel that their integrity has been violated. This was confirmed by the many speakers from the audience, who had the opportunity to make comments after the consumers had finished their conversation. And I think that all of those who were present in the audience were left with a more profound understanding of the nature and effects of coercion on human beings.

The final conversation between decision-makers also turned out to be different. It is rare to attend sessions were people with so much power appear so humble, so soft-spoken, and with little intention of disqualifying the criticism they had heard listening to the groups and to the general debate. One of them summarized his experience of being present in a way I guess many others in the audience would endorse: "Of course, I knew everything from before, but today I have achieved a different and more profound understanding of what it means to be subjected to coercion. I doubt if the same burdens or 'side-effects', as I have understood is inherent with the use of coercion, would have been accepted if they had occurred in somatic care."

I shall stop here. The conference was different. It was a bold experiment where the audience was invited to listen to small groups discussing experiences and emotions among themselves. Nothing more—but at the same time more than you usually get when you attend a conference. People who participated remember the conference, and it has made an impact on decision-makers that can be traced in new governmental plans to reduce coercion in the delivery of mental health services.

And, most encouraging: the format worked. I even think it was a necessary precondition for the strong and profound understanding we all experienced of the impact of the use of coercion on persons subjected to psychiatric treatment. All members of the planning group did a great job, but I think the conference would never have been the success it proved to be without Tom Andersen's initiative and ideas. Most disappointing? The almost complete lack of psychiatrists attending the conference.

CHAPTER 16

# A small "musical" greeting from "The Chamber Music Group, *Seven Sisters*"

*Rebekka Alne, Heidi Susann Emaus, & Anki Godø Giæver, together with Liv Marit Edvardsen, Åsrun Gjølstad, Gry Årnes, Tone Vangen Fagerheim*

We called our group *Seven Sisters* since we were seven women. All sisters of someone, most of us were even big sisters. Some of us were also sisters professionally, as "søster" is a Norwegian term for nurse. Now we were to meet frequently for two years in a study group with Tom Andersen and Fay Wilhelmsen as supervisors. In this rewrite we have chosen to call ourselves "The Chamber Music Group, *Seven Sisters*", addressing here what the training in "relations and network collaboration" has meant to us.

This metaphor has possibilities and limitations, in similarity to all metaphors. Chamber music is played by small crews. Often the members of these small crews also participate in other and larger orchestras, just as we worked in our designated jobs and departments and were students on the side. *Seven Sisters* played instruments by repertory from three different professions. The instruments were well-tuned in advance, pure sounding after our several years of professional education, many more of practice, and by the combined experience of seven lives. By viewing ourselves according to the principles of chamber music, we see that the question of a common repertory probably was not present as a matter of course. However, after a great deal of practice we learned to improvise.

The conductor and first violinist in our chamber ensemble likely led us less than they might in a usual ensemble. The most important lesson was to meet well prepared and well-tuned within ourselves to be able to intone together with the others we were to play with. One has to be well prepared to be able to meet the unforeseen: what has never before been heard. On one occasion we asked Tom how he was able to sit and listen to all the things people were able to come up with. Tom replied that his thinking was: "By saying it, it must be important for them." In a performance of a musical piece, all the tunes are not as important all of the time; one has to know when one's own part is only an accompaniment for others to perform their solo parts.

Accompaniment in the chamber group has several possibilities. If well performed, the soloist is able to present her part of the piece with glamour and bravura and stand out as a star. If those accompanying become too eager to present their own parts and instruments, they may drown out the soloist. As in the art of reflecting, a reflection may contribute to increasing the main character's own knowledge, to bring out new questions, expand horizons, and open new rooms. It may contribute to making both new and other internal and external dialogues. In the language of football, one often says "we make each other good". However, reflections may also be used primarily to present one's own views, without sufficient attention to the main character and his or her expressions and needs. In those cases, both reflections and accompaniment are poorly presented.

In the chamber group *Seven Sisters* we eventually discovered a great repertory among us. We played classical music by strictly prescribed rules, jazz with a lot of improvisation, and sometimes rock and roll with power and nerve. Which tone to strike up depended most often on the soloist or the soloists who were invited. One time, a soloist came with his own instrument and performed a full solo concert for our chamber ensemble with us as the audience. The soloist played self-composed music, and for the first time we were total amateurs. When the soloist, the conductor, and the first violinist said goodbye and left the stage, the cacophony tore loose within our own chamber group. Great disharmony, disagreement, and differences suddenly appeared. Was this too different for us? Several questioned their own instrument. Taking close care of our own instruments one by one and together, we suddenly discovered a greater understanding and gained new experience. Again, we could intone with a greater security.

We played together. We became seven chamber musicians. We performed primary subject and secondary subject. Well, sometimes we were more a trio or a quartet, sometimes longer or shorter soloist performances appeared, and sometimes a duet. We would have totally abandoned our own ear had it not been for Tom and Fay. Maybe that was the point—to become conscious of our own ear and to breathe right with and into our instruments?

CHAPTER 17

# Thank you, Tom

*Eva Albert*

The day before I was asked if I would contribute with these words, I had for the first time in twenty years been interviewed while being observed by a reflecting team, and I felt I was back where it all started. Maybe it is not correct to use the word "started". Let me say that I felt back in a setting where my interest in people, their lives and stories had been cultivated in a most inspiring and nourishing way.

Where and when and by whom was this? The answer is Tromsø in the 1970s, and the creator and cultivator was Tom Andersen, professor in psychiatry.

The university had opened in 1972. The medical school started in 1973, and I began studying in 1974. I would not say that Tom was like a father to us—that sounds too patronizing. Let me say that he was like a charming, unpredictable uncle or older brother. In the beginning he was a bit frightening—I did not always understand why he laughed, and probably I did not always understand what he meant either. But as we got to know him through interaction groups, lectures, seeing him with patients and families, and going through the course in muscle tension and respiration where the legendary physiotherapist Aadel Bülow-Hansen appeared, I understood that this was a rare, vivid, broadminded, and serious man. His respectful and open way of listening (and talking) to all kinds of people was an eye-opener. The way he intervened in families with conflicts and problems could, at first glance, seem mysterious, but it was never condescending. He taught by doing, not by telling us what to do. His respectful attitude is what I remember most, and I hope this has left its stamp on my way of communicating with patients and their families as well.

My professional field has mostly been gynaecology and obstetrics, but for the past three years I have ended up in palliation and grief. This shift from birth to death might also have to do with Tom.

He was my tutor when doing my *Hovedoppgave*—my "main project" or thesis—the last year of my studies. I wanted to do something that involved me as a person and affected me emotionally and prepared me as a doctor to deal with separation and death. I asked Tom to help me do this. And he did!

He presented me with a 57-year-old, divorced woman with pancreatic cancer who had four young sons. I had several interviews with the woman before she died, and the sons were interviewed both before and after their mother's death. I gave the project the title "After All, What More Can You Do About Grief Than Respect It?" which was a quotation from the Marilyn French novel *The Women's Room*. Even though the title is formed as a question, it expressed my professional ambition then and now: to show respect for a person's way of reacting when confronted with death and loss, rather than interpreting what they say and do. Again, I feel the strong influence of Tom.

It is strange, but two years after this woman died during Easter, my own mother who was divorced, died on Good Friday of the same disease. I took care of her for the last three months of her life. We went for walks as long as she was able to. We sat in front of the open fireplace, and we talked. For the first time she was able to empty her soul of the painful feelings that had been hidden since the break-up of her marriage. Finally, the constant nightmares that for twenty years came when she was left alone disappeared. It is not too much to say that I felt Tom had helped me to prepare not only for my professional life, but also for life itself.

After having started writing these words to you, Tom, I was asked to do some teaching in a day-care group for cancer patients with short life-expectancies. The doctor in such a context is often expected to talk more about "hard facts" rather than existential or emotional issues. As I could choose the subject myself, I was tempted and felt free to take "After all, what more can you do about grief than respect it?" out of the drawer. I chose to do some reading aloud from the part where the woman herself was interviewed.

There were only women in the group, and I told them in advance what I planned to do and asked if they were interested. They nodded eagerly. I stopped a few times to check whether they still wanted to hear more, and apart from one patient who fell asleep, they all seemed interested in listening to the story of how this woman lost both strength and appetite, that she started vomiting and got swollen legs. How she changed her attitude from complaining about the noise from her sons' stereo sets, to pitying them for not being able to use their expensive equipment because they did not want to disturb her. That she, as time passed, accepted that "others" had to take over responsibility for her youngest son of 15 and, finally, how and when she died.

"After all", as one of the group members said, "this is a true story." Another added, "It is strange that you can talk of everyday life subjects on one day and be dead on the next." And a third woman, who had no children of her own, commented on the positive aspect that the ex-husband re-entered the family and took over responsibility for the young sons.

Facing death is not easy. For the women sharing their forthcoming fate, this story seemed to ease their minds. Thanks to you, I felt confident in bringing up with them the subject you had encouraged me to confront personally and professionally almost thirty years ago.

Once again, thank you Tom.

CHAPTER 18

# Movements of life

*Berit Ianssen*

In the late days of Christmas in 1990, Tom Andersen wrote a letter to me. He had read my written exam in Norwegian psychomotor physiotherapy. He liked the way I had written about the treatment of a patient—first describing what we did and what happened, and then afterwards trying to understand.

He wrote, "what about writing a book in this way—first describe what we did and what happened—and then try to understand?" And so we did. I invited different physiotherapists to participate, and Gudrun Øvreberg and four of my colleagues agreed.

We lived far apart, over the whole of Norway. The distance between us was like that of Oslo to Rome. We worked in private practice. So how to manage a book together—woven into our daily life?

We met in Harstad, in the north of Norway, several times. The first occasion was in September 1994. Here we talked about each others' writing. We had a tape recorder on the table and changed tapes when we changed subject from the work of one to another. Then we brought home our tape—and the others' voices on the tape—to help us when we sat working, sometimes late at night, on our own chapter in the book.

We also had telephone meetings—all seven of us together.

We worked for three years, and in 1997 the book *Bevegelse, liv og forandring* [Movements of life] was published (Ianssen et al., 1997).

The best thing I learned through this process was to listen to what one person at a time wanted to say, to wait until he or she had finished talking—took a pause—perhaps said something more—paused, and finished. And then listen to the next person. Not to rush out to be sure I would be heard. I knew my time would come. That made a good rhythm: both inspiration and expiration and a pause in-between. To talk to others is often too much inspiration.

CHAPTER 19

# Our inspiration to write a book together: clinical experience and reflections in psychomotor physiotherapy

*Gudrun Øvreberg*

The birth of a book can be a process with many ingredients. Our book *Bevegelse, liv og forandring* [Movements of life] had a very long pregnancy. It never seemed to get properly started, and we sometimes wondered if it would end up in a miscarriage. In any case, we kept on working through a sense of loyalty and, above all, curiosity.

Professor Tom Andersen introduced us to a new way of working together that was quite unusual. Our meetings together—six physiotherapists and Tom—and talks were profound, open, filled with respect, and completely without negative feelings or stress. Initially the work proceeded towards an aim that was almost invisible to us and perhaps one that we didn't quite believe.

Tom challenged us to write from our work with patients who had been prescribed psychomotor physiotherapy. This would be a clinical case report, including our thoughts and reflections. At our meetings, everyone took time talking about their special case. After each individual talk, everyone in turn reflected on the case presented, as well as the presenter's reflections and writings. This helped us to get going. As writing was not a lonely affair, we were inspired to find new angles and a broader perspective. In fact, for a couple of years we were just discussing, talking, and making small notes. Slowly the ideas in our heads matured enough to put words on paper, even though everyone felt a kind of thrilled discomfort.

Between meetings we emailed our writings and reflections to each other according to an agreed upon agenda. Mostly we worked in pairs, and telephone meetings were added in-between to keep spirits high.

As we proceeded, meetings became more productive. Then Tom began to put a tape recorder in the middle of us all. As each one talked in turn, revealing their reflections, hesitations, and even problems such as "I can't do this", it was all taped. In that way each of us could bring a tape home to help us with the process. On the tapes there were voices from fellow writers and words of direction on how to move forward. Following such a process, we all became givers and receivers.

We managed to meet, although we lived in different parts of Norway and despite Tom's busy travel schedule. A bonus that these years of work has given us is an unbreakable team that has made close friends out of good colleagues. And, as colleagues, we have in our minds a care and dedication to our special form of physiotherapy.

We continued to meet, to telephone, and to send emails. The more we met, the more the creative kettle was kept warm and simmering with new ideas. Just to meet became an inspiration.

The height of our meetings was our trips to Provence in September 2002 and 2005, when we stayed at colleague Eli's summer house. What a place for joy, reflection, and talks this was! In addition to our luggage, we all brought some thoughts and ideas to share through quiet nights and bright mornings. We fell into a similar way of working through talking about our ideas, then listening to the thoughts of the others. Under the warm sun of southern France, concrete fruits came from our works, and what we collectively believed to be true found its way as words on paper. There are many kinds of fruits, and this book is one that now, finally, after careful growing is ready to be consumed.

Our current working project involves one of the group members gathering all written material from and about Aadel Bülow-Hansen. Before she died a few years ago, at the age of 95, she had single-handedly developed this special form of Norwegian physiotherapy. In March 2006, a seminar was held in her memory marking the one hundred years since her birth. It has been our wish to have all the material ready for this commemorative seminar. Aadel Bülow-Hansen has been the crucial inspiration for us all, including Tom, of a very special way of working, thinking, and reflecting in our profession.

In addition to the written material, two from the group are planning a film project, covering the movements in our physiotherapy. For the time being, I am working on the recordings I have from Bülow-Hansen's numerous visits to Harstad, a little town in the north of Norway. She presented several clinical cases here in which our own patients were studied hands-on and with dialogue.

These recordings are of great value, both historically and professionally. Again, it was Tom who became so inspired, thoughtful, and impressed that he started recording her work in 1980. Afterwards he wrote down all that occurred and was said in seven clinical cases, including the ensuing discussions. He made a book of it, adding illustrations, a foreword, and so on. It is an extraordinary and impressive piece of work, and it is now compulsory literature in our postgraduate training. I was inspired by this to buy my own camera, and I continued recording cases and discussions when she was here.

The current plan is to donate these videos, now also converted to DVD, to the University Library in Bergen. Since this is sensitive material for those involved, we are in the process of establishing agreements with the patients involved on how the videos are to be handled.

We call us "the book group". One or maybe even two of us have just started thinking about writing another book about psychomotor physiotherapy. Our next meeting is planned for the end of November 2006, here in the north of Norway. Then we will see where our inspiration will take us. Most important is "to be on the road together". May it never end—this road of inspiration.

CHAPTER 20

# An expanded framework: employing psychomotor physiotherapy in arenas other than the treatment of individual patients

*Eli Rongved*

Since 1982, I have worked as a psychomotor physiotherapist in Melbu, a small coastal town on an island in Vesterålen, in northern Norway.

Working as a psychomotor physiotherapist in a small town, mainly conducting individual consultations and treatments, sometimes gives you the feeling that you're working inefficiently.

Great resources are used on treating each individual patient. Your waiting list expands. The need for help seems to increase proportionately to the collective understanding of how problems and symptoms develop and of how everything is interconnected. Another problem is the double and sometimes triple relations you build to several of your patients; in a small town, where everybody knows everybody, they are no longer only your patients but also your neighbours, friends, and people you meet in other realms of everyday life. It can therefore be difficult sometimes to draw the line between your role as a professional and your role as a private person.

In 1994, a colleague and I started to work with preventative health care within businesses. After some time, we gradually realized that this work opened new doors for us, into new arenas, where we would be able to meet more people simultaneously. At first, we just saw this as an incredibly useful opportunity to communicate our knowledge and offer guidance. However, we also soon understood that we would now need to meet people in new contexts, in their own realities. The people we were supposed to help let us into their own sphere, and we participated there. We went to them—they no longer came to us.

This contributed greatly to our understanding of our clients' realities, their personal relations, and their everyday contexts. The individual actually became more important to us. Gradually, we saw that our relationship to the client had changed; where before we would take on the role of the expert, and the client would be the weak and needy one, now the client would invite us into his or her world, and we would work together towards some form of change.

We found ourselves moving around more carefully, and acting with a new-found form of respect. This new respect came to us when we found that *we* were the ones "not knowing". The client would be our guide into a world that we would gradually and increasingly understand. This development represented a qualitative change in the relationship between us and the client.

In short, we found ourselves in a relationship where the client helped us to realize or understand things, with the resulting process then consisting of guided interaction, either with individual clients or in a group. Our main task was to be present, or nearby, in situations of evaluation or choice.

Our genuine curiosity, our newfound perspective as the ones "not knowing", and our humility all became significant factors that contributed to change. Alternative solutions could be discussed, tried, or rejected. There would be no single, correct solution, but many alternative paths to take.

CHAPTER 21

# What does it mean to be human?

*Barbro Collén, Curt Westin, & Madeleine Thörnlund*

"What is it like to be called disabled? What does the word mentally retarded mean? What does it mean to be human?"

These are questions we took up in a series of reflective dialogues held at the Rehabilitation Service of Uppsala County Council. The dialogues about what it is like to live with a diagnosis of being mentally retarded are the latest and very inspiring phase of the collaboration we have had with Tom Andersen over the past ten years or so. With Tom's help we have, over the years, tried to identify those qualities that have been important to our service users and to our staff in achieving a good mutual working relationship and in ensuring that the effort put into rehabilitation is of the greatest possible help in the service users' lives.

When Tom visits us in Uppsala, he has often come from or been on the way to other places, both far and near—everywhere from the prison in Kalmar to a children's centre in São Paolo. This has given us a sense of connection with these glimpses of other distant realities, which nevertheless have so much in common with our own.

Occasionally, we have with a mixture of fear and pride asked ourselves why Tom has chosen to come back and work with us during all these years. Perhaps the answer is to be found in the fact that our work together has been so valuable to both Tom and us. We feel enriched by what we created together at the time, and which none of us could have achieved on our own.

A group of people, who are called mentally retarded, and the rest of us, who in this context are called professionals and work with rehabilitation, took part in the dialogues that we now describe. The need to talk about their disability came from the service users themselves, while the form—the reflective dialogue—was introduced by the rehabilitation service.

Tom Andersen has taken an active interest in the process both by participating in several of the dialogues and by studying and giving his views on recordings of the dialogues when he has not been able to participate himself. He has contributed to making the dialogues exciting, alive, and hopeful due to his warmth of interest, experience, and authority. He has also encouraged the participants to make a film of their own story—a film that would be greatly enjoyed by many who are in the same situation and provide inspiration for new dialogues.

## *A selection from some of the dialogues*

Tom: "The word 'mentally retarded'—is it a good word or a difficult word?"

Lisen: "It's a good word, and I think you should tell other people that you are mentally retarded because then there won't be any misunderstandings. People know too little about disabilities. It's a good experience to be able to talk about it. I feel safe then."

Her husband Jimmy is more doubtful. He is afraid then that people will think that you can do less than you actually can, so he adds:

"I can talk about hearing difficulties, but it's more difficult with brain damage. . . . Sometimes I hear that they are talking, but, you know, the words don't get through to me. I usually ask what the words mean if I don't understand."

Ove: "Mentally retarded is surely a bad word. Intellectually disabled is a nicer word than mentally retarded."

Albert: "Yes, saying intellectually disabled sounds better."

Inga: "I don't like the word mentally retarded. I don't think you should have a different name for a disabled person—these people should be just the same as everyone else. You shouldn't label them as mentally retarded. When you say mentally retarded, you mean people. People can be good at different things. There is no special name for an ordinary person, or a special group."

Jarl: "In FUB [The Swedish National Association for Persons with Intellectual Disability], we usually bring it up, changing the name. It's difficult, it's difficult to talk about it. But it's alright now, because I'm prepared now. Before I wasn't prepared, so I was unhappy."

Albert: "You're an ordinary person even if you go to a special school."

Jarl: "Yes, you can do more than you think"

Sofie: "I was born mentally retarded, but not my sister."

Inga: "But then it depends, of course, on how you feel about it. I don't feel particularly different even though I was born with a disability, not any more different than my brothers and sisters. Perhaps they can do things that I can't; they've had children, for example. I've thought a lot about those sorts of things, and it feels, of course, hard to talk about. But now it feels better; before it was harder. You can be good, of course, at different things. I'm good at cooking. We travel, we go out dancing, which my brothers and sisters can't do.

Eli: "You hear words sometimes—disability words—that you can't do anything, that you have something wrong with you. There are a lot of people who talk about it. There are some words that I don't understand—'What idiots', I think. It's nothing to worry about. When I can't answer, there's a complete halt. Sometimes I don't listen if a person isn't nice or if he is stressful. I try to listen when we're talking, I try to understand. Last time I couldn't answer at all. I listened instead."

Sara: "I find it difficult with words that are difficult to understand. Sometimes everything goes too fast, then it goes in one ear and out the other—'Listen so it goes into your thick head', they say. But it's difficult to listen. Sometimes I don't know what I should say. But it's fun hearing others talk and describe things."

Eli: "It's easier to listen to a person who is nice. I try to listen a lot to Tom. He is really nice to listen to. Kind, and he makes eye contact and wants to understand. Then there's nothing to worry about! At work I have someone who understands me really well. I try to get on as best as possible in life."

Niklas: "I don't understand some words, but I don't worry about it. It's been fun to talk with you and Tom. Can't explain why, but I've been happy when I go home. It has worked well with people listening. I was a bit nervous at first, but then it got easier."

Ann-Marie: "Sometimes you don't concentrate. Then it's difficult to understand."

Eva: "I become more of a person because of my boyfriend. I'm accepted."

Eli (*addressing Eva when she wants to say something but remains silent*): "Have you lost the words, Eva? Just say it—you can do it!"

Our thoughts about the dialogues:

Barbro: "When I thought about writing something in connection with Tom Andersen's 70th birthday, it was only natural that it should be about our latest collaboration, and that was the dialogues with people who have a mental retardation—what they think about words like 'mentally retarded' and 'disabled' and what it's like to live with these words. I believe the meetings have touched us deeply and have been enriching for all who participated. Perhaps because they've been about simple and basic human themes that touch our own innermost concerns: to understand and be understood, to like and be liked, to need and be needed."

Curt: "I agree. And they've also been about the humanity that lies behind the simple and everyday, and which touches us all. I have been greatly inspired by the respect shown for the meeting, the dialogue, and for all those taking part. There is a real strength in that. It is easy not to take what a person says seriously. And this applies not least when talking to people with mental retardation. Like when Sara in one of the dialogues talked for a long time about her cat, or when Lisen says that she thinks I have a warm voice. But Tom takes all the people and what they say seriously. This has been instructive."

Barbro: "And he tries to see everyone and give everyone the opportunity to say something, or make some other contribution."

Madeleine: "Tom approaches everyone with the same kind of expectancy and curiosity, at least as far as one can see. He talks to each person about what is important to that person. This has taught me to pay attention to how I listen to and treat others. Both theory and practice must be there. What looks really simple and ordinary in the dialogues actually involves great knowledge and awareness."

Curt: "I have also become much more aware of how I act in the dialogues. Do I talk too much? Do the participants in the dialogues keep up with what is being said? Do I give them the chance to understand the words being discussed? Or am I too taken up by my own words?"

Madeleine: "Some of it goes to the brain, some to the heart."

Barbro: "We don't, of course, always understand either the content of, for example, articles about systemic thinking on a more scientific level, where the language can be really abstract. Even so, we seem to have the ability to take in the essence of what is being expressed. I'm also thinking about the last times, when there were two of us who reflected after the dialogues. I don't think all the participants fully understood all the words, but they liked listening to how we reflected on what they said. They were very quiet afterwards."

Madeleine: "I think that the people we met in the group are very respectful towards and listen to each other. Perhaps it is the situation that creates this attitude among the participants."

Curt: "That's when there can be a dialogue. When Niklas says that he listens and thinks but can't explain, I think that even if he doesn't say much and can't explain, it's nevertheless important that he take part. Dialogue is, of course, not just words, but so much more."

Madeleine: "Yes, it can, of course, be about capturing sighs and breathing and facial expressions when people speak or listen. I think about how the participants' body language has changed during this journey. They wouldn't come back several times and see Tom and us if they didn't think it was valuable."

Barbro: "I think that these dialogues have a dimension that it is difficult to put a name to. We usually feel happy and uplifted and then fulfilled when they're over. A little bit like how you feel after a moving theatrical or musical performance. I'm thinking of words like beauty and culture."

Madeleine: "Perhaps those emotional moments are when it is beautiful—which makes you grow."

Curt: "Yes, many have felt really inspired. I have thought about this and believe it may be due to a feeling that we have created something together."

Madeleine: "Perhaps that's what Tom means when he talks about dialogue as peace work. Everyone shares with the others and wants to talk. Somebody thought that she could perhaps help others by telling her story, so that they wouldn't have to go through the same thing."

Barbro: "Yes, sharing their experiences and thoughts with others seems to be important and gives purpose to all the participants in these dialogues. They're really enthusiastic about making a film about their experience of living with mental disability. A story that can be of help to themselves and also a help to others."

The dialogues have affected our ideas about people with mental retardation, ideas that we believe are deeply rooted in us all and are reinforced by the diagnostic culture and legislation that, for better or worse, we have in our society to ensure that people with disabilities receive the resources they need. These people, whom we at first thought of as a group united by their common limitations, proved during the dialogues to be multifaceted individuals. They showed humour, strength, compassion, pride, anger, rebellion, and dignity and a strong desire to talk and explain. During the dialogues they also appeared to change their self-image on the basis of what they themselves and their companions said, and the responses they got from the whole group.

The difficulties that they found they had in common were important and affected their everyday lives, but they were, despite everything, only a small part of each person and his or her life. They all had difficulty counting, which could lead to problems in keeping time and managing money. And words needed to be explained sometimes, as when they rushed past too quickly. To dare to ask and demand an answer was a wish shared by most of them, as well as a longing to be allowed to decide more over their own lives.

They also had different opinions on what were, for them, important questions—for example, the value of words such as "mentally retarded" and "disabled". The question about what it means to be disabled or mentally retarded gradually came to include what it means to be human, a question that we all, of course, ask and have in common. And this is what it's all about. We are all human beings who have the potential to grow together. Tom said in one of the dialogues:

"What does it mean to be human? When you talk to somebody, it's in a way almost a human responsibility to make sure that the other person has grasped what you are saying. If you are uncertain and see that the other person doesn't understand the words, you can say—'Was it difficult to grasp what I said? It's quite alright to ask.' And if the other person dares to say—'No, I didn't grasp what you said', then you can try and find other words. And it's this, I believe, that's really important. Being human is talking and speaking in such a way that others can understand."

## *Finally*

We know that Tom Andersen doesn't like to have attention drawn to him, and we share his conviction that you become somebody when you interact with other people. But now, on the occasion of his 70th birthday, we are taking the liberty to explain how the group of clients and professionals who took part in these dialogues experienced Tom when he was interacting with us. He was kind, cheerful, and agreeable, with a warm handshake and pleasant voice, a sensitive listener who takes what one says seriously and doesn't interrupt. A person whom it is a true experience to talk to, a genuine and impassioned authority. A calm, thoughtful, discreet person with a helpful manner, straightforward and ordinary, focused and attentive. He makes the humdrum exciting, inspires and gives you a lift, and helps people understand their own thoughts. A modest, unpretentious person who makes people feel that they are seen and acknowledged, which means that they grow when he is there.

Madeleine: "I think I expected that a person with so much knowledge, a professor who travels around the world and lectures, would be of a certain type, but instead a man comes to us who behaves in such a simple, attentive, and respectful way that everyone feels they are important."

Thank you, Tom, for the collaboration we have had and still have with you. It has been invaluable to us, both professionally and personally.

CHAPTER 22

# A tribute to Tom— humbly, from the heart of the Norwegian Family Therapy Association

*Pål Abrahamsen, Kirsti Ramfjord Haaland,*
*& Hans Christian Michaelsen*

> "Little that is meaningful can be said about such matters,—they can only be shown."
>
> Ludwig Wittgenstein

In the centre of the edge—that is where Tom Andersen moves, wherever he is; in Tromsø, in our Norwegian Family Therapy Association (NFFT), or anywhere in the world. Inside, but outside, looking for ways to find the unheard voices, ways to help us all go on. It is all about looking, he says, looking to move and get moved.

In the heart of the NFFT, which is at Markveien 23 in Oslo, gathered together at the penthouse flat of Pål Abrahamsen are Kirsti Haaland (founder and Chair for many years), Hans Christian Michaelsen (present Chairperson), and Pål (General Secretary throughout NFFT's existence), looking for the best words to describe Tom. Partly we are looking for them in the fireplace, where flames flicker and make thoughts find their own paths through memories and language games, partly in a pile of eighteen annual volumes of *Metaforum*, the journal of the NFFT, and in its predecessor, *Tannhjulet*.

Here we will describe how our meeting proceeded, suddenly realizing that we were fulfilling one of Tom's sentences: "We will be what we are when we convey what we convey. Internal and external voices challenge and oppose each other; we are to create a balance. We *are* not; we *will be*, as Tom might have voiced it. What will we be—who will we be, with whom? Let's see where our meeting takes us.

In many ways Tom is here with us; we find him in words and pictures in many of the issues of our journal, and even between it all. We reflect: Tom has been with our association from the beginning, when NFFT was founded in December 1983, and he has never left us. On the contrary, his interest and participation is always expressed in his generous contributions to our meetings; never has he forced an intrusion upon us, but often he acts with the gentle provocation that comes only from a true friend.

Words are bricks. They can be used for building walls or building bridges. A bridge-builder across huge distances in time, space, and ideas with tools from language and emotions, Tom himself is also a builder in wood and stone. Furniture, tables made of natural stones, even a summer cabin by the sea are material products of his thoughts and not least by his hands.

## *A practical philosopher, a philosophical practitioner*

Tom goes against the currents of the stream, he makes choices, and he is hurt, time and again. He challenges all "truths" and dogmas, he is much more devoted to encounters than to ideas, and thus the ideas that exist within us are constantly challenged. He never throws away experiences, but preserves them for a future occasion, even if they create noise and stir up people.

Is he doing therapy? If not, what is he doing? "It is all about to touch, to be touched, to move and to be moved", he says. Tom is a collector of words that come by in conversations, putting them into his box, looking at them to see what they are. Not really, though—he is, rather, inviting *us* to look *into* the words with fresh eyes. This stirring-up makes ways for new possibilities. Now the three of us are looking upon our own conversation: what words may we find about what Tom is doing? Magic? Art?

Pål runs to the kitchen and produces a couple of coffee mugs—with the printed words, "Den gode samtale" [The good dialogue]—that he acquired from a meeting in Steinkjer, Norway, in October 2001. The conference focused on conversations in prisons between prisoners and their guards, the intent being to replace the harsh, disrespectful, and often degrading exchanges carried out in most places and much of the time in such extreme places as prisons. Tom told the participants of the seminar: "It took me a while and a lot of thinking to come to grips with my prejudices about the dangerous criminal and replace him with a human being." Was this, then, therapy? "Therapy is being with others", Tom told us on this occasion (see *Metaforum,* Vol. 4, 2001). In the same issue of *Metaforum* is a synopsis of Tom's seminar in Sulitjelma, North Norway, in June of that year and also his impressions of a Turkish bath (Rudas) on the bank of the Danube in Budapest, Hungary—all showing the many-faceted impressions that Tom wants to share with us. The Hungarian letter is, in fact, one in a series of letters from his extensive travels. For instance, three years earlier he told the *Metaforum* readers about his journey to South Africa, which in turn resulted in an invitation and a very moving opening plenary dialogue on reconciliation, with Mmatshilo Motsei, from South Africa, at our International Congress in 2000.

Artists are often lonesome—and very vulnerable. Their way is never easy, but difficult and thorny. The artist must *see* and *perceive* and must train his or her abilities in this respect. Tom sees people in a way that makes both parties moved by each other. He brings about encounters; his ability seems simultaneously intuitive and conscious.

But what if the encounters do not develop? Tom's advice: Take some deep breaths from your belly, slow down your tempo and your pitch of voice. It is mandatory to go into the situation, to participate; standing on the outside will prevent you from the magic, from the touch of words that makes us move.

Pål is inspired at this point. He grabs a deck of cards and starts to show the others some magic tricks. The situation is obviously inspiring him to contribute in this way—choosing the occasion to show what is obvious but not obvious unless you really *see* it. Pål says afterwards: "I cannot explain why I did this just then. But explaining is not of any particular importance, is it?" The others agree wholeheartedly. In fact, beforehand the three of us had planned to meet for an intellectual survey on the influences Tom has given us, and—we ended up playing language games with toys of images. It is all there, just before our eyes, though most of the time we do not see it. Our thoughts shadow our awareness about *what really is* there in front of us. Don't think. Look. It is all about looking. And "then shall we be moved", as Tom says.

We were also reflecting on the fact that Tom often focuses on the body—and on breathing in particular. His *inspiration* from the Norwegian physiotherapist Aadel Bülow-Hansen has made quite a new impact on his way of *seeing* people's communication as bodily expressions as well as verbal ones. But Tom is hesitant in commenting on such bodily reactions, because he feels he may touch upon something for which there are as yet no words. The body has its own language, in which they may speak more directly to each other than going via words. To be struck by the moment, the way the moment expresses itself, is, however, a guideline for Tom, giving him clues as to where to turn his focus next, where the conversation may continue, how to make a new distinction. The body is there, telling directly; our respiration, the first and last movements in life. It never lies, but goes on until it dies.

On this note Pål brings (for the body) a rare drink of "mjødurt"—a drink made from a herb originating from Pasvik in North Norway near the Russian border, a taste very special and intense and not easily forgotten. And upon tasting it and bringing in and focusing on bodily sensation, we reflect.

The NFFT is far from being a congregation. People come in and go out all the time. They learn from each other (particularly from Tom, we must admit) and then often rearrange their ideas—about reflecting teams, about cooperation, by some called therapy, by some called supervision, according to what is the context. Tom himself never objects to people wanting to try to develop his ideas further. His way is basically the challenge–and he challenges himself as well as others, maybe even more. To doubt one's original beliefs seems to be one of Toms' few dogmas. Doubt all of that which is handed over to us, whether it is from former generations or from present scholars, always question the unquestionable, Tom urges. We should even question our own language games—perhaps they only create more knots in our relations, not fewer. Maybe our language is our greatest deception; we believe in it for clarity, as it weaves us into its web of mystery. Tom's self-questioning gives us faith to go on in this mystery, sorting out ways of going on in life. Thank you, Tom, for your inspiration, for your artistry, for your humanity and your sincerity, and for your generosity in dealing with us, your true friends in the NFFT!

### *Tom in the NFFT*

When the NFFT was founded in 1983, there were strongly opposing opinions on the nature of such a venture. Was this to be an association for psychiatrists and psychologists only with particular interest in the field, or should all interested parties be allowed to join? Tom was very much in favour of the latter alternative, although the "approved" professionals very much doubted the idea—which, however, was accepted and has been the foundation for the years that followed. Tom was always very much supporting ideas and practice coming from innovative people, regardless of their background and formal training. And so Tom has always been a very strong force and supporter of our endeavours to make the family therapy field a useful arena for both therapists and those supposed to benefit from therapeutic action.

Tom is a modest man—never putting himself in front of others, never participating unless he believes he is asked and his ideas are wanted by those who invite him. In the NFFT, however, he just *knows* he is in demand—and he always participates at our meetings and gives his contributions, knowing as he does that he is always wanted—by those who know him and those who are new to him and the field of family therapy. The marriage between the NFFT and Tom is a strong one and seemingly never ending. He meets colleagues interested in development in the field of therapy based upon relational and context-oriented therapy. He has on a number of occasions presented thoughts in plenaries, workshops, and in private talks when we hold our annual conference—always adding a new dimension by videotapes and his own words to us. In 2004 a participant described Tom's workshop that year with the following words:

> To enter Tom Andersen's universe is a journey into becoming more perceptive, more reflective, and more present in oneself and in the encounter with The Other. With his mild, slow voice he brings us in contact with new sceneries, oscillating between reflection and observation, at large and into the details. Some times he is putting his points directly to us, at other times we may catch glimpses of the wisdom he is presenting. Like a Zen-master he directs us, by words, videos, music, and pauses. A lot is never even said. Sometimes we are shaken, sometimes confused, sometimes we discover new connections and understandings with or without using words to acknowledge. [*Metaforum*, Vol. 2]

Tom never opposes us—he always contributes and promotes to enrich the way people think and act. He never will question and criticize; he will add his voice to others' voices to enlarge the field. His extensive travels bring together all parts of the country—particularly the South to the North, in the latter part of which he lives, even if he originally came from the former.

We particularly remember his contribution when we were to host the 2000 International Family Therapy Congress but lacked the funds. He offered to give a two-day seminar, free of charge, in December 1998 on New Perspectives in the Work with Psychiatric Disorders. Two hundred and ten participants found their way to the event, and, needless to say, the economic base for our congress was secured. Language, therapy, and research were subjects elegantly blended in a performance praised as poetic, aesthetic, and emphatic. No wonder we love him!

## *Tom in Tromsø*

Tom has lived most of his adult life in Tromsø, a city of sixty thousand inhabitants in the far north of Norway, above the Arctic Circle, with midnight sun in summer and near-complete darkness in winter. It is a small but industrious society, with great humans in great nature. This is, indeed, where Tom is right in the centre of the edge. He has never ceased to feel responsibility for this remote, but very alive part of the country, and he has arranged numerous seminars, workshops, and other events, particularly for professionals and others living in the north. Generously he has also invited people from the south, as well as from our neighbouring countries, to a number of events. North Norway has, with his initiatives, become very exotic, as he has invited quite a few of his international friends to come—for example, to a "Greek Kitchen in the Arctic" and to other very tasty encounters for all of us to join in.

In addition to his teaching activities, since 1981 he has acted as a professor of social psychiatry at the University of Tromsø, the northernmost university in the world. He has thus created bridges between all types of health workers in various contexts and has been especially eager to connect professional people inhabiting the north of Norway to those of northern Sweden, Finland, and Russia. His seminars at the university level have become very popular and have attracted—and still attract—students from many countries. To us he seems to carry out a never-ending schedule of activities to benefit all those who want to expand their views and learn more about how focusing on relationships may increase their skills and open up to new qualities, both in them and in those whom they want to help. He is now 70 and officially becoming an emeritus, but you can never tell with Tom!

## *Tom in the world*

Most of all, Tom is a citizen of the world. He has travelled extensively to all corners of the world and has kept us informed and invited us to join his efforts to serve the underprivileged, to unite the affluent world in solidarity with the less fortunate parties. For some time he has also been a member of the board at IFTA (the International Family Therapy Association) and he has pointed out the need for global views. In the IFTA conference in Istanbul in March 2004, he reminded the participants of reciprocity and wideness of scope:

> I must comment upon something we all heard yesterday. First the words: "Terrorism as a weapon." Speaking this way can easily contribute to escalation. It would be safer to balance

> the word by saying: "Terrorism as a weapon and terrorism as an answer." I also felt uncomfortable that September 11th was so much in focus. It was actually abbreviated to 9/11 several times. For many, September 11th 1973, when Allende died, was a harder day than September 11th 2001. We must remember that. So, every time we speak of 9/11 we should add if we mean 1973 or 2001. [*Metaforum,* Vol. 3, 2004]

In discussing forthcoming international events, instead of asking those lacking money to come to us for meetings and congresses, Tom suggests that we should go to their countries, to see, observe, and contribute He himself is doing what he preaches, often visiting less fortunate parts of the world and giving speeches, seminars, and demonstrations, some of which he tells us about when he returns "home" to the NFFT. His message is always: "We need to be present where we are needed!"

Nevertheless, he helped us tremendously when the NFFT was to host the IFTA Congress in Oslo in 2000, where sixteen hundred guests from sixty-five countries were gathered, many of whom were invited by Tom, who also initiated a "solidarity fund" for travel and accommodation for people from countries with fewer resources due to their financial status. We—and Tom, we know—are very proud of this work, which is now extended to the IFTA Congress in Iceland.

When Tom was asked by Ukrainian colleagues to visit them in order to develop family and relational therapy there, he generously invited the NFFT to be represented with him, and two of us together with Tom visited Kiev in April 2002 and also later. The interpreter was a very important person and concluded: "I am privileged to live in a time when my country is offered new possibilities and I may contribute to the new developments!" (*Metaforum,* Vol. 4, 2002).

Even being a very well known person himself, Tom is never in favour of guru-ism. It is the *ideas*—the carrying-out of meetings between people, not those who introduce such practice—that are of interest, he says. By contributing to this book, we, however, slightly disagree with him. As a plain matter of fact, we—as do the other contributors to this book—think Tom deserves a tribute also for who he is and for what he has done and still does to our therapeutic community!

### *How Tom presents and conveys his work, and how he will, time and again, inspire us*

> "The light of work is a beautiful light, which, however, only shines with real beauty if illuminated by yet another light."
>
> Ludwig Wittgenstein

"The light of work" is obvious in the video presented by Tom in a workshop that he presented at the Nordic Congress of Family Therapy in Elsinore, Denmark, on 19 August 2005.

> Three generations of women are presented to us; they are obviously restlessly awaiting the session to start. Tom is with them, and he is attentively listening to their talk. The therapist, Pat, is about to prepare a conversation with Grandma Therese, the daughter Maureen, and the granddaughter Theresa, the latter in her teens. Maureen's sister is also present, but she excuses herself by saying: "I'm just the driver."
>
> Tom tells us: just look, don't think; just observe, don't interpret; just listen to the words, don't make opinions. And what we see on the video is that Tom is closely watching all of them, listening to the noise that we also may hear; the ladies are very talkative, noisy, laughing, and he tells us that at this point he was somewhat restless, thinking where and how to begin talking with them. The conversation eventually begins, and the women say that little Theresa is mean and ungovernable. Her mother is very worried about this and doesn't know what to do, grandma is very angry and very silent, and Aunt Tina is still just the driver. Situation: Noisy. Locked. Frozen.

Is it possible to turn this into an exchange with other movements than those that we have just observed? What can be done here?—any therapist is bound to throw questions like this. "What is your method?" people from the audience ask Tom. And he answers calmly and steadily: "None". What? None whatsoever? Is that possible—there has to be a manual, a method, a way to go?

Well, yes, in the sense of movement. One has to move, Tom admits. In this case, one has to move within the language presented, move like a fish in the water. A predestined rigid method would only add more noise and put up a filter that would prevent us from really *seeing* what we hear. In order to see what is there just in front of us, we have to be awake and perceptive. It is the description of all that is seen and heard that constitutes the movements, the co-movements—in fact, the healing process called treatment. These descriptions are our voices, both the internal ones and those that are expressed externally. The voices may be in opposition to each other, but together they may create a sort of a balance, like muscles in the body. By talking to each other, we talk to ourselves—"we will become what we become when we say what we say", Tom elaborates. In fact, we *are* not—we *may become*. But who may we become—and with whom? He emphasizes this as a very central point and a very crucial question, both in this videoed conversation and in life in general.

> Tom proceeds by asking himself: "In a situation: what makes one choose one and not the other? Why does one choose to talk to one person and not the other?" He asked himself this question when being confronted with the noise from the women. He talks to them for a while, and proceeds to ask them what they fathom one might talk about in this room; he asks who wants to speak and when do they want to do so. He listens closely to what they say, not to what is *not* said. More and more the development favours his direct dialogue with Grandma Therese, who had been very silent at the beginning of the session and had said very little in the opening minutes. Why did you pick her, the audience wanted to know. Tom answers: "I believe it is as simple as this: My feelings. I felt sorry for her. I also felt that I had to talk to all persons present in order to facilitate the situation for Pat to find the answer she was there to find."

Feelings? Can therapists learn to use feelings in their therapies? How can that be done? Well, no, we cannot learn to use them. We have to *be* there. When we, as therapists, participate in interactions that create movements within and between persons, we need to be open to the possibility of becoming moved ourselves. Movements come from within, triggered by what we perceive, hear, and see externally. We must pay close attention to what others are trying to say and then see what they are in fact saying to us. This is far more valuable than the use of any method. It is the attitudes that are of importance. Our own internal dialogues and movements will have to connect to the voices of the others present. "My task is to answer the answers that they give", Tom says. He has demonstrated this attitude in meetings with people in despair and in troublesome situations. He summarizes it:

- Notice and comment upon what they say that is important to them.
- Repeat what they say using their own words and expressions ("remember their use of words and bring them back to when they were expressed").
- Work with their expressions and idioms, walk into them, so to speak, and examine them closely.
- Avoid expressing your own opinions, use the way of reflections.

Tom told us he had borrowed ideas for his own attitudes from language philosophers like Mikhail Bakhtin and Ludwig Wittgenstein. From the latter he quotes: "Like everything metaphysical, the harmony between thought and reality is to be found in the grammar of the language" (*Zettel* 55) and: "The question 'What do I mean by that?' is one of the most misleading of expressions. In most cases one might answer: 'Nothing at all—I *say* . . .'" (*Zettel* 4). Thus, listen and observe what is said. There are the answers—and the questions.

Wittgenstein says that to *describe* people is the beginning of the treatment. The description is in itself promoting a change. In an "either–or" world that deals with that part of reality that is visible and static, it is dangerous to create non-living descriptions of living creatures. But when dealing with the invisible and moveable aspects of life, the world will be "both–and". Tom remarks that this is also the case with language, like an extension of our physical body, like the hands of a child exploring the world.

In her exchange with Tom, Grandma Therese has told him about incidents in her own life that up to now she has kept to herself. The granddaughter has listened intently to the dialogue. Grandma then addresses her directly, tells her she is angry, that she loves her, but hates what she is doing. The grandchild is moved, new voices emerge, voices about longing and yearning.

> "What we [say and] do is an answer to something that has just happened to us."
>
> Mikhail Bakhtin

All languages and expressions contain rhythms and pauses. The intervals, the pauses, may be of equal importance to the words themselves. Tom plays music for us during intervals, not to disconnect from something but to connect to something—the music, in-between the words. On this occasion, Tom plays *Litany,* written in 1996 by Arvo Pärt, a 70-year-old Estonian composer. The music has pauses that may be perceived as more characteristic than the music itself, but in this way the pauses give more character to the music, which is also how the composer himself has described it. The pauses play the greater part. And when this music is playing, the video shows a frozen picture: Grandma Therese looking into the air as if she is seeing something in her life for the first time. Tom has his eyes on her, with a look shining from deference for her life. This is the beautiful light of work—which, in turn, is illuminated by yet another light.

# *REFERENCES AND BIBLIOGRAPHY*

Andersen, T. (1987). The reflecting team: Dialogues and meta-dialogues in clinical work. *Family Process, 26*: 415–428.

Andersen, T. (1991). *The Reflecting Team: Dialogues and Dialogues About the Dialogues*. New York: W. W. Norton.

Andersen, T. (1992). Reflections on reflecting with families. In S. McNamee & K. J. Gergen (Eds.), *Social Constructionism as Therapy*. London: Sage.

Andersen, T. (1994). *El Equipo Reflexivo: Diálogos y diálogos sobre los diálogos*. Barcelona: Editorial Gedisa.

Andersen, T. (1995a). A linguagem não é inocente. *Nova Perspectiva Sistêmica, 4*: 7.

Andersen, T. (1995b). Reflecting processes. Acts of informing and forming: You can borrow my eyes, but you must not take them away from me! In: S. Friedman (Ed.), *The Reflecting Team in Action*. New York: Guilford Press.

Andersen, T. (1996). Language is not innocent. In F. Kaslow (Ed.), *The Handbook of Relational Diagnosis* (pp. 119–125). New York/Oxford: Wiley.

Andersen, T. (2003). *Reflekterande Processer Samtal och samtal om samtalen*. Stockholm: Mareld.

Andersen, T. (2005). The network context of network therapy. In: A. Lightburn & P. Sessions (Eds.), *Handbook of Community-Based Clinical Practice*. New York: Oxford University Press.

Andersen, T., & Epstein, E. (2002). Contribuciones de Harry Goolishian. *Sistemas Familias, 18* (3): 42–56.

Anderson, H. (1987). "Therapeutic Impasses: A Breakdown in Conversation." Unpublished manuscript, adapted from paper presented at Grand Rounds, Department of Psychiatry, Boston, MA (April 1986).

Anderson, H. (1991). Opening the door for change through continuing conversations. *Family Therapy Approaches with Adolescent Drug Abusers*. Massachusetts: Allyn & Bacon.

Anderson, H. (1997a). *Conversación, Lenguaje y Posibilidades*. Buenos Aires: Amorrortu.

Anderson, H. (1997b). *Conversation, Language and Possibilities: A Postmodern Approach to Therapy*. New York: Basic Books.

Anderson, H. (2003). A postmodern collaborative approach to therapy: Broadening the possibilities of clients and therapists. In: R. House & Y. Bates (Eds.), *Ethically Challenged Professions: Enabling Innovation and Diversity in Psychotherapy and Counseling*. Ross-on-Wye: PCCS Books.

Anderson, H. (2005). Myths about "not-knowing". *Family Process, 44*. 4: 497–504.

Anderson, H., & Burney, P. (1996). Collaborative inquiry: A postmodern approach to organizational consultation. *Human Systems: The Journal of Systemic Consultation and Management*.

Anderson, H., & Goolishian, H. (1988). Human systems as linguistic systems: Preliminary and evolving ideas about the implications for clinical theory. *Family Process, 27* (4): 371–393.

Anderson, H., & Goolishian, H. (1991). Thinking about multi-agency work with substance abusers and their families. *Journal of Systemic and Strategic Therapies, 10*: 20–35.

Anderson, H., & Goolishian, H. (1992a). The client is the expert: A not-knowing approach to therapy. In: S. McNamee & J. K. Gergen (Eds.), *Therapy as Social Construction*. London: Sage.

Anderson, H., & Goolishian, H. (1992b). *Från påverkan till medverkan: Terapi med språksystemiskt synsätt*. Stockholm: Mareld.

Anderson, H., & Goolishian, H. (1995). El cliente es el experto: un enfoque de la terapia del "no saber". *Sistemas Familiares, 11* (3).

Anderson, H., Goolishian, H., & Winderman, L. (1986). Problem-determined systems: Towards transformation in family therapy. *Journal of Strategic and Systemic Therapies, 5*: 1–13.

Anderson, H., & Rambo, A. (1988). An experiment in systemic family therapy training: A trainer and trainee perspective. *Journal of Systemic and Strategic Therapies, 7*: 54–70.

Anderson, H., & Swim, S. (1994). Learning as collaborative conversation: Combining the student's and the teacher's expertise. *Human Systems: The Journal of Systemic Consultation and Management, 4*: 145–160.

Anderson, H., & Swim, S. (1995). Supervision as collaborative conversa-

tion: Combining the supervisor and the supervisee voices. *Journal of Systemic Therapies*, 14: 1–13.
Bachelard, G. (1964). *The Poetics of Space*. Boston, MA: Beacon Press.
Bakhtin, M. (1981). *The Dialogic Imagination*, ed. M. Holquist, trans. C. Emerson & M. Holquist. Austin, TX: University of Texas Press.
Bakhtin, M. (1984). *Problems of Dostoevsky's Poetics*, ed. and trans. C. Emerson. Minneapolis, MN: University of Minnesota Press.
Bakhtin, M. (1986). *Speech Genres and Other Late Essays*, trans. V. W. McGee. Austin, TX: University of Texas Press.
Bakhtin, M. (1991). *Dostojevskijs poetik*. Stockholm: Anthropos.
Bakhtin, M. (1993). *Toward the Philosophy of the Act*. Austin: University of Texas Press.
Bateson, G. (1972). *Steps to an Ecology of Mind*. New York: Ballantine.
Bateson, G. (1979). *Mind and Nature: A Necessary Unity*. London: Fontana/Collins; New York: Bantam Books, 1980.
Bateson, G. (1991). Propósito consciente y naturaleza. In: *Pasos hacia una ecología de la mente*. Buenos Aires: Carlos Lohlé.
Bateson, G. (1998). *Mönstret som förbinder*. Stockholm: Mareld.
Bateson, G., & Bateson, M. C. (1987). *Angels Fear*. New York: Macmillan.
Benhabib, S. (2002). *The Claims of Culture: Equality and Diversity in the Global Era*. Princeton, NJ: Princeton University Press.
Benhabib, S. (2004). *Jämlikhet och mångfald: Demokrati och medborgarskap i en global tidsålder*. Göteborg: Daidalos.
Bernardes, C., Barbas, M. C., & Pereira, M. (2001). Multiplicadores reflexivos. *Cadernos de Familiae*, *17*: 33–38.
Caminha, P. V. (1500). *Carta do descobrimento do Brasil* (available at: http://orbita.starmedia.com/~hpcaminha/).
Cecchin, G. (1989). Nueva visita a la hipotetización, la circularidad y la neutralidad: Una invitación a la curiosidad. *Sistemas Familiares*, 5 (1).
Cecchin, G. (2002). *Irreverencia. Una estrategia de supervivencia para terapeutas*. Barcelona: Paidós.
Cecchin, G., Lane, G., & Ray, W. (1993). *Irreverence: A Strategy for Therapists' Survival*. London: Karnac.
Collins, C. (1993). *Truth as a Communicative Virtue in a Postmodern Age: From Dewey to Rorty* (available at http://www.ed.uiuc.edu/EPS/PES-Yearbook/93_docs/COLLINS.HTM).
Conan, N. (2003). The Quilts of Gee's Bend. *Talk of the Nation*. National Public Radio, 4 February.
Damasio, A. (1994). *Descartes' Error*. New York: Putnam.
de Shazer, S. (1994). *Words Were Originally Magic*. New York: W. W. Norton.
Fraser, N. (2003). *Den radikala fantasin: Mellan omfördelning och erkännande*. Göteborg: Daidalos.
Freire, P. (1970). *Pedagogia do oprimido*. São Paulo: Paz e Terra.

Freire, P. (1985). *La educación como práctica de la libertad.* Buenos Aires: Siglo veintiuno editores.

Freire, P. (1997). *Pedagogía de la autonomía.* Buenos Aires: Siglo veintiuno editores.

Freire, P. (1998). *Pedagogy of Freedom: Ethics, Democracy, and Civic Courage,* trans. P. Clarke. Lanham, MD: Rowman & Littlefield.

Freire, P. (2001). *Pedagogia da autonomia, saberes necessários à prática educativa.* São Paulo: Paz e Terra.

Galeano, E. (1981). *Las venas abiertas de América Latina* (5th edition). Madrid: Editorial Siglo Veintiuno.

Geertz, C. (1983). *Local Knowledge: Further Essays in Interpretative Anthropology.* New York: Basic Books.

Gergen, K. (1997). La comunicación terapéutica como relación. *Sistemas Familiares, 13* (3).

Gleick, J. (1999). *Faster: The Acceleration of Just About Everything.* New York: Vintage Books.

Goolishian, H. (1988). "A Starting Point for Conversation." Opening address to the GFI Galveston Conference (25–26 October).

Hoffman, L. (1990). Constructing realities: An art of lenses. *Family Process, 29*: 1–12.

Hoffman, L. (1993). *Exchanging Voices: A Collaborative Approach to Family Therapy.* London: Karnac.

Hoffman, L. (2002). *Family Therapy: An Intimate History.* New York: W. W. Norton.

Hoffman, L. (2005). A communal perspective for the relational therapies. In: A. Lightburn & P. Sessions (Eds.), *Handbook of Community-Based Clinical Practice.* New York: Oxford University Press.

Ianssen, B., Øvreberg, G., Andersen, T., Kvebæk, I., Ottesen, A., & Rongved, E. (1997). *Bevegelse, liv og forandring.* Oslo: Cappelen akademisk forlag.

Katz, A. M. (1991). Afterwords: Continuing the dialogue. In: T. Andersen (Ed.), *The Reflecting Team: Dialogues and Dialogues about Dialogues.* New York: W. W. Norton.

Katz, A. M., & Shotter, J. (1996). Hearing the patient's "voice": Toward a social poetics in diagnostic interviews. *Social Science and Medicine, 46*: 919–931.

Katz, A. M., & Shotter, J. (1998). "Living moments" in dialogical exchanges. *Human Systems, 9*: 81–93.

Katz, A. M., & Shotter, J. (2004). On the way to "presence": Methods of a "social poetics". In: D. A. Pare & G. Larner (Eds.), *Collaborative Practice in Psychology and Psychotherapy.* New York: Haworth Clinical Practice Press.

Katz, A. M., Shotter, J., & Seikkula, J. (2004). Acknowledging the otherness of the other: Poetic knowing in practice and the fallacy of misplaced systematicity. In: T. Strong & D. A. Pare (Eds.), *Furthering*

*Talk: Advances in the Discursive Therapies*. New York: Kluwer Academic/Plenum Press.

Keränen, J. (1992). The choice between outpatient and inpatient treatment in a family centred psychiatric treatment system. [English summary.] *Jyväskylä Studies in Education, Psychology and Social Research, 93*: 124–129.

Kinman, C. (2001). *The Language of Gifts*. Vancouver, B.C.: Rock the Boat Publications.

Kjellberg, E., Edwardsson, M., Niemelä, B. J., & Öberg, T. (1995). Using the reflecting process with families stuck in violence and child abuse. In: S. Friedman (Ed.), *The Reflecting Team in Action*. New York: Guilford Press.

Larson, G., & Martin, S. (2003). *The Complete Far Side*. Kansas City, KS: Andrews McMeel.

Lévinas, E. (1993). *Etik och oändlighet*. Stockholm: Symposion.

Lowe, R. (2005). Structured methods and striking moments. *Family Process, 44*: 65–75.

Lysack, M. (2004). *Reflecting Processes as Practitioner Education in Andersen and White through the Lens of Bakhtin and Vygotsky*. Unpublished Ph.D. Thesis, McGill University.

Martel, Y. (2002). *Life of Pi*. Edinburgh: Canongate Books.

Maturana, H. (1992). *El sentido de lo humano*. Santiago: Ed. Hachette.

McNamee, S., & Gergen, K. (1996). *La terapia como construccion social*. Barcelona: Paidós.

Meyerhoff, B. (1992). *Remembered Lives: The World of Ritual, Storytelling, and Growing Older*. Ann Arbor, MI: University of Michigan.

Minuchin, S. (1999). *Familias y Terapia Familiar*. Barcelona: Editorial Gedisa.

Ochoa, M. G., Olaizola, J. H., Espinosa, L. M. C., & Martínez, M. M. (2004). *Introducción a la psicología comunitaria*. Barcelona: Editorial UOC.

Pearce, W. B. (1994). Nuevos modelos y metáforas comunicacionales: el passage de la teoría a la praxis, del objetivismo social y de la representación a la reflexividad. In: D. Fried Schnitman, *Nuevos Paradigmas, Cultura y Subjetividad*. Buenos Aires: Paidós.

Penn, P. (1998). Rape flashbacks: Constructing a new narrative. *Family Process, 37* (3): 299–310.

Penn, P. (2000). Metaphors in region of unlikeness. *Human Systems: The Journal of Systemic Consultation and Management, 10* (1).

Penn, P., & Frankfurt, M. (1994). Creating a participant text: Writing, multiple voices, narrative multiplicity. *Family Process, 33*: 217–231.

Rankin, J. (1999). Ancestral voices, spirits and magic do a new dance in the family therapy room. *Journal of Contemporary Family Therapy, 21* (2). (*Special Issue on Family Therapy in South Africa.*)

Seikkula, J. (1991). Family–hospital boundary system in the social network. [English summary.] *Jyväskylä Studies in Education, Psychology and Social Research, 80*: 227–232.

Seikkula, J. (1993). The aim of the work is to generate dialogue: Bakhtin and Vygotsky in family session. *Human Systems: The Journal of Systemic Consultation and Management, 4*: 33–48.

Seikkula, J. (1996). *Öppna samtal: Från monolog till levande dialog i sociala nätverk.* Stockholm: Mareld.

Seikkula, J. (2002). Open dialogues of good and poor outcome in psychotic crisis: Example on family violence. *Journal of Marital and Family Therapy, 28*: 263–274.

Seikkula, J., Aaltonen, J., Alakare, B., Harakangas, K., Keränen, J., & Sutela, M. (1995). Treating psychosis by means of open dialogue. In: S. Friedman (Ed.), *The Reflecting Team in Action: Collaborative Practice in Family Therapy* (pp. 62–80). New York: Guilford Press.

Seikkula, J., Alakare, B., & Aaltonen, J. (2001). Open dialogue in psychosis II: A comparison of good and poor outcome cases. *Journal of Constructivist Psychology, 14*: 267–284.

Seikkula, J., Alakare, B., Aaltonen, J., Haarakangas, K., Keränen. J., & Lehtinen, K. (2006). Five years' experiences of first-episode non-affective psychosis in Open Dialogue approach: Treatment principles, follow-up outcomes and two case analyses. *Psychotherapy Research, 16* (2): 214–228.

Seikkula, J., Alakare, B., Aaltonen, J., Holma, J., Rasinkangas, A., & Lehtinen, V. (2003). Open Dialogue approach: Treatment principles and preliminary results of a two-year follow-up on first episode schizophrenia. *Ethical Human Sciences and Services, 5* (3): 163–182.

Seikkula, J., & Olson, M. (2003). The open dialogue approach to acute psychosis. *Family Process, 42*: 403–418.

Selvini-Palazzoli, M., Boscolo, L., Cecchin, G., & Prata, G. (1980). Hypothesizing–circularity–neutrality: Three guidelines for the conductor of the session. *Family Process, 19*: 3–12.

Shotter, J. (1993). *Conversational Realities: Constructing Life through Language.* London: Sage.

Shotter, J. (2001). *Realidades Conversacionales. La construcción de la vida a través del lenguaje.* Buenos Aires: Amorrortu.

Shotter, J. (2004). *On the Edge of Social Constructionism: "Withness-thinking" versus "Aboutness-thinking".* London: KCC Foundation.

Shotter, J. (2005). "Wittgenstein, Bakhtin and Vygotsky: Introducing Dialogically Structured Reflective Practices into Our Everyday Life." Presentation at Special Education Conference, Copenhagen, Denmark (May).

Shotter, J., & Katz, A. (1998). "Living moments" in dialogical exchanges. *Human Systems, 9*: 81–93.

Shotter, J., & Katz, A. (2005). "Poetics and 'Presence' in Practice." Presentation for Kensington Consultation Centre Summer School, Kensington, UK (July).

Sluzki, C. (1994). Violencia familiar y violencia política: implicaciones terapeuticas de un modelo general. In: D. Fried Schnitman, *Nuevos Paradigmas, Cultura y Subjetividad.* Buenos Aires: Paidos.

St. George, S. A. (1994). Multiple formats in the collaborative application of the "as if" technique in the process of family therapy supervision. *Dissertation Abstracts International.*

Tutu, D. (2000). *No Future without Forgiveness.* London: The Mars Agency.

Wagner, J. (1997). Vad regionen vill veta om samtalsverksamheten på KVA Kalmar? *Rapport KVM Kalmar (Sweden).*

Wagner, J. (1998a). Are dialogical conversations possible behind Walls? *Human Systems: The Journal of Systemic Consultation and Management, 9* (2): 95–112.

Wagner, J. (1998b). Samtal innanför murarna: Återblickar och betraktelser. *Fokus på familien, 3*: 131.

Wagner, J. (1999). Sind dialogische gespräche hinter Gittern möglich? *Zeitschrift für systemische therapie, 17* (3).

Wagner, J. (2000). Son posibles las conversaciones dialógicas detrás de los muros de ona cárcel? *Sistemas Familiares, 16* (3).

Wagner, J. (2001). Nät, nätverk och det skrivna språket 2001. *Svensk Familjeterapi, 1*: 12–22.

Wagner, J. (2002). Kalmar-Sulitjelma/tur-retur 2002. *Svensk familjeterapi, 3–4*: 12–21.

Wagner, J. (2006a). Reflekterande team, processer gjennom 20 år. In: *Reflekterande team, processer i praksis Del fyre. Arbeide med större system. Fångad i samtal.* Oslo: Universitetsförlaget.

Wagner, J. (2006b). Trialogues and answerability: Reflecting conversations with incarcerated youth. In: H. Anderson & D. Gerhart (Eds.), *Collaborative Therapy.* New York: Routledge.

Waldegrave, C. (1990). What is just therapy? *Dulwich Centre Newsletter, 1*: 10–16.

Weisenburger, G. A. (2003). *Dialogical Conversations in Community Transformation.* Thesis, Universidad de las Americas, Mexico City, Mexico.

White, M. (1990). *Narrative Means to Therapeutic Ends.* New York: W. W. Norton.

White, M. (1995). *Re-authoring Lives: Interviews and Essays.* Adelaide: Dulwich Centre Publications.

Wittgenstein, L. (1953). *Philosophical Investigations,* trans. G. E. M. Anscombe. Oxford: Blackwell.

Wittgenstein, L. (1980). *Culture and Value,* trans. P. Winch, with introduction by G. Von Wright. Oxford: Blackwell.

Wittgenstein, L. (1995). *Észrevételek.* Budapest: Atlantisz könyvkiadó.

Wright, von, G. H. (2002). *Sobre la libertad humana.* Barcelona: Paidos.

Zevallos, R., & Chong, N. (2002). Terapia familiar en contextos de pobreza. *Revista Sistemas Familiares, 18* (3).

# INDEX

www.ingramcontent.com/pod-product-compliance
Ingram Content Group UK Ltd.
Pitfield, Milton Keynes, MK11 3LW, UK
UKHW022024061126
477531UK00002B/26

*9780367105754*